SECURITY SCIENCE

SECURITY SCIENCE

The Theory and Practice of Security

CLIFTON L SMITH
Electron Science Research Institute
Edith Cowan University

DAVID J BROOKS
School of Computer and Security Science
Security Research Institute
Edith Cowan University

AMSTERDAM • BOSTON • HEIDELBERG • LONDON • NEW YORK • OXFORD
PARIS • SAN DIEGO • SAN FRANCISCO • SINGAPORE • SYDNEY • TOKYO

ELSEVIER   Butterworth-Heinemann is an imprint of Elsevier

Acquiring Editor: Pamela Chester
Editorial Project Manager: Amber Hodge
Project Manager: Priya Kumaraguruparan
Designer: Alan Studholme

Butterworth-Heinemann is an imprint of Elsevier
225 Wyman Street, Waltham, MA 02451, USA
The Boulevard, Langford Lane, Kidlington, Oxford, OX5 1GB, UK

Notices
Knowledge and best practice in this field are constantly changing. As new research and experience broaden our understanding, changes in research methods or professional practices, may become necessary. Practitioners and researchers must always rely on their own experience and knowledge in evaluating and using any information or methods described herein. In using such information or methods they should be mindful of their own safety and the safety of others, including parties for whom they have a professional responsibility.

To the fullest extent of the law, neither the Publisher nor the authors, contributors, or editors, assume any liability for any injury and/or damage to persons or property as a matter of products liability, negligence or otherwise, or from any use or operation of any methods, products, instructions, or ideas contained in the material herein.

Library of Congress Cataloging-in-Publication Data
Application submitted

British Library Cataloguing-in-Publication Data
A catalogue record for this book is available from the British Library.

ISBN 978-0-12-394436-8

For information on all Butterworth–Heinemann publications
visit our website at store.elsevier.com

Printed and bound by CPI Group (UK) Ltd, Croydon, CR0 4YY

Transferred to digital print 2013

To my dearest wife Maree and daughters Fiona and Amanda who always supported me
   in my endeavors.
To Professor John De Laeter who showed me how to be a scientist.

—*Clifton L. Smith*

To my darling wife Glenda, for the hours that this work has taken me from you. You are
   still my world.
To Professor Clifton Smith, coauthor and mentor, who inspired me to reach this place.
To my Australian and United Kingdom families, my foundation.

—*David J. Brooks*

Contents

Acknowledgments

We wish to express our gratitude to a number of people and organizations who have assisted us by thought and deed over the duration of the planning, development, and production of this book.

- Mr. Jeffery Corkill, who was always willing and able to provide us with his detailed knowledge of intelligence and input into the future of security.
- Mr. Chris Cubbage from MySecurity, who provided valuable comment and was always most optimistic about the validity of this book.
- Professor Martin Gill from Perpetuity Research for his contribution of support in the Foreword of this book.
- Professor Rick Sarre of the University of South Australia for providing valuable feedback on portions of the book.
- Mr. Bruce Braes for being a sounding board for security risk management, business continuity, and his considerable research into organizational resilience.
- Pam Chester, our acquisition editor, who acknowledged the value of our idea in writing this book, and her very supportive staff.
- To the (too few) academics striving to elevate this unique area of security into a true discipline.
- Finally, to the progressive security practitioners who strive to improve their industry for those following behind.

About the Authors

Professor Clifton L. Smith, PhD, MAppSc (Phys)

Dr. Clifton Smith is currently an honorary professor at the Electron Science Research Institute at Edith Cowan University (ECU), and a visiting professor at the Imaging Group at Nottingham Trent University (NTU). He initiated the establishment of the Australian Institute of Security and Applied Technology at ECU in 1987, and he developed research profiles in security imaging, biometric imaging, ballistics identification, infrared sensing, and security education. Over the duration of a decade, Clifton developed the first bachelor of science (security) program in Australia, a BSc (security) honors degree, a masters of science (security science) research degree, and a doctor of philosophy (security science) research degree. In 2004, Professor Smith established the Security Systems Research and Test Laboratory at ECU for the design and testing of security technology. The security systems evaluated and tested included intelligent CCTV and access control through biometric systems. In 2005, Professor Smith developed the masters of security management coursework degree, which is now delivered online to all continents. Dr. Smith retired from ECU in 2006, and continues to supervise PhD students at ECU and NTU in security-related topics.

Dr. David J. Brooks, PhD, MSc (Security Science), BSc (Security), ADipEng (Electronics)

Dave has a 33-year security career having served in the U.K. Royal Air Force, held positions in the Australian Department of Defence, as an academic at Edith Cowan University (ECU), with private security consultancies, and currently for WorleyParsons as a project manager of security. During his career, Dave has worked in all parts of the security industry gaining insight that such experience provides.

Dave maintains a role as a research leader within the Security Research Institute at ECU, specializing in security knowledge, security risk management, technology evaluation, and security decay. He is the academic chair and editor of ECU's annual Security and Intelligence Conference and is on the editorial committee of the Security Journal. Dave has a PhD in security risk management, a masters by research on psychometric risk, and a bachelor of science (security).

Foreword

It is possible that on a list of all the topics of central importance to our well-being and yet have been subjected to a low amount of scholarly research, security would appear near the top. Indeed, there have been few good attempts to develop the science of security, not because there are not good scientists interested in security, but it is more that by and large they have written different types of books. This is why this text is important. It is written by two leading researchers, indeed household names in security research, who are able to speak the language of both science and security.

Moreover, this text is written to engage. It starts with a critique of the concept of security. Most books of this kind start that way, but often progress little more than reminding us that the word "security" has several meanings and in some languages is interpreted as the same as "safety." Clifton Smith and David Brooks take us far beyond that—the body of knowledge of security is defined and critiqued and we are invited to understand how the current state of security knowledge relates to the requirements of a discipline (to which it surely aspires). I hope all students—and for that matter, practitioners too—will take a special interest in their discussion of the scientific method. This is fundamental to fully understanding how security as a subject needs to evolve and develop. Personally, I would not mind if it became a requirement, and at the very least an expectation, that all students of security management should read at least the first chapter, but they would be wise if they read the whole text.

In so doing, they will be able to learn how different theories apply to security, including management theories and systems theories, and how these inform the practice of security and relate to planning, metrics, ethics, and cost benefits, to highlight just some examples that practitioners need to engage with. The authors offer us 10 key principles that they present as guides to practice. Not everyone will view these as complete, but they have set a framework for others to critique. I am sure the authors hope, as we all should, that future researchers will engage with that task.

Indeed, in an array of areas, for example, risk management, business continuity management, facilities management, routine activities theory, defense-in-depth, and crime prevention through environmental design, concepts are examined and shown how they can and do relate to security not from the perspective of a criminologist, as so often is the case, but rather from the viewpoint of a scientist. Their discussion of the role of technology offers a benchmark against which the progress of security can be measured in the years ahead, and they devote a chapter to highlight the ways in which they believe technology is likely to develop and security is likely to change. Throughout, the authors keep their audience engaged with important insights and critiques and never lose sight of their goal of providing a better understanding of what security is and how it functions, or should function. The inclusion of a whole chapter on knowledge management is further testament to that.

The authors are surely right in presenting security as an emerging discipline, and right too in suggesting that properly directed, it has a bright future. Crucially, this is the important point: developing better theories provides a more solid foundation for informing and guiding security work and moving the world of security practice from its current state of "chaos" to a recognized profession. This book is likely to become a major influence in guiding us in the right direction—I hope it will be heeded, it needs to be.

Martin Gill

Preface

The writing of this book has been a true adventure, as we believe that we have made a quantum step in the understanding of the design, application, operations, and education of security by having a theoretical foundation for our security content. We consider that a theoretical foundation to the understanding and application of security at the national and commercial levels will enhance the future development of the discipline.

Professional development is an essential component of professional employment, as it allows individuals to maintain currency in their chosen career field. A characteristic of professional development is that it is both ongoing and directed—that is, to maintain the confidence of the community in the knowledge and skills base of a profession, an individual must continue to strive to be at the leading edge of knowledge in his or her chosen discipline.

The security industry has become an integral part of business enterprise and human activities, wherever businesses engage in wealth-creating activities and people congregate into groups for leisure or living. The functional aspects of security are necessary to ensure protection and safety of individuals and assets. The security of persons, assets, and information remains the responsibility of government, large organizations, and the community. At best, the study of security can only be considered as an emerging discipline, and in some minds still a component of criminology. However, over the past decade sufficient new knowledge in the domain of asset protection has been published that there is

a case for the claim of security to be considered as a distinction and discrete body of knowledge.

The purpose of this book is to seek regularity and internal consistency within the knowledge domain of security, and to demonstrate the underlying principles applied in the understanding of security to those of the scientific method. That is, much of the knowledge domain of security can be discussed in terms of theory, either as newly developed paradigms for asset protection or as well-established theories within other disciplines. Thus, by borrowing theories from other disciplines, it may be possible to enhance the understanding and therefore development of the emerging discipline of security science.

Using theories to apply methods of protection allows a degree of prediction and provides a robust test for the discipline. Nevertheless, for security and, in particular, the security industry to reach such a state requires further professionalization at many levels. To be considered a profession requires defined concepts that form a body of knowledge that has structure. Knowledge is being defined within the broader context of security; however, the relevance and relationship of such knowledge has to be determined. If security is an emerging discipline, what concepts are more related to security than others and how do they relate to the knowledge structure? An understanding of how security knowledge is structured, and its interrelationship and interdependencies, are an important element in achieving regularity and consistency. Ultimately, a structure of security knowledge may be formed that supports a discipline of security science.

The principal themes of this book are according to our philosophy of the structure of knowledge in the discipline of security science, and, as such, will influence the arguments and discussions on the future directions in the study of the protection of assets. These themes of the book include an understanding of the concept and management of security, together with security risk and the management of security risk. Thus, by developing a theoretical context for these principal themes of the knowledge base, it is possible to build a knowledge structure that can be applied to security aspects that can be operationalized to fulfill the function of protecting an organization's assets. According to these themes, the understanding of the ideas of asset protection has been strongly influenced by Bloom's taxonomy, where a hierarchy of understanding of concepts and principles has been presented to ensure that advanced-level thinking is applied to the preservation of well-being and safety.

This book presents a case for the future direction in the development of security science through the understanding of the knowledge associated with asset protection and the processes to achieve asset protection. On the concept of security, Chapter 1 discusses the notion of asset protection according to sociological traits, and the perceptions of the functions of security. A description of the scientific method is presented to establish the basis for theories of security. Chapter 2 discusses the principles of security management within the concept of resilience applied to asset protection. The principles of risk, security risk, and security risk management are presented and applied in Chapter 3. The social and cultural theories associated with the risk management process are considered to evaluate the theories that underlie decision making within security risk management. Chapter 4 compares and contrasts the security strategies that may be used to improve the built environment, considering such techniques as physical measures, crime prevention through environmental design, lighting and the landscape, and the interrelationship between facilities and security.

Chapter 5 presents the need for physical security for the protection of assets, and considers the defense-in-depth principle as an important approach. The applications of the routine activity theory through defense-in-depth and crime prevention through environmental design are appropriate applications in security. The applications of critical path analysis and universal element conceptual mapping in Chapter 6 are suitable strategies for assessing physical attacks on facilities. Also the types and functions of detection systems are discussed, with understanding of the possibility of being defeated. Furthermore, Chapter 7 describes the principles of access control with an emphasis on biometric identification. The modes of attack on biometric systems are considered in order that these might be prevented. Chapter 8 discusses knowledge management as strategies and practices in an organization to consolidate the corporate understanding of its information. The importance of security intelligence applied to the security management plan is presented, together with some discussion on espionage and insider security threats. The importance of the four stages of business continuity management in the context of a crisis is presented in Chapter 9. Finally, Chapter 10 discusses the future of the concept of security in short-, medium-, and long-term predictions for its future directions and outcomes.

The foundation for the continued development of formal knowledge of security and its applications for the protection of assets in the national and international contexts will depend on understanding the principles and concepts of the emerging discipline of security science. A theory-driven learning program at the undergraduate and graduate levels of study will ensure that the formal understanding of security will prevail. The knowledge base for the emerging discipline of security will be enhanced by ongoing research, both in the fundamental context of theory development and the applied context such as knowledge management and business continuity management. Such emergence will provide the foundation for the formal discipline of security science, providing organizational security with an element in becoming a profession.

Clifton L. Smith & David J. Brooks
September, 2012

CHAPTER

1

Concept of Security

OBJECTIVES

- Discuss what constitutes a traditional approach to the nature of security.
- Critique the scientific method and engineering design process for the study of security science.
- Examine the diverse and interrelated disciplines and practice domains of security.

- Evaluate theories or concepts that provide definitions of security.
- Appraise the need to provide context when defining the concept of security.
- Defend a framework that supports a contextual definition of security science.

INTRODUCTION

The traditional academic disciplines have evolved and developed over centuries to reach their current state of refinement. These traditional disciplines, such as astronomy, physics, mathematics, medicine, and, more recently, biology and environmental science, exhibit a set of characteristics by which each can be designated as a discipline. Some of the characteristics of a discipline would include:

1. *Body of knowledge:* A well-defined and inclusive body of knowledge.
2. *Structure of knowledge:* An internal structure of the knowledge, achieved through internal relationships between concepts so that consistency and logic prevail.
3. *Concepts and principles:* The building blocks of the knowledge of a discipline are concepts, and the relationships between concepts are governed by principles.
4. *Theories:* Theories are predictive in function and provide the ultimate test for a discipline, as outcomes can be predicted.

The knowledge domain of security has yet to achieve the status of being designated an academic discipline, as it lacks validity in the characteristics of the traditional disciplines. However, the emerging security science discipline will aspire to these characteristics with future

Security Science – The Theory and Practice of Security
http://dx.doi.org/10.1016/B978-0-12-394436-8.00001-1

ongoing research applied to the characteristics of a discipline, to provide the context for knowledge, structure, principles, and predictive theories.

Security lacks definition and, therefore, lacks structured knowledge. In addition, security is diverse, cross-disciplined, and without a defined or specified knowledge or skill structure (Hesse and Smith, 2001). Nevertheless, this should not lead to a conclusion that security does not contain a definable knowledge structure. The diversity and cross-disciplined nature of security will evolve as the discipline becomes more professional, concepts are developed and defined, and tertiary education programs increase. Professional development is an essential component of professional employment, as it allows the individual to maintain currency in their chosen career. Thus, professional diversity has to be bounded by structured knowledge concepts. A characteristic of professional development is that it is both ongoing and directed—that is, to maintain the confidence of the community in the knowledge and skills base of a profession, you must continue to strive to be at the leading edge of knowledge in your chosen discipline.

The foundation for the continued development of formal knowledge of security and its applications for the protection of assets in the national and international contexts will depend on an understanding of the principles and concepts of the emerging discipline of security. Research and development in the structure of the discipline of security is crucial for the professional application of a new generation of conceptual principles of security for the protection of assets. As Fischer et al. (2008, p. 482) suggested, the future of security is very positive considering the growth indicated in the discipline.

Security lacks characteristics of a discipline, with a defined and inclusive definition, as the *concept* of security is diverse and multidimensional. Nevertheless, security can be defined given context. Therefore, this chapter introduces the concept of security and provides definition through context and the presentation of supporting theories, models, and frameworks. Thus, a definition goes some way in achieving such understanding as to why security is multidimensional in nature through a staged approach, commencing from security of the individual to security of national and international systems. Security is a human characteristic that is objective, perceived, expected, and demanded by people in many different forms. It is perhaps one concept that over many decades has not changed in its original use; rather, it has become more broadly used to encompass greater and more diverse meaning.

SCIENTIFIC METHOD IN SUPPORT OF SECURITY SCIENCE

The development of the knowledge base in security science depends on its advancement as a discipline, and the extent of interaction between academia and professional practitioners of the security industry. The knowledge base for the emerging discipline of security will be enhanced by ongoing research both in the fundamental context of theory development and the applied context of asset protection. It is necessary for government, academia, and the commercial security industry to contribute to this knowledge base.

The stages in the development of a scientific discipline depend on the application of the scientific method to the knowledge base under consideration. The scientific method is a process for experimentation to seek cause-and-effect relationships between observable factors in the information of data gathered. For example, does the presence of a person in an e-field detector distort the field so that intrusion can be registered? From a social perspective, do people use utility theory when accessing security risk or do they take a heuristic approach? Whether in the hard or soft sciences, the scientific method seeks the cause-and-effect relationship by controlling the variables in the experimentation of the phenomenon.

A definite feature of a science is that there are a set of procedures that demonstrate how outcomes are produced, and these procedures are sufficiently detailed so that others may replicate the process to verify or refute the outcomes. The scientific method is a process of inquiry that regards itself as fallible, and as a result purposely tests itself and criticizes its outcomes to correct and improve itself. Although there are several versions of the scientific method, a basic approach involves a four-stage model to develop knowledge of a natural phenomenon:

1. Gather data by measuring or recording the observations of the phenomenon.
2. Construct an idea of how the phenomenon operates or functions in the form of a hypothesis.
3. Test or evaluate the idea or hypothesis by designing an experiment to show the operation or function of the phenomenon.
4. Analyze the results of the experiment to see if the hypothesis is true or false; if it is true, then the idea may be formalized as a theory.

Scientific Method

The model of the scientific method can be expanded with preplanning for background research or information seeking before the hypothesis testing stage, and the model can be extended with an outcomes communication or reporting stage after the analysis to disseminate findings to practitioners and interested people (Figure 1.1). The strength of the scientific method is that a formalized process is applied to the problem, and an outcome will either be gained or rejected. A feature of the scientific method is that the hypothesis of the problem can be tested time after time, and if the hypothesis continues to be accepted then it is accepted as knowledge. However, if the hypothesis is rejected once, then the model will not be accepted. The strength of the scientific method is that anyone can conduct the hypothesis testing for the problem, and thus establish the validity of the model.

The regularization of observations of a phenomenon can eventually be presented as a theory, provided the phenomenon is scrutinized many times from a variety of viewpoints and with the same outcomes for each experiment. Figure 1.1 shows that if the result of hypothesis testing is false or partially true, then a modified hypothesis must be tested. When consistency of testing the hypothesis is obtained, then the idea becomes a theory and provides a coherent set of propositions that explain a class of phenomena. The theory can be considered as a framework to explain further observations, from which predictions can be made.

The strength of the scientific method is that it is unprejudiced—that is, it is not necessary to believe the results or outcomes of a particular researcher, as one can replicate the experiment and determine whether the results are true or false. The outcomes of the hypothesis testing do not depend on a particular experimenter, so that faith or belief does not play any part in the logical proof or material evidence on whether a scientific idea or theory is adopted or discarded. Thus, a theory is accepted, not based on the proponent, but rather on the quality of the results obtained through observations or experiments. Results obtained through the process of the scientific method are repeatable and reproducible.

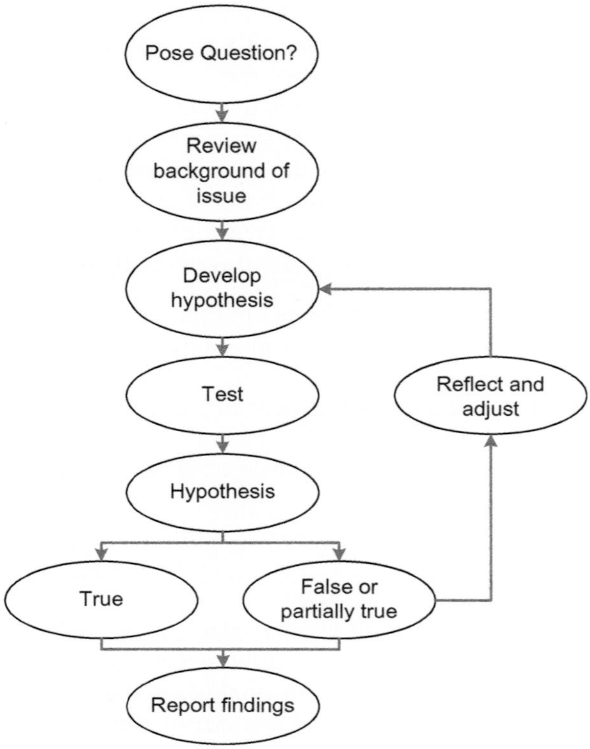

FIGURE 1.1 Stages of the scientific method showing the hypothesis testing of an idea.

An important characteristic of a scientific theory or hypothesis is that it must be *falsifiable*. That is, if any single experiment relevant to the hypothesis is shown to be negative or untrue, the hypothesis must be rejected. Thus, theories cannot be proven when the hypotheses are tested, but only rejected when a negative test results from an experiment. The philosopher Wittgenstein (1953) in his analyses of experimentation claimed that "there is no independent criterion of correctness," so that the scientific method must continue to test the validity of its knowledge.

In a tested scientific hypothesis, a prediction is a rigorous, often quantitative, statement forecasting new outcomes under specific conditions of the idea being considered. The scientific method is formulated on testing assertions that are logical consequences of scientific theories, developed through repeatable experiments or observational studies of a phenomenon. Thus, a scientific theory of which the assertions are contradicted by observations and evidence will be rejected. The ability of an idea or hypothesis to predict further outcomes is a strength of the scientific method in its regularization of information from observation of experiment. Therefore, the power of the scientific method is to be found in the ability to predict further outcomes from the original hypothesis of the phenomenon. This important outcome of prediction from the scientific method is a strong indicator of validity of the process, as logical predictions of an idea can then also be hypothesis tested for acceptance or rejection. The philosopher Karl Popper (1963) sought to show that challenges to the scientific method are based on a series of misconceptions about the nature of science, and about the relationship between scientific laws and scientific prediction.

The application of the scientific method to ideas in natural phenomena has scientific researchers propose hypotheses as explanations of the phenomena. Thus, they are able to design experimental studies to test these hypotheses and make predictions that can be derived from the hypotheses. The process must be repeatable, to safeguard against mistakes, confusion, or prejudice by a particular experimenter. Theories that embrace wider domains of knowledge from similar fields of study may coalesce several or many independently derived hypotheses together in a coherent supportive knowledge structure. These knowledge structures are the foundations for the development of an academic discipline and are particularly relevant to security science.

The scientific method is an enduring cycle that constantly develops more accurate and comprehensive methods and models. For example, when Einstein developed the special and general theories of relativity, he did not refute or discount Newton's principia, which was the foundation for Newtonian mechanics in physics. Newtonian physics was correct in its day and was true for the observations in nature. But Newton's equations could not cope with the enormity of mass in the universe, the tininess of particles in the atom, and the huge speeds of objects in space, which became observable data in the twentieth century. So Einstein's theories are extensions and refinements of Newton's theories, and therefore increase our confidence in Newton's ideas of the natural world.

Engineering Design Process

The application of the scientific method has evolved over centuries, but interestingly, the engineering design process has more recently been developed to service the needs of the engineer who creates new products or processes. For engineers, the engineering design process is a set of phases or actions that establishes a need for a product, system, or environment. Table 1.1 shows the methodology of the engineering design process, and also the correspondence with the scientific method.

TABLE 1.1   Scientific Method versus Engineering Design Process

Scientific Method	Engineering Design Process
State a question or problem	Define a problem or need
Gather background information	Gather background information
Formulate hypothesis; identify variables	Establish design statement or criteria
Design experiment, establish procedure(s)	Prepare preliminary designs
Test hypothesis by doing an experiment	Build and test a prototype(s)
Analyze results and draw conclusions	Verify, test, and redesign as necessary
Present results	Present results

The engineering design process defines the problem by seeking responses to the following questions as a reason to engage in the development of a product, system, or environment:

1. What is the problem or need?
2. Who has the problem or need?
3. Why is the problem important to solve?

The engineering design process rarely proceeds in a linear manner through stages, but rather moves back and forth while converging to a solution. Thus, feedback loops in the logic of the design process are an important characteristic of the procedure. Table 1.1 demonstrates that similar logic is presented in each of the methodologies for science and engineering. The rigor of both of the processes is the strengths of the approaches for testable outcomes. While the scientific method modifies hypotheses that do not test positive and are hence rejected, the engineering design process features iterations between stages to achieve design outcomes that are both logical and sustainable.

Security science will use both scientific and engineering design methods. However, due to the applied nature of security science, it would be expected that the engineering design method is equally relevant in developing the discipline. Such applied research allows directed evaluation of real problems within the social environment rather than theoretical research, better supporting the security industry.

Security science is an emerging discipline that is developing its own theories for the structure of knowledge within the context of its knowledge domain. Although some theories in security science are discipline specific, generally current theories are adapted from other disciplines and knowledge domains for the security context, such as criminology, psychology, and engineering, where relatively strong theoretical contexts have been developed. However, security science is in its formative phase, and will evolve over the next decade into an accepted science. Thus, evolution will be based on rigor and logical application through science and technology theory and principle. The emergence of security science as an accepted discipline will herald the advancement of security as a profession.

DEFINING THE CONCEPT OF SECURITY

To varying degrees, we all have a concern for our well-being. These concerns extend to our family, friends, colleagues, the environment, and the world we occupy. The need to address these concerns is generally labeled *security*. The concept of security takes numerous forms within the wide spectrum of society. As Zedner (2009, p. 22) suggests, *security* is a powerful term that has a strong emotional appeal arising from its capacity to bear multiple meanings simultaneously. Furthermore, the rhetorical allure of security has seen it attach to a long line of neologisms (global security, international security, cooperative security, and human security) that deliberately use the term to mobilize political support and economic recourse.

Security is multidimensional in both concept and application; however, we can define security and understand its nature when we consider it from a contextual perspective. For example, security is comprehensible when we consider a lock and key, but less so when we consider the fight on terrorism. The meaning of security can be unbounded, for example, in the past decade the increasing world exposure to terror attacks has raised social concern over the ability of nation-states to protect its citizens. When we use the term *security* without context, it can and does mean many things to many people.

Security may be considered assured freedom from poverty or want; precautions taken to ensure against theft or espionage; or a person or thing that secures or guarantees (Angus and Roberston, 1992). Furthermore, Fischer et al. consider that security "implies a stable, relatively predictable environment in which an individual or group may pursue its ends without disruption or harm and without fear of such disturbance or injury" (2008, p. 31). A traditional definition of security may be the provision of private services in the protection of people, information, and assets for individual safety or community wellness. In addition, private or commercial security may be considered the provision of paid services in preventing undesirable, unauthorized, or detrimental loss to an organization's assets (Post and Kingsbury, 1991).

Nevertheless, security has to be expanded to consider national security and the defense of a nation-state through armed force or the use of such force to control its citizens. Security may also imply public policing by state-employed public servants. Still others consider security as crime prevention, secure technology, risk management, or loss prevention (Brooks, 2009). The *Protection of Assets Manual* (Knote, 2004, pp. 1–2) states that the title was chosen because the term *security* is too narrow a definition, whereas the title of *protection of assets* better describes the function of security; however, it is argued that the reverse holds greater validity. Asset protection does better define the function of a part of security, but it is only one part of many.

Security may be considered to be all of these statements; however, such diversity results in a society that has no clear understanding of security, with a divergence of interests from many stakeholders (Manunta, 1999). As ASIS International stated, "every time we think we've got the definition of the security field nailed, somebody . . . starts taking some of the nails away" (2003, p. 10). Security has to have a shared definition among the many disciplines that incorporate and contribute to security. However, security does present rather different meanings to different people (Davidson, 2005), given time, place, and context.

As shown in Table 1.2, the *nature* of security has to be considered. Security may be extensions—namely, security of international systems, nation-states, and groups and individuals (Rothschild, 1995). In addition, the aspect of security can be an objective concept (e.g., a lock and key), subjective and driven by our perceptions (e.g., the installation of public CCTV to make a community feel safer), or symbolic (e.g., aviation security restricting passengers taking excessive liquids airside). We need to consider security from the individual to international, as well as the objective, subjective, and symbolic aspects.

TABLE 1.2 Nature of Security

Security Extensions	Security Aspects
Security of individuals	Objective
Security of groups	Subjective
Security of nation-states	Symbolic
Security of international systems	

SECURITY OF INDIVIDUALS

Security of individuals can be discussed within the context of a number of theories. These theories include Maslow's hierarchy of human needs (1943), the related but distinct concepts of security and safety, and, finally, the risk effect. Risk has always been closely related to the concept of security, but it is only in recent times that the management of risk has played such a significant role in applied security.

Hierarchy of Human Needs

In 1943 Maslow proposed the theory of hierarchy of human needs, ranking an individual's motivational needs within a priority schema. The theory is often presented as a triangle (Figure 1.2), with five successive stages. Maslow integrated two distinct groupings, being deficiency of needs and growth needs. Deficiencies at each stage must be satisfied by the individual before they can proceed to the following level, resulting in the higher needs only being considered once the lower or more basic needs are satisfied. Once these lower needs are achieved, creativity, self-fulfillment, and realization of one's potential may be reached. However, if lower-level needs are no longer being achieved, the person will temporally refocus on such lower needs and not regress to the lower levels.

Physiological needs are concerned with human survival—breathing, homeostasis, water, sleep, food, and excretion. Once these physical needs are satisfied, safety needs are considered. The safety level is often presented as *safety and security*, with an individual's needs for personal security and extending to aspects such as order and control, financial security, job security, health, and well-being.

Once physiological and safety needs are reached, the need of love and belonging follows. This third stage involves emotional-based relationships and a sense of belonging, such as friendship, family, affiliation, intimacy, and love. The next level, esteem, considers an individual's need to achieve, seek, and gain peer approval and recognition, gain self-value, and respect others. Finally, the highest level is actualization, where one gains self-fulfillment, understanding, and realizes one's potential. Such actualization leads to creativity, morality, spontaneity, problem solving, and acceptance of others (Huitt, 2004; Maslow, 1943).

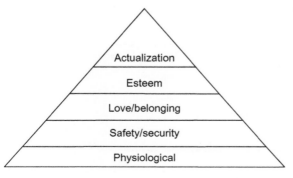

FIGURE 1.2   Maslow's hierarchy of human needs.

As Maslow's hierarchy of human needs demonstrates, safety and security is a primary need for the individual. Without feeling safe and secure, our ability to cooperate as a cohort and achieve creativity is restricted. Thus, such an understanding leads to the conclusion that security should be an important focus within an organization, allowing employees to be as efficient as possible. As Huitt (2004) states, Maslow's—and more recent research in this area—is important for anyone concerned with developing and using the human potential.

Safety versus Security

Safety is freedom from danger or risk of injury, which reflects a past definition of security. Notwithstanding Maslow's view on the relationship of safety and security, these two concepts are distinct from each other. They do have a degree of relationship, but should be considered as unique concepts. Safety focuses on hazards that tend to suggest an accident or an internal threat. As Ale states, "safety is associated with incidents and accidents. Security deals with malicious acts, such as sabotage and terrorism. There is a grey area, however, where the distinction between security and safety, between accident and criminal act, is difficult to draw" (2009, p. 12).

Nevertheless, the distinction between the concepts of safety and security is the added emphasis on being protected from dangers that originate from outside. A security threat or risk is someone or something that intends to or could cause harm (see Chapter 3 for a more extensive discussion of threat and harm), applied from the external (the idea of external threat should not be taken literally). Safety focuses on the process within the internal environment. It could be considered that security threats and risks are far more difficult to address, as the attacker will try to use his or her human ingenuity to bypass any protection system put into place.

Risk-driven Security

Security is considered a form of risk, applied within the management approach of risk management. All activities carry some form of risk and, thus, one makes a decision as to whether to conduct an activity based on the utility of the activity. In other words, does the risk of an activity outweigh the benefit? Demands for ever greater reductions in risk exposure—from a cultural, social, community, corporate, and individual basis—can proceed beyond the point of overall benefit and become counterproductive. There are three significant points about how people determine the acceptability of risk:

1. Risk is generally less accepted when imposed by external factors over which people have little or no control. People demand higher safety standards at work and risks in the workplace are not well accepted, because people cannot control their exposure.
2. Risks stemming from identifiable activities are not as accepted. Incidents such as the Exxon Valdez oil spill are less accepted because someone is at fault.
3. Simple numbers and probabilities are inadequate to represent reaction to incidents of different magnitude. Catastrophic events are given far more attention than more frequent, but lower consequence, events.

Nevertheless, risk is the possibility of incurring loss or misfortune, which is distinct from security. There is a degree of interrelationship, but risk management takes an actuary approach to security. An actual or perceived risk will eventuate in the need for some form of security, whether that is at the individual, group, or nation-state levels. Security is an outcome of risk, and in today's world, the concept of risk could be considered to take precedence over security (see Chapter 3).

SECURITY OF GROUPS

The security of groups extension can be discussed within the context of the law and public security. For example, the underlying nature of the law and social contract, where law is the foundation of our society, and security is the maintainer or enforcer. In addition, the function of public security (e.g., police) as both policing and private security are becoming more reliant on each other and converging.

The Law and Social Contract

Driving and developing public security was the most significant aspect that led to our current social construct, namely the phenomenon of the social contract between the individual and the nation-state. This contract was perhaps a fundamental aspect that shaped and defined the broader concept of security as we know it today. We, as individuals, surrender some of our rights for protection by our nation-state, and in exchange the nation-state expects us to support it.

Society, as a whole, defines social expectations or norms. The law is the foundation and articulates these social norms. If an individual or group operates beyond those social norms, they are considered to be breaking the social contract and therefore breaking the law. To maintain the social contract requires a reaction—in general, defined public security or, more commonly, policing. Therefore, security is the enforcer or output of the social contract.

Public Security (Policing)

The primary public security function is to maintain accepted behaviors among the community, upholding law and regulations, and protecting a nation-state's' general public (Zedner, 2009). Nevertheless, public security is often considered a form of security and is developed hand-in-hand with other practice areas of security. While one security practice area may have been more dominate than the other at some point in time, each rose concurrently, supporting each other and with members moving between areas. While it is considered that private security developed first, it is important to consider that security reflects society and aims to meet the needs of its society. Western views suggest that security may have first been documented in medieval England, with programs to clear the king's roads of brush to serve as a precaution against highway robbery.

As society changes, so does security, and there are extensive discussions on public security verses private security. It would be highly unlikely that nation-states would wholly replace their public security functions for wholly private security services. In the past where this has been attempted, the results have been for a short-term financial state benefit, public discourse, and contract termination (Knote, 2004). Nevertheless, both relationships and contractual partnerships have and will continue to be successful and expand. Relationships between public security and private security have been growing for many years. In the past, this has been through second-career police officers moving from one career to the other. Both public security and other security practice areas can see the benefits of such a relationship. In addition, contractual partnerships have been increasing, where private security complement and allow sworn public officers to be more effective in frontline public security functions.

Distinct differences between public security and private security are their philosophy, principles, authority, and status (Table 1.3), where public security has the obligation of egalitarian service but private security obligations are client exclusive (Knote, 2004, pp. 2–22; Sarre and Prenzler, 2011, p. 83). In other words, public security upholds the social contract, whereas private security protects one's own assets. Private security's primary function is to protect their client's people, information, and assets. Such an approach does lead to varying needs between very similar organizations, resulting with inconsistencies. In addition, the debate in regard to a profit or nonprofit approach should be considered, but this may reduce with increasing financial pressure in many public departments. Nevertheless, public security and private security have quite a different intent.

Public security has many similar functions to the other practicing security domains; however, it is quite distinct. Public security reacts to an event, with the function to enforce social law. The reactive nature distinguishes public security from private security, which attempts to prepare for an event to protect one's own property.

TABLE 1.3   Public Security versus Private Security Functions

Private Security	Function	Public Security
Client	Input	Citizen
Selective	Service	Equal
Profit-driven	Delivery resourcing	Tax-funded
Undetermined	Finance	Predetermined
Fragmented	Structure	Centralized
Citizen	Power	Legislated
Limited	Training	Intensive
Loss prevention	Role	Law enforcement
Protection	Orientation	Offender
Specific	Target	General
Private	Space	Public
Restricted	Regulated	Heavily
Wide	Discretion	Limited
Asset protection	Output	Enforcement
Proactive	Stance	Reactive

Private Security

A significant development in security has been the growth of private security, which has grown into a large and international industry that can be broadly defined as an industry devoted to crime prevention. Private security is also known as organizational security, corporate security (Brooks, 2009), commercial security, asset protection, and security management.

Private security officers outnumber public security (police) officers at the estimated global average of 348 to 318 per 100,000 of population (Prenzler et al., 2009, p. 4). In the United States, there are 10,000 security companies employing 1.8 million security guards, equating to almost three private security officers to every public security officer, and this ratio is expected to increase (Hemmens et al., 2001). Cities in the United States are spending $70 million per week on security services (Fischer et al., 2008).

The private security industry is an emerging and relatively young discipline and the traditional distinction between past security entities of public security, private security, and defense are merging. The expansive nature of private security has resulted in limited and diffuse understanding, even though extensive resources are being expended. The role of private security has further expanded, and "there is now an acknowledged role for commercial security in actions against global security threats, national security concerns, local community safety needs, as well as the requirements of the corporation and the individual" (Wakefield, 2007, pp. 13–14).

Combining the findings of several studies (Bradley and Sedgwick, 2009; van Steden and Sarre, 2007), it has to be noted that the strong growth of private security can be attributed to the following factors:

- The reduction in the public provision of services by nation-states.
- The general increase in the fear of crime.
- The transfer of noncore public security tasks to the private sector.
- Growing value and portability of assets requiring more protection.

Within many parts of the world, the security industry is not classified as one industry; rather, its members are spread across many associated practice areas that include many occupations. Private security's prime purpose is to maintain corporate activity, allowing output and support profit. Thus, such purpose may be applied to not only private organizations but also public organizations. However, to sustain security requires the cost to be spread between receiving beneficiaries or stakeholders of the mitigating strategies. In addition, such security has to consider intangible aspects of social and community issues, a difficult task when dealing with such diverse stakeholders with competing views.

The growth of private security will continue and its importance strengthened within the broad spectrum of security. Therefore, there is a greater need to better understand and develop a scientific foundation for the security science practice area.

SECURITY OF NATION-STATE AND INTERNATIONAL SYSTEMS

Security extensions of both nation-states and international systems can be discussed within the context of the traditional approaches to international security, such as defense or military power. In addition, international systems may include national security, which is focused on local and regional nation-state protection. A more recent approach to nation-state security is homeland security, the convergence of traditional security practice areas such as defense, public security, and private security. Finally, the politicized approach to some or all of these security extensions is considered with securitization.

National Security and Defense

Security has strong parallels with defense, as once groups formed and became nations, these had to be protected and expanded; nevertheless, defense cannot explicitly define security. The recent international security environment has witnessed the erosion of traditional nation-states with increased globalization and access to worldwide information networks that have further merged defense and security (Stapley et al., 2006). The conventional view of security in defense concerns the survival of the nation-state and the preservation of its sovereignty (Hettne, 2010, p. 33). Revolving around this view are definitions that are "more concerned with redefining the policy agendas of nation-states" (Baldwin, 1997, p. 5).

Defense, as with other related practice areas, is often considered security. An example of such parallelism may be demonstrated through public security and military organizations, and the increasing convergence in their response to homeland security challenges. Nevertheless, opposing such convergence is still the large number of different state agencies that may respond. Thus, such diverse and multidisciplined views of security cannot support a single definition of security.

Homeland Security

An applied extension of security of nation-state is homeland security. Homeland security incorporates and attempts to integrate diverse domains of security such as defense, national security, private security, and public security. National and public security also integrate first responders and disaster recovery departments such as fire and emergency, medical facilities and staff, and other state departments such as intelligence agencies.

An example of such integration can be seen in the United States, where the Department of Homeland Security (DHS) was formed as a result of national security events and directed threats. Many other nation-states have not been so direct in their attempt to reconstruct their approach to national security and the need for greater convergent security. Nevertheless, many nation-states have shifted their approach to national security to better integrate their broad security domains, attempting to ensure that they can better tackle their changing national threats. As Fischer et al. suggest, more nation-states are now experiencing greater government control in establishing and maintaining the nations' security (2008); however, much of this security is supported by the private sector.

In the United States, homeland security is officially defined by the National Strategy for Homeland Security as "a concerted national effort to prevent terrorist attacks within the United States, reduce America's vulnerability to terrorism, and minimize the damage and recover from attacks that do occur." The DHS includes the Federal Emergency Management Agency, which has responsibility for preparedness, response, and recovery to natural disasters. The scope of homeland security includes emergency preparedness and response for an all-hazards approach to such events as terrorism to natural disasters. In addition, domestic and international intelligence activities, critical infrastructure protection, and border security that includes land, maritime, and nation borders.

World nation-states react to local, state, and regional threats and situations, resulting in political agendas where policy is developed and driven by many vectors. Such policy drives the domains of security to varying degrees, based on their own and competing factors. Thus, the affect is seen not only in national security, but in all aspects of a community from transit security, public and private utilities, public buildings, and private facilities.

Securitization

The concept of *securitization* was put forward as a means to better understand security, based on the notion of different sectors of security drawn from speech act theory (Buzan et al., 1998). Securitization highlights the intellectual and political aspects in using the term *security* for an ever wider range of issues. The idea argues that it is essential that an analytical grounding or principle has to determine what is and what is not a security issue. If this approach is not taken, there is a danger that the concept of security will be applied to any issue and hence becomes effectively meaningless. Furthermore, the concept of security is directed to survival; therefore, an issue is represented as an existential threat to the survival of an object.

Securitization is achieved when an issue comes to be treated as a security issue and it is reasonable to use exceptional political measures to deal with it, thus the issue has been "securitized." We can think about the process of securitization in terms of a spectrum that extends from nonpoliticized (meaning that an issue is not a political issue), through politicized (meaning it is part of a public debate), to securitized (meaning that the issue is thought of as an existential threat and therefore justifies responses that go beyond normal political practices) (Peoples and Vaughan-Williams, 2010, p. 77). Securitization can be extended to all sectors of security such as the military, environment, economic, and societal, and of course its focus being the political arena, although it has not been extended to the individual.

CONCEPT OF SECURITY MATRIX

Security has been considered within the context of its extension, namely of the individual, group, nation-state, and international. Various theories have been used in an attempt to define the concept of security; nevertheless, security is not easy to define. As Manunta and Manunta state, "security is both a need and philosophical idea" (2006, p. 631).

One approach to better understand the concept of security and provide understanding is through the articulation of context or practice areas. Such an approach can be more clearly demonstrated when considering some of the applied domains of security, using and increasing the "extensions" of security. Table 1.4 is not comprehensive, but it demonstrates the more popular view of security within a matrix format.

However, Table 1.4 does demonstrate, to some degree, the importance of understanding the context of security. Where, as with risk, a definition of security is dependent on a clear

TABLE 1.4 Applied Security Matrix

by/for	Defense	Public Security	Homeland Security	Corporate Security	Private Security	Individual
International	X					
Regional	XX		X			
Nation-state	XXXX	XX	XXXX			
Community	XX	XXXX	XXX	X	X	
Organization	X	XX	X	XXXX	XXX	X
Group		XX	X	XX	XX	X
Peer		X		X	X	XX
Family						XXX
Individual						XXXX

Note: X indicates the strength of the relationship between the security provider (by) and the receiver of security (for), with XXXX having the strongest and X having the weakest relationships.

articulation of context to gain understanding. With this in mind, there needs to be a definition that provides a more appropriate context for security, which in this case commences with defining security science.

SECURITY SCIENCE: CONTEXT DEFINES CONCEPT DEFINITION

When considering a definition of security science, one approach is to view security within a practise area or with context. Such an approach allows a review of what *functions* security practitioners perform and leads to an understanding of its body of knowledge. There has been past studies (ASIS International, 2010; Brooks, 2009; Hesse and Smith, 2001) that have taken such an approach to develop a security science body of knowledge; nevertheless, before these studies can be considered a final definition will be presented.

Theoretical Definition of Security

Manunta (1999) put forward a definition of security that encompasses the *natures of security* (Table 1.2), as it can be applied across the many extensions of security from the individual to national defense. In addition, the definition allows, to some degree, the aspects of security to be addressed, namely the objective, subjective, and symbolic nature of security. The definition uses a formula that combines a number of mutually inclusive components:

$$\text{Security} = \int (A, P, T) Si$$

where A is asset, P is protection, T is threat, and Si is situation.

For security to be considered there must be an asset (*A*), and there is an individual, group, or nation-state who wish to provide some level of protection (*P*), with an actual or perceived threat (*T*) against the asset. In addition, the sum of these components has to be considered within a certain environment or situation (*Si*), giving the definition context. Thus, the formula provides the elements of security; nevertheless, the formula is deficient in several aspects. First, let us consider that for security to be addressed, the asset has to have value (whether actual or intrinsic). Second, and an issue with many security definitions, the formula does not assist in a consensual understanding of security. The ability to define security still requires context, thus placing security within a situation.

Studies in a Body of Knowledge

Traditional academic disciplines exhibit characteristics that designate them as a discipline. One of the more significant characteristics is a *body of knowledge*, which needs to be well defined and inclusive. Supporting and integral to a body of knowledge is the *structure of knowledge*, which provides internal structure of the knowledge through conceptual relationships that exhibit consistency and logic.

The knowledge domain of security has yet to achieve the status of being designated an academic discipline, as it lacks validity in the characteristics of a definable and defendable body of knowledge. This is an area that researchers, educators, industry, and government have been progressing; nevertheless, slowly due to the inability to define the many domains of security. Such issues include an understanding of what this practice area encompasses and also semantics—for example, is it security management or protection of assets?

Notwithstanding these issues, research groups (ASIS International, 2010; Brooks, 2009; Hesse and Smith, 2001; Kooi and Hinduja, 2008) have begun to progress a defendable body of knowledge. One such group is ASIS International, at their annual practitioner/academic symposia. An outcome of their annual symposium has been the development of a security model containing what the group believed were the core elements of security, which has within the United States provided a baseline for tertiary-level course development (ASIS International, 2003). For example, the 2009 symposium attempted to gain an understanding of the security body of knowledge, understand what disciplines security may extract its knowledge categories from, what knowledge categories are core, how these knowledge categories can be used, and to consider if consistency and consensus can be gained. In addition, a list of 18 knowledge categories (ASIS International, 2009, p. 44) was put forward as a security model (Table 1.5).

TABLE 1.5   ASIS International Symposium Security Model

Physical security	Personnel security	Information security systems
Investigations	Loss prevention	Risk management
Legal aspects	Emergency/continuity planning	Fire protection
Crisis management	Disaster management	Counterterrorism
Competitive intelligence	Executive protection	Violence in the workplace
Crime prevention	Crime prevention through environmental design	Security architecture and engineering

Kooi and Hinduja (2008, p. 299) summarize their experience of teaching security to criminal justice undergraduates where they considered the wider understanding of the art and science of security, resulting in the recommendation of 19 topic areas (Table 1.6). Nevertheless, it could be argued that many of these proposed topics—for example, retail, casino, Olympic, nuclear, and museum security—are practice areas rather than security knowledge.

Security education, from the perspective of criminal justice and social science, can be beneficial in further validating security categories and the body of knowledge; however, such studies may also increase confusion as to what may constitute security and reduce the ability of achieving consensus in the near to medium term.

In a study to define security, Brooks (2009) put forward a list of 13 security knowledge categories (Table 1.7). The list was extracted and developed from a critique of 104 international undergraduate tertiary security courses from Australia, South Africa, United Kingdom, and the United States.

Thus, listings from these many groups begin to support a common body of knowledge. Such security knowledge categories provide a number of benefits, such as providing a degree of contextual understanding and the commencement of a security science body of knowledge, supporting a contextual definition. Furthermore, these categories allow a consolidated framework of security science to be presented. Nevertheless, security science will be prone to a

TABLE 1.6   Security Course: Components in the Context of a Criminal Justice Undergraduate Degree

The origins and development of security	Security education, training, certification, and regulation	The role of security
Proprietary vs. contract security	Risk analysis and security survey	Perimeter and exterior security
Interior security and access control	Transportation/cargo security	Computer and information security
Security and the law	Internal and external fraud	Personnel policies and human relations
Workplace violence	Retail security	Casino security
Olympic security	Nuclear security	Museum security
Continuity of operations		

TABLE 1.7   Security Knowledge Categories

Criminology	Business continuity management	Security management
Facility management	Industrial security	Security technology
Investigations	Physical security	Law
Risk management	Safety	Fire science

Source: Adjusted from Brooks, 2009.

suffering from a fluid body of knowledge due to such issues as knowledge structure, terminology, differing context, and practice domains and academic disciplines that feel that they have some ownership of security knowledge.

Consolidated Framework of Security Science

The integration of the 13 knowledge categories from Table 1.7 leads to a framework of security science (Figure 1.3). Such a framework considers the breadth of security science, whereas traditional security knowledge has generally focused on electronic, manpower, and physical security categories and not the range of security-related functions. As the security science framework indicates along its upper axis, core security knowledge categories comprise of risk management, business continuity management (BCM), security technology (encompassing traditional electronic security, but also IT and computing), physical security, personnel security, and industrial security, all applied at operational, tactical, and strategic levels. Industrial security encompasses security requirements in unique environments such as nuclear, aviation security, maritime security, and critical infrastructure. Many of these industries have legislative security requirements.

The model may overlap other disciplines, which is appropriate as other disciplines can and do support security science with allied theories. Supporting security knowledge categories include investigations, law, criminology, facility management, fire and life safety, occupational safety and health, and intelligence. Such an approach supports what more mature disciplines do—that is, selectively draw from related disciplines to append their unique offerings (Young, 2007, p. 84). In addition, the tabulated knowledge categories and integrated framework provide some degree of concept definition, assisting in understanding organiational security and commencing knowledge structure.

Thus, organizational security operates at many levels within an organization, such as operational, tactical, strategic, and governance. At the operational level, the day-to-day practice of security ensures that the function of security is achieved and maintained at the appropriate level to counter the threat, and meets the organization's expectations and legislative compliance. Nevertheless, effective security should also operate at a tactical level, seeking methods

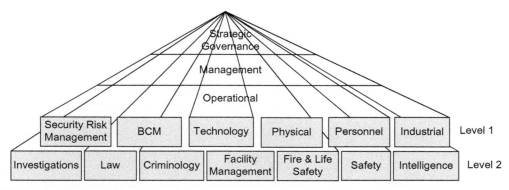

FIGURE 1.3   Integrated knowledge framework of security science. (Used with permission from Brooks, 2012, p. 10.)

to improve performance and provide tangible benefits to the organization. Perhaps the most important level in developing a true security profession is the ability of practitioners to be effective at the strategic security level. Such an approach aligns security with the group's core goals and future directions, allowing proactive management and supporting the group. As Langston and Lauge-Kristensen state, "it is this [strategic] level that separates the routine from the dynamic, and justifies the emergence of . . . a professional discipline in its own right" (2002, p. xv).

There have been a number of assumptions made within this integrated framework and other security models presented. These assumptions considered that some knowledge categories are more relevant to security than others; therefore, this framework incorporates a hierarchy of knowledge categories. Level 1 may be considered core security knowledge categories, whereas level 2 is noncore knowledge categories. The noncore knowledge categories may be allied disciplines, practice domains, or industries informing or supporting the general function of security. In addition, the fluid nature of a defined security science body of knowledge can be overcome. The acceptance of such a framework and its knowledge has to go through iterations, until international consensus can be demonstrated. Nevertheless, with the increasing tertiary offerings, and a greater research commitment, such consensus will be achieved.

SECURITY SCIENCE

Security science is an idea that brings together many concepts and principles—with some, in the future, becoming theories—into a developing and structured body of knowledge. Such convergence is the beginning of an academic discipline in the traditional sense. Nevertheless, security science is still in its formative years with a developing set of characteristics that will, in the future, make it a profession and an academic discipline.

It is important that security science develops a structured and defined body of knowledge, with a clear context or practice definition. A more simplistic view of security science—beyond the integrated knowledge framework—can be presented as a Venn diagram, which integrates the concepts of security management, the built environment and security principles, informed and directed by security risk management (Figure 1.4). Security management encompasses the human function of security, including tasks like management, business,

FIGURE 1.4 Primary concepts of security science.

finance, administration, awareness, and policy and procedures. The built environment includes the physical and technological environment we live, work, and play in. Principles are related security strategies, including allied academic theories appropriate in supporting the function of security. Such principles may include the functions of deter, detect, delay, respond, and recover to criminology offender studies. Finally, security risk management directs, informs, and, to some degree, quantifies the security mitigation strategies. Thus, such a model may provide some overview of the function of security science.

Nevertheless, we must always be aware that we are attempting to counter at the extreme, motivated attackers with the intent to use knowledge and resources to circumvent our mitigation strategies. In addition, being secured is a paradox as it is "measured by the absence of activities which would have negative effects on the corporation if they occurred" (Challinger, 2006, p. 587). When security controls are working, it appears as though nothing is happening, and to some degree there lies the paradox.

CONCLUSION

Security is diverse and multidimensional, leaving the ability to define and understand the concept of security open to debate. Nevertheless, security can be contextually defined, once the practice domain and its functions have been articulated. Many parts of the practice domains of security lack definition and are defuse, yet are distinct fields of practice and, to some degree, academic disciplines.

As a broad concept, security can be defined in many ways. One such method is the nature of security, where security can be considered as international systems, security of nation-states, security of groups, or the security of individuals (Rothschild, 1995). In addition, security has to be considered from an objective, subjective, and symbolic perspective. Such duality allows theories and ideas to more effectively consider all parts of security. For example, the security of the individual may use Maslow's hierarchy of human needs (1943), or the related but distinct concepts of security and safety, or, finally, the effect of risk. Risk has always been closely related to the concept of security, but it is only in recent times that the management of risk has played such a significant role in applied security.

Security of groups has to consider the underlying nature of law and the social contract, where law may be considered a foundation of society and security is an output, being a maintainer or enforcer. The security maintainer has, for over 100 years, been considered the function of public security (policing), although private security is becoming more relevant and both domains are converging. The security of nation-states and international arenas include military defense, which is one of the more traditional views of security. More recently, homeland security has been applied at the nation-state level, converging traditional security practice areas such as defense, public security, and private security.

The security industry requires, among other characteristics, a dedicated academic discipline to support its professional development. A dedicated academic discipline can validate and structure the growing body of knowledge through the scientific method, seeking cause and effect. Whether such research uses the scientific method or an engineering design approach, either will suit the diverse strategies applied in security and develop the discipline of security science.

Security science is an emerging academic discipline that brings together concepts into a structured body of knowledge. At its most simplistic, knowledge areas include security management, security theories and principles, the built environment, and security risk management. These concepts can be expanded into an integrated framework that also includes business continuity, security technology, physical and personnel security, and industrial security (see Figure 1.3). Thus, context provides many parts of security with clear understanding of its operating boundaries, from which further consensus in a body of knowledge can be achieved.

Further Reading

Button, M., 2008. Doing Security: Critical Reflections and an Agenda for Change. Palgrave Macmillian, Houndmills, Basingstoke, UK.

References

Ale, B., 2009. Risk: An Introduction—The Concepts of Risk. Sanger and Chance, Routledge, Abingdon.

Angus and Roberston, 1992. Dictionary and Thesaurus. HarperCollins Publishers, Sydney.

ASIS International, 2003. Proceedings of the 2003 Academic/Practitioner Symposium. University of Maryland, College Park, ASIS International.

ASIS International, 2009, July 29–31. 2009 Academic/Practitioner Symposium. Paper presented at the 2009 Academic/Practitioner Symposium, University of Maryland, College Park.

ASIS International, 2010. 2010 Academic/Practitioner Symposium. Paper presented at the 2010 Academic/ Practitioner Symposium Hilton Old Town, Alexandra, VA.

Baldwin, D.A., 1997. The concept of security. Review of International Studies 23 (1), 5–26.

Bradley, T., Sedgwick, C., 2009. Policing beyond the police: A "first cut" study of private security in New Zealand. Policing and Society 19 (4), 468–492.

Brooks, D.J., 2009. What is security: Definition through knowledge categorisation. Security Journal 23 (3), 229–239.

Brooks, D.J., 2012. Corporate security: Using knowledge construction to define a practising body of knowledge. Asian Journal of Criminology, http://dx.doi.org/10.1007/s11417-012-9135-1.

Buzan, B., Waever, O., de Wilde, J., 1998. Security: A New Framework for Analysis. Lynne Rienner, London.

Challinger, D., 2006. Corporate security: A cost or contributor to the bottom line? In: Gill, M. (Ed.), The Handbook of Security. Palgrave Macmillian Ltd, Basingstoke, UK, pp. 586–609.

Davidson, M.A., 2005. A matter of degrees. Security Management 49 (12), 72–99.

Fischer, R.J., Halibozek, E., Green, G., 2008. Introduction to Security, eighth ed. Butterworth-Heinemann, Boston.

Hemmens, C., Maahs, J., Scarborough, K.E., Collins, P.A., 2001. Watching the watchmen: State regulation of private security, 1983–1998. Security Journal 14 (4), 17–28.

Hesse, L., Smith, C.L., 2001. Core Curriculum in Security Science. Paper presented at the Proceedings of the 5th Australian Security Research Symposium, Perth, Western Australia.

Hettne, B., 2010. Development and Security: Origins and Future. Security Dialogue 41 (1), 31–52.

Huitt, W., 2004. Maslow's Hierarchy of Human Needs. Retrieved March 1, 2009, from http://chiron.valdosta.edu/whuitt/col/regsys/maslow.html.

Knote, M.E., 2004. Part 1: Introduction to assets protection. In: Williams, T.L. (Ed.), Protection of Assets Manual. POA Publishing, Los Angeles.

Kooi, B., Hinduja, S., 2008. Teaching security courses experientially. Journal of Criminal Justice Education 19 (2), 290–307.

Langston, C., Lauge-Kristensen, R., 2002. Strategic Management of Built Facilities. Butterworth-Heinemann, Boston.

Manunta, G., 1999. What is security? Security Journal 12 (3), 57–66.

Manunta, G., Manunta, R., 2006. Theorizing about security. In: Gill, M. (Ed.), The Handbook of Security. Palgrave Macmillan, New York, pp. 629–657.

Maslow, A.H., 1943. A theory on human motivation. Psychol Rev 50 (4), 370–396.

Peoples, C., Vaughan-Williams, N., 2010. Critical Security Studies: An Introduction. Routledge, Oxon.

Popper, K., 1963. Conjectures and Refutations: The Growth of Scientific Knowledge. Routledge, London.

Post, R.S., Kingsbury, A.A., 1991. Security Administration: An Introduction to the Protection Services, fourth ed. Butterworth-Heinemann, Boston.

Prenzler, T., Earle, K., Sarre, T., 2009. Private security in Australia: Trends and key characteristics. Trends and Issues in Crime and Criminology 374, 1–6.

Rothschild, E., 1995. What is security. Daedalus 124 (3), 53–98.

Sarre, R., Prenzler, T., 2011. Private Security and Public Interest: Exploring Private Security Trends and Directions for Reform in the New Era of Plural Policing. Australian Research Council, Caberra.

Stapley, C., Grillot, S., Sloan, S., 2006. The study of national security versus the study of corporate security: What can they learn from each other? In: Gill, M. (Ed.), The Handbook of Security. Palgrave Macmillian Ltd, Basingstoke, UK, pp. 45–65.

van Steden, R., Sarre, R., 2007. The growth of private security: Trends in the European Union. Security Journal 20 (4), 222–235.

Wakefield, A., 2007. The study and practice of security: Today and tomorrow. Security Journal 20, 13–14.

Wittgenstein, L., 1953/2001. Philosophical Investigations. Blackwell Publishing, Oxford.

Young, L.J., 2007. Criminal intelligence and research: An untapped nexus. The Journal of the Australian Institute of Professional Intelligence Officers 15 (1), 75–88.

Zedner, L., 2009. Security: Keys Ideas in Criminology. Routledge, London.

2

Security Management

OBJECTIVES

- Be able to critically discuss the management issues and benefits of security management planning.
- Understand systems theory for the design and implementation of security management plans.
- Outline and be able to apply within a security context the five management functions of plan, organize, staff, lead, and control.
- Critique the four underlying methodologies in the design and implementation of security management plans, being risk-based, quality assurance, governance, and strategic security management frameworks.
- Establish a broad understanding of the concept of resilience and how it may apply to organizational security.

- Integrate the functions of organizational security into a security management plan, including governance, metrics, performance, cost analysis, training and awareness, and succession planning.
- Recognize the features and formulate comprehensive security policies and procedures.
- Compare and contrast the 10 principles of organizational security.
- Examine why ethics is an important concept for security.
- Evaluate the concept of entropic decay, how it affects the security management plan, and how directed inputs can maintain the efficacy of security strategies.

INTRODUCTION

This chapter takes a systems approach to organizational security management. A system is considered to be an organized collection of components, elements, or functions that are integrated and operated at their optimum level, without disorganization or decay. The security management system needs to use people and resources to achieve and maintain the desired security and, primarily, an organization's outcomes.

Based on a systematic framework of controlled organizational security, effective security management may be achieved through appropriate inputs and deliverable outputs. These inputs include various security enablers such as strategic and tactical direction and alignment, leadership, governance, accountability, ethics, culture, sustainability, and resilience. Finally, outputs need to be clearly articulated inasmuch as what should be achieved from security management. These outputs include the protection of people, information, and assets, as well stakeholder assurance, maintained capability, legal and social compliance, and confidence in the organization so that isomorphic learning is achieved.

For organizational security to be on par and gain acceptance with an organization's decision-makers, the security manager must understand the organization's culture, clearly define the security role, and know when or when not to raise alarm bells. In today's competitive and ever-changing threat environment, there is a need for a more dynamic and proactive security management. Security management mitigates negative risks; puts in place response, control, and recovery plans should prevention measures fail; and does not overlook or jeopardize potential business opportunities. All of these factors and more can only be brought together through competent security management.

Where related functions, such as information communication and technology (ICT) security, preemployment screening, and fraud management, are performed beyond the control of organizational security, a strategic security management plan can afford significant value in aiding the development of a comprehensive understanding of overall program architecture. Such an increase in common understanding and language can aid communication across many functional boundaries, encourage cooperation among staff, close gaps caused by internal silos, and provide for more accurate development of security metrics to support the security business case (Buczynski, 2011, p. 1).

There is no single security management framework that can be used by all organizations and in all environments; rather, any framework should be adjusted to suit the contextual requirements of an organization based on their operating and strategic environment. In addition, security management plans are not explicit functions, but rather an overarching process that integrates the many and diverse security (and in some cases, nonsecurity) functions.

SECURITY MANAGEMENT ISSUES

The written literature on security management "tends to focus on the operational or micro-issues, rather than on strategic matters" (Buczynski, 2011, p. 13). But, security management is not just about policy and procedures, setting the shift roster, resolving an employee's problem, or submitting an annual budget. Such views effect the perception of security, where:

- Security is considered a cost center rather than a profit center.
- Security comes at a cost.
- Being reactive rather than preventative to events.
- Being negative (pessimistic) rather than business focused.
- Not having a direct line of reporting to the senior members of an organization.
- Security mitigation strategies applied in a piecemeal approach.

- Managing at the operational rather than strategic level.
- The security budget is the first to be reduced when the projects overruns.
- Being seen in the greater organization as "guards and guns."
- Limited literature, either text or standards, on strategic security management.
- Effective security leads to a reduction in the perceived need for security.

At the corporate level, security is often considered a cost center, rather than a profit center. Nevertheless, "good security is expensive, but bad security can be even more costly. The question is, what portion of security resources should companies spend on defending against threats, and what portion should they spend pursuing them?" (IBM, 2008, p. 24). Such questions are often difficult to define, unless effective security management is applied that is proactive and directed with a business language.

There is limited literature on how a security manager should design, implement, and manage a security management plan. Fay provides supporting concepts and theories that focus on the design of a security management plan comprising of components and other supporting elements (2006), yet this forms only a limited entry in what is a comprehensive text. Consistent with the majority of literature, most management plans focus on operational and process levels, such as physical security, preemployment screening and guarding operations. Robertson's (2006) work again highlighted the focus of many today, primarily delivering information based around operational outcomes rather than issues of strategic management concern.

Today, a security manager should be a business leader who champions the security cause for the greater benefit of an organization. Such an approach can only be achieved if the security manager presents a well-defined understanding of the threat with a cost-benefit mitigation strategy that will protect an organization's critical functions within a business language. Any other approach and the ability to be successful are greatly diminished.

A SYSTEMS APPROACH

Previous management theories, such as classical, behavioral, and management science, were limiting as they did not take a holistic view of an organization and its independencies. Classical theory took the approach that the best way to manage an organization was to focus on the jobs and structure. Thus, reducing the organization into isolated departments or groups leads to an understanding of how a department or team works, but not how they interrelate to the greater whole. Behavioral theory attempted to better manage people to be more productive. Whereas, management science theory used mathematics and later computers to aid with problems and, ultimately, decision-making (Lussier, 2009). As with classical and behavioral theories, similar issues apply in such a reductionist approach to the complex and contextual environment of an organization.

Systems theory focuses "on viewing the organization as a whole and as the interrelation of its parts" (Lussier, 2009, p. 42). An organization is a system that has inputs (resources) that are transformed through manufacture, production, or service into outputs (Figure 2.1), which are goods or services.

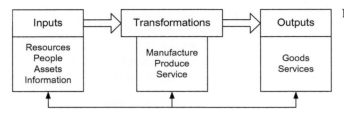

FIGURE 2.1   Systems theory approach.

General Systems Theory

Bertalanffy explains systems theory as "principles which apply to systems in general, whatever the nature of their component elements, or of the relations or forces between them" (1968, p. 139). In applying a system approach to physical security, Garcia (2001, p. 6) defines a system as an "integrated collection of components or elements designed to achieve an objective according to plan." Nevertheless, there are many different types of systems with a number of dichotomies, each considering a particular aspect of systems thinking. The most significant development in scientific method toward systems thinking has stemmed from the open versus closed dichotomy.

Closed systems are those considered isolated from their environment. For a closed system, whatever matter-energy is within that system is finite, and overtime that energy gradually becomes disordered and decays. Closed systems therefore emphasize the tendency toward equilibrium that attain a time-independent equilibrium state, with maximum entropy and minimum free energy (Bertalanffy, 1968).

In contrast, open systems are not isolated from their environment. Open systems consider a system's interaction with its environment as crucial to the adoption and evolution of complex systems. Open systems depend on their environment for resources and are constrained by its influence. For an open system, the ability to change in response to environmental pressures ensures the system's long-term viability. An open system may attain (certain conditions presumed) a stationary state where the system remains constant as a "whole," referred to as a steady-state condition.

Security management systems are open systems that attempt to maintain a steady state, but are affected by their internal and external environment. For example, if an organization's research and development group wins a contract to develop a new defense device, the decision to sign the contract will affect the financial, information technology, and security departments. If the marketing department wants to move into a new region, this decision will effect most other departments, and managers have to consider the greater organization in their decision-making. For security, systems theory can assist in developing a scientific approach to security management.

Benefits of a Systems Approach

The adoption of a systems approach to security management should provide the following:

- Simpler to define a common lexicon and understanding among stakeholders.
- Act as an aid to defining the security program architecture.

- Generate awareness of system design principles to establish senior management support.
- Provide the basis for conscious divergence from a common philosophy.
- Assist communication across traditional and functional boundaries.
- Promote the regard for security management through adoption of mature concepts.
- Provide flexibility within what might be regarded as an otherwise rigid framework.
- Reliability, maintainability, and the ability to be upgraded.
- Flexibility and resilience.
- Provide the basis for gap analysis with existing systems (adjusted from Buczynski, 2011, pp. 10–14).
- Support performance and effective resource allocation.
- Provide explicit senior management support.

An organization's management should concentrate on reducing risks, but also know that the risk level is consistent with the business. It is the security manager's role to ensure that security is effective, does not waste resources on security items, and uses current security systems to their full potential. The provision of sound security analysis and management proposals to the executive management allows the company to consider and approve a balanced security plan. Such balance promotes efficient spending to reduce 'under-' or 'over'investment in security management, and provide approved security to counter risks that can impact the company's reputation, intellectual and physical assets, and the ability to recover from a crisis (Cubbage and Brooks, 2012).

SECURITY MANAGEMENT

Management is a method to plan, organize, and control every aspect of an organization's strategy and operations to improve the way in which it does business. Organizations must identify the threats and risks they may face, and attempt to reduce these to meet the objectives of the organization by detecting vulnerabilities, whether these are people, processes, or technology. Therefore, a security management plan is an overall model or framework for developing comprehensive security programs that underpin the organization's approach to security (Talbot and Jakeman, 2008, p. 368).

A formal approach to security management can contribute directly to the business capability and credibility of an organization (International Organization for Standardization, 2007, p. vi). The development of a security management plan provides a formulated strategy that helps to gain and allocate organizational resources into a viable posture, based on its relative internal competencies and shortcomings, anticipated changes in the environment, and dynamic actions by intelligent opponents. Strategic plans determine the overall direction of an organization and its subsequent divisions, shaping the organization's goals and direction.

Management Functions

Any manager, whether they are a security manager or not, have to effectively apply five distinct functions for success: planning, organizing, staffing, leading, and controlling (Table 2.1; Lussier, 2009, pp. 11–12).

TABLE 2.1   Management Functions

Function	Descriptor
Plan	Setting objectives and defining in advance how these are to be met
Organize	Structure in delegating and coordinating tasks, and allocating resources
Staff	Selecting, training, and evaluating employees
Lead	Influencing staff and stakeholders
Control	Establish and implement metrics to ensure objectives are met

Planning is the a priori process of setting out a detailed scheme or method to attain an objective. In general, planning is the starting point in management that allows people to strive toward. Organizing is the process of designing and implanting plans into a structured whole, which requires delegation and the coordination of resources and people. Staffing is the selection, training, and evaluation of employees by an organization.

Leading is the ability of a manager to inspire, guide, or show others the way forward. These include internal staff within the security department, but also executives, directors, other departmental heads, and external stakeholders. Leading requires managers to influence and motivate employees in achieving planned goals, which requires appropriate interpersonal skills. Finally, controlling is the ability to command, rule, or direct employees. Such control is achieved through establishing and implementing metrics to measure and monitor achievement toward objectives, and when these objectives are not being achieved, take the necessary corrective action (Lussier, 2009).

A security manager will require a broad set of knowledge categories across the organizational security domain. Such broad corporate understanding of security has to ensure that they have technical and decision-making skills (Figure 2.2). Technical skills are not considered the ability to install and cable a CCTV system; rather, it is the technical understanding of how to gain efficacy from such technology. Likewise, decision-making skills are the transfer of specialized security knowledge into a business language that senior management can understand.

FIGURE 2.2   Security management skills.

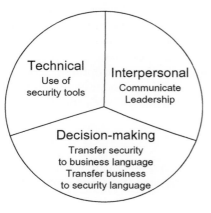

The functions of planning, organizing, staffing, leading, and controlling assist security management in understanding what they need to do. Furthermore, the ability to have technical, interpersonal, and decision-making skills aids a security manager in how he or she may progress his or her personal development strategies. Nevertheless, neither the functions nor skill of management removes the need for a strategic management framework or planning.

Security Planning

A critical component of security management is the planning phase for the protection of an organization's assets. The purpose of planning is to prepare for future events and their management that may impact the organization's operations. Planning can be conducted at several levels and can be classified as:

1. *Strategic planning:* Developed by senior management for broad and long-term goals.
2. *Tactical planning:* Developed by middle management for specific objectives, usually developed within set timeframes.
3. *Operational planning:* The success of strategic and tactical plans is reliant on operational planning. Operational planning is concerned with the immediate functioning of the organization.

The planning process commences with an analysis of the relevant security requirements in terms of its mission. From the mission statement, the goals need to be set that are challenging, attainable, specific, measurable, relevant, and timely. The aim of setting goals is to develop an end-state that is beneficial for the organization.

To achieve the goals of the organization, the security manager needs to develop processes to operationalize and achieve the established security goals of the entity. This decision-making process can be described as:

- Identify the problem.
- Generate alternative solutions.
- Evaluate and choose among the possible solutions.
- Implement and monitor the chosen solution.

Plan implementation is an important phase of the security planning process. Effective implementation will require attention to the following four areas:

1. Acquisition and deployment of organizational security resources.
2. Development of an appropriate organizational security structure.
3. Establishment of appropriate organizational security systems.
4. Development of a strategic supportive culture.

The implementation of the security management plan, according to the achievement of the established goals, needs to be evaluated to assess its effectiveness. That is, does the implemented plan contribute toward the achievement of the acknowledged goal? Thus, the evaluation and monitoring of the plan will be a continual process, with the effectiveness of the security plan of importance to the organization. If the effectiveness of the plan is lacking, then the planning cycle should commence again with missions, goal setting, and implementation. For security to be effective, the security planning for the organization must be thorough and will be achieved by a well-structured process or framework to deliver strong outcomes for the organization.

STRATEGIC SECURITY MANAGEMENT FRAMEWORKS

The complexity of the security management plan will depend on organizational expectations and requirements. The management plan provides a structured framework that integrates the many functions and practicing areas of organizational security, although in more simplistic plans these may not be inclusive. Each plan or part of a plan is to some degree modular, where a framework should be built to best suit an organization and its operating and strategic environment.

If the management functions of planning, organizing, staffing, leading, and controlling are considered again, the organizational type, size, location, and culture all play some part in the final acceptance of a successful security management plan. For example, with planning, a large organization will more readily accept a comprehensive and formal written plan, whereas a smaller or entrepreneurial organization are generally informal and may only require a one-page plan. A larger organization tends to have three levels of management and formal policy and procedures, whereas a smaller organization has an less formal structure and limited policy and procedures (Lussier, 2009, p. 19). When controlling, a larger organization will have a single and computerized reporting system, whereas a small organization will tend to focus on direct management observations with a wider span of hands-on control.

Security management plans do not provide a how-to approach to security management; rather, they set out a clear framework that informs the security department, senior management, and others within and outside the organization on the approach of corporate security. The how-to elements are embedded into the various parts of the security plan at the operating or practicing level. For example, policy provides intent for the executive managers and procedures inform guards on what they need to do.

Security management plans can be categorized into four discrete types, based on their underlying methodology as shown in Table 2.2.

TABLE 2.2   Security Management Frameworks

Framework	Methodology
Risk-based	Use of risk management as the informer and driver
Quality assurance	Plan, do, check, and act
Governance	Advisory boards or teams
Strategic security management	Use of knowledge categories or practice domains

Risk-based Framework

The risk-based framework (Figure 2.3), as the name suggests, takes a risk approach to the security management methodology. Risk management is the primary input and drives all mitigation strategies, resulting in risk-informed outputs.

The risk-based plan commences with the strategy and planning stage, articulating the context and legislative platforms. Rationale is the reason for the plan, considering the strategic and operational contexts and legal requirements. Stakeholders list the internal and external stakeholders, always a useful task in any risk management function. Risk management defines the proposed security framework and other aspects, such as appetite and evaluation process. Finally, planning defines timelines, roles and responsibilities, and other project management tasks. the risk management stage follows a security risk management process (see Chapter 3).

The design and enable stage applies the past input stages and transforms these stages to propose risk mitigation strategies. Strategies are aligned with security practice areas or outputs, including physical security, procedural security, personnel security, and process control, that attempt to detect, delay, respond, and provide resilience. Finally, the implementation and review stage is the procurement and application stage, where selected strategies are implemented, tested, and have ongoing maintenance applied.

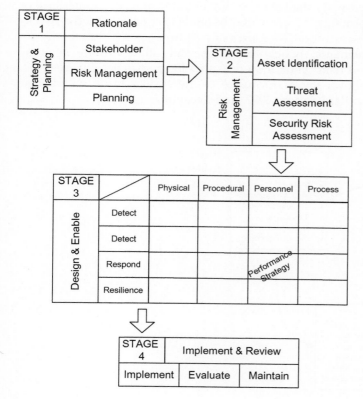

FIGURE 2.3 Risk-based security management framework.

Quality Assurance Framework

A quality assurance methodology applies a process approach to security management, based in part on ISO 9001:2000. Such an approach allows an organization to use their existing management system as a foundation for security management, along with other business functions. The underlying approach is the method known as plan, do, check, and act, which incorporates into the quality assurance framework (Figure 2.4).

Security planning (plan stage) establishes and authorizes the overall security management policy, as well as the security management objectives and a commitment to continual improvement. Risk management is carried out, using security risk management. Security targets are identified and documented to align with the security objectives, which are appropriate and measurable.

Implementation and operation (do stage) provides a project management approach, which details structure, expected timelines, roles, responsibilities, and authorities. A senior staff member is assigned responsibility for the overall security management system, where available resources are provided. Communication of the plan should be considered, so that relevant internal employees, contractors, and stakeholders are aware of the plan (International Organization for Standardization, 2007). Documentation should include the scope of the plan, each part of the plan, and formal document control and recordkeeping. Finally, operational control considers the more significant risk mitigation or security strategies.

Checking and reporting (check stage) establishes, maintains, and reports the measure of security management system performance. Measure may be qualitative or quantitative, whatever is most appropriate for the organization. Measures of performance should identify security-related decay, failures, incidents, nonconformance, and other factors, such as changing environmental threats and risks. Thus, system evaluation allows periodic reviews, red-teaming, and learning that allows the performance of the system to be maintained (International Organization for Standardization, 2007) and decay managed.

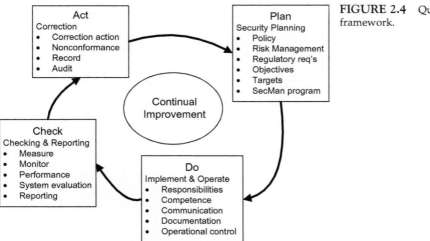

FIGURE 2.4   Quality assurance framework.

Correction (act stage) is informed by the check stage, where nonperformance needs to be addressed and corrective action taken to rectify the problem. Records need to be kept to show what and why a certain decision was made. Finally, an audit on a periodic basis, incident-instigated basis, or when there are changing organizational aspects allows the efficacy of the security management plan to be maintained.

Governance Framework

The governance framework provides a mechanism for senior management, as well as those at the operational level, to have a clear understanding and oversight of each other's expectations, objectives, performance, risk appetite, and reporting requirements. In addition, that these aspects are effectively communicated to relevant persons in the organization. Thus, the governance framework is a "guidance system composed of standard management practices within the governance framework designed to suit the organization" (Talbot and Jakeman, 2008, p. 63). The corporate governance framework sets objectives, policies, values, culture, accountabilities, and performance. Risk management and security risk management are integral components of effective corporate governance.

The security management plan that takes a governance approach (Figure 2.5) should align itself with the corporate governance process. At the most senior level, the security plan should

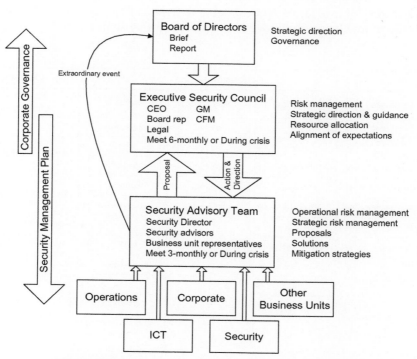

FIGURE 2.5 Governance security management framework.

report to the board level on a regular basis. For extraordinary items, there should be a process where the executive security council can gain reporting access to the board.

The executive security council is made up of senior executives and a representative from the board. The council's focus is to receive proposals from the security advisory team and provide strategic direction back down to management and also upwards to the board. Their considerations include aspects such as corporate policy, risk management, standards, business opportunities, operational and strategic alignment, and legislative obligations.

The security advisory team is the security management plan's working group environment, made up of senior security executives representing each business unit or working group. The senior security manager should chair this group. The advisory team's focus is to receive operational information from the various business units, and provide proposals and solutions, reporting these to the executive security council. On direction from the council, they propagate advice to the various business units.

Strategic Security Management Framework

The strategic security management framework (Figure 2.6) incorporates the many practicing or knowledge categories of organizational security integrated into a system. The methodology focuses on the interrelationship between the different functions and departments within an organization.

Inputs are the business enablers such as leadership, strategic knowledge, management, and understanding of legislative requirements to business accruement. In general, these requirements are more business management focused, rather than a security specialization. As

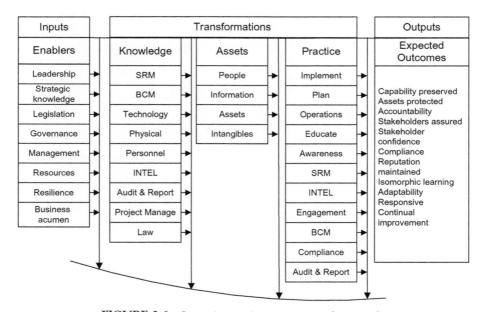

Inputs	Transformations			Outputs
Enablers	Knowledge	Assets	Practice	Expected Outcomes
Leadership	SRM	People	Implement	Capability preserved Assets protected Accountability Stakeholders assured Stakeholder confidence Compliance Reputation maintained Isomorphic learning Adaptability Responsive Continual improvement
Strategic knowledge	BCM	Information	Plan	
Legislation	Technology	Assets	Operations	
Governance	Physical	Intangibles	Educate	
Management	Personnel		Awareness	
Resources	INTEL		SRM	
Resilience	Audit & Report		INTEL	
Business acumen	Project Manage		Engagement	
	Law		BCM	
			Compliance	
			Audit & Report	

FIGURE 2.6   Strategic security management framework.

Dalton (1995) suggests, a security manager is first and foremost a business manager, and second a security manager.

Transformation comprises of specialized security knowledge, corporate assets, and security activities. Specialized security knowledge was discussed in Chapter 1 and will not be discussed further, except to highlight the additional skills and knowledge such as auditing and project management. Corporate assets comprise of people, information, physical assets, and intangible assets such as reputation and partnerships. Finally, security activities include such processes as planning, implementation, education, and awareness. Engagement should include both internal and external stakeholders, such as other departments and contractors.

The strategic framework outputs are expected outcomes or output principles of organizational security. To some degree, these outputs are similar to the ISO 31000:2009 risk management principles (see Chapter 3); nevertheless, in the strategic framework some form of benchmarking or measurement needs to be designed, implemented, and reported.

ORGANIZATIONAL RESILIENCE

Organizations are using greater resources to raise levels of governance and security protocols, under the term *resilience*. Nevertheless, organizational resilience is vague, and the concept implies multidisciplined and diverse strategies, requiring a diversity of skills and knowledge that reaches beyond either security or governance. The resilience domain is still developing; however, initial embodiments of organizational resilience originate from both the United Kingdom rebranding business continuity management, and the United States rebranding security management (Braes and Brooks, 2011).

Resilience

The term *resilience* has been used with increasing popularity across many disciplines including health, medicine, information management, and economics. For example, in the field of psychology, resilience is a well-researched phenomenon with such understanding that *resiliency* and *resilience* are two different concepts. Resiliency relates to a personality characteristic and resilience refers to a dynamic developmental process (Luthar et al., 2000).

Resilience is a common capacity possessed by individuals, groups, or communities that allow them to prevent, minimize, or prevail in the face of adversity. Resilience is often developed in expectation of foreseeable hardship. In the past, major disasters that occurred in one nation-state had minimal effects on other distant nations. Today, organizations may transcend the globe and function across multiple nations-states.

Resilience capacity is a multidisciplinary quality that allows an organization to successfully withstand, respond to, and potentially capitalize on disrupting events (Hamel and Valikangas, 2003). Resilience provides an underpinning of insight, adaptability, and robustness that enables an organization to bounce back and create new ways to thrive when faced with uncertainty and adversity within its environment. Such capacity is embodied in organizational routines and processes that an organization continually prepares itself, to act decisively and move forward, and establishes a culture of diversity and adjustable integration that empowers it to overcome the potentially incapacitating consequences of a disruptive shock (Lengnick-Hall and Beck, 2005).

Organizational Resilience

Organizational resilience can be considered a philosophy, achieved by a number of functional processes (Figure 2.7) rather than a "management system." Resilience within an organization is multifaceted and heterogeneous, both a top-down culture (value, leadership, accountability, flexibility) and bottom-up functions, delivered by a number of processes such as management, governance, risk management, security management, situational awareness, and business continuity (Braes and Brooks, 2011).

FIGURE 2.7 Organizational resilience framework.

Organizational Resilience Planning

The planning process needs to consider a number of aspects, and like a security management plan, the extent and complexity of the resilience plan will depend on the expectation and type of organization. Nevertheless, there are indicators (Stephenson et al., 2010, pp. 35–37) that allow an organization to assess its level of resilience within a planning and adaptive capacity (Table 2.3).

According to Stephenson, et al. (2010, p. 35), *planning indicators* are defined by a number of planned activities. Planning strategies are the identification and evaluation of organizational plans that are designed to identify, analyze, and manage vulnerabilities in the business environment. Participation in exercises considers the degree by which organizational members are involved in simulations or scenarios designed to enable the organization to rehearse plans that would be instituted during a crisis response. Proactive posture is the ability of an organization to respond to the unexpected and to use "near misses" as triggers for evaluation, rather than confirmation of success. Capability and capacity of external resources is the ability to manage and mobilize external resources as part of an interdependent network. Finally, with planning indicators, recovery priorities is the organization's awareness of what their

TABLE 2.3 Organizational Resilience Indicators

Planning	Adaption
Planning strategies	Free from silo mentality
Participation in exercise	Capability of internal resources
Proactive posture	Staff engagement and involvement
Capability of external resources	Information and knowledge
Recovery priorities	Leadership, management, and governance structures
	Innovation and creativity
	Devolved and responsive decision-making
	Internal and external situation monitoring and reporting

priorities would be following a crisis and its minimum operating requirements, defined at the critical organizational level.

Adaptive indicators are a capability defined by a number of organizational factors. To be free from silo mentality requires an organization that attempts to eliminate cultural and behavioral barriers that can be divisive within and between departments, which manifest as communication barriers creating disjointed, disconnected, and detrimental ways of working. Capability and capacity of internal resources is the ability to manage and mobilize an organization's physical, human, and other resources to address the operating environment. Staff engagement considers the degree at which employees are responsible, accountable, and occupied with developing the organization's resilience through their work, and that they understand the links between the organization's resilience and its long-term success.

The sharing of information and knowledge through the organization ensures that decision-makers or those managing uncertainty have as much useful information as possible. Leadership, management, and governance structures balance the needs of internal and external stakeholders and business priorities, which would be able to provide appropriate decision-making during crisis. Innovation and creativity are consistently encouraged and rewarded, where the generation and evaluation of new ideas is recognized as key to the organizations future performance. Devolved and responsive decision-making, formal or informal, is where employees have the authority to make work decisions and where, when higher authority is required, this authority can be obtained quickly and without excessive bureaucracy. Finally, there needs to be internal and external situational monitoring and reporting of human and environmental sensors to continuously identify and characterize the organization's internal and external environment, and proactively report (Stephenson, et al., 2010, pp. 36–37).

Building Resilience

Resilience is as much a philosophy as it is a function; therefore, to build a resilient organization requires the desire to be resilient at the highest level (Critical Infrastructure

Resilience Branch, 2008). Key action that an organization's executive can take to develop and maintain a resilient organization includes:

- Identify a direct line of responsibility for driving resilience.
- Treat the risk-based functions (risk management, governance, business continuity, security management) as senior management tasks.
- Integrate risk and business components.
- Remove silos between operating areas and functions.
- Invest in building existing functions, such as risk management, governance, business continuity, strategic planning, and security management.
- Develop outcomes based and align key performance indicators around resilience.
- Integrate a management approach in strategy and express that to internal and external stakeholders (Critical Infrastructure Resilience Branch, 2008).
- Devolvement of decision-making in a crisis.
- Tailor the process to your organization and its expectations.

SECURITY MANAGEMENT FUNCTIONS

An effective security manager is first a business manager, then a security manager. Therefore, to ensure that the management functions of planning, organizing, staffing, leading, and controlling are achieved, a number of functions are necessary. These functions include security governance, implementation of controls, metrics and performance management, security risk management, succession planning, education and training, applying cost-benefit analysis, and setting budgets.

A security manager needs to develop security governance within the corporate governance process, and to support this need, develop and implement controls using metrics and performance management. Furthermore, a security manager needs to develop and maintain a strong relationship with the human resources department, and have a robust and corporate wide security risk management process. The department should ensure that each core security role has a successor, security staff has the opportunity for education and training, and finally, that a cost-benefit analysis for security strategies is applied and that these strategies are budgeted and presented in a business format.

Security Governance

Governance is a framework of rules and practices used by an organization to ensure accountability, fairness, and transparency among an organization's stakeholders. Organizational stakeholders may consist of the board, executives, management, employees, financiers, customers, government, and the community. The corporate governance framework consists of explicit and implicit agreements between the organization and stakeholders, for distribution of responsibilities, rights, and rewards. Thus, the framework provides procedures for reconciling the sometimes conflicting interests of stakeholders in accordance with their duties, privileges, and roles, with procedures for proper supervision, control, and information flow.

Controls

Whatever security management plan, security governance system, or other systems are put into place, there needs to be a priori developed, defined, and measurable controls. Controls and their measurement are perhaps the most difficult processes to achieve in security management. It is often suggested that success in security leads to a reduction in the perceived need of security and, therefore, resources. Thus, without such measurable controls, there is little to counter such resource reductions.

Security professionals and some security management plans tend to discuss controls as if they were only physical security strategies. However, controls are as much about developing, defining, measuring, and adjusting the performance of the whole system, using people, processes, and physical and technological elements.

There are defined steps in the control system process, which commence with setting objectives and standards followed by measuring performance, that are compared against the predefined standards from which corrective or reinforcement can take place (Figure 2.8).

Objectives and standards is the commencing point, which needs to measure performance in the areas of quantity, quality, time, costs, and behavior:

- Quantity considers the metric output of people, processes, or functions; for example, the number of words a secretary types or the number of classes a teacher teaches.
- Quality considers how well a job or task has been performed. For example, for a secretary the number of typed errors, or for a teacher the level of student evaluation. Quality is perhaps the most difficult to establish and the most subjective, but can be the most insightful and relevant for security.
- Time considers how quick a task was completed or whether it met a deadline; for example, the number of words per minute a secretary types or the time period a teacher takes to return assessments.
- Cost considers the monetary value of completing a task. For example, how much does it cost for a secretary to type x number of words, or for a teacher, the funding provided per student.

FIGURE 2.8   Setting controls within security management.

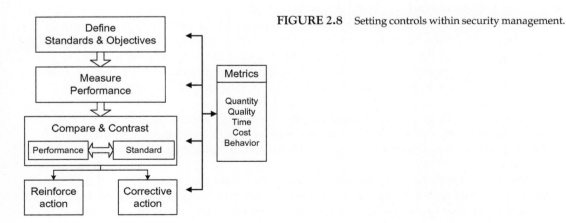

- Behavior considers what employees should or should not do? For example, a secretary may be required to answer a telephone call with a specific response, or a teacher's relationships with students (Lussier, 2009, pp. 452–453).

Following the a priori development of standards, measuring performance needs to be achieved. Considerations include how often you measure performance and what methods are used. Once performance is measured, these data have to be compared with the predefined standards. Comparison highlights achievement and failures, which allows corrective or reinforcement action to take place during the transformation process.

Security Metrics and Performance Management

Metrics, as defined by controls, allows a systems performance to be measured. Nevertheless, measuring security is perhaps one of the most difficult management functions to achieve, in part, due to its very nature and subjectivity. The ability to measure more traditional elements, for example loss prevention, is valid, but in the corporate environment security has to be more strategic. Therefore, subjective processes such as security risk management, business continuity, value of security, and reputation have to be measured in some meaningful way.

Metrics should be contextually specific to allow decision-makers to understand and take action. Thus, a metric should be a consistent measurement, cheap to extract, and expressed in a quantitative format and in at least one unit of measure (Jaquith, 2007, p. 22). One method is to consider parts of the security management plan, for example, the physical security components (Figure 2.9).

Using the control standards of quantity, quality, time, costs, and behavior, security metrics can be developed and measured:

- Quantity (quantitative and metric) considers the metric output of people, processes, or functions. For example, what was the recovered value in monetary terms achieved by the internal investigations team in a month? How often was the security risk management threat assessment reviewed?
- Quality (subjective and qualitative) considers how well a task has been performed. For example, is the threat assessment meeting the needs of the security advisory team?
- Time (quantitative and metric) considers how quickly a task was completed or whether it met a deadline. For example, was the threat assessment completed within the prescribed man-hours period or was the assessment completed by the project goal date? What was the downtime of the CCTV system, from first reporting to fully operational?
- Cost (quantitative and metric) considers the monetary value of completing a task. For example, was the contracted maintenance of security technology in budget? How many man-hours did the threat assessment take at x cost per person and was it in budget?
- Behavior (quantitative and qualitative) considers what employees should do. Did the security guards respond and take the prescribed action when responding to a call? Did the security manager or supervisor take effective control in managing an evacuation?

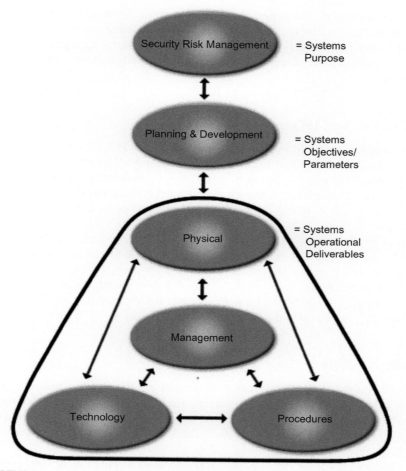

FIGURE 2.9 Physical security management system. (*Adjusted from Coole and Brooks, 2011.*)

Security Risk Management

Security risk management is a core knowledge category of the security function. Such a function should provide the organization with articulated and consensual threats and risks that inform and direct the security effort. In some organizations, the security manager can become the risk driver for the greater organization. Such an approach certainly elevates the security manager from his or her perceived function of "guards and guns."

Succession Planning

The importance of succession planning should come with the realization that progressive employees will not remain indefinitely within a position due to promotion, seeking greater challenges, or leaving an organization. Core positions that are crucial for security functions because of skill, seniority, and experience required could be hard to replace. Therefore, succession planning needs to be carried out, which allows security staff to see that there is progression and a career in security. Security management must put in place a succession plan, which may include personal development, training, education, temporary assignments, and special projects.

Security Training and Education

Security managers are realizing that directed education and training programs are needed to elevate the recognition of security professionals among senior management. Tertiary security education has just begun to be more commonly available, although some are little more than rebadged criminology, social justice, or political science courses (Brooks, 2012). Nevertheless, such tertiary education is better than nothing and does add a broader view to the security function.

Specific security science programs add considerably more training for a security professional, from which a business or management master's degree can follow. Training has, in general, been relatively well catered for in a silo approach, where courses are offered for guarding, alarm installation, CCTV, and lock-smithing, but such vocational education should be seen as a steppingstone of staff development. Unfortunately, many organizations see vocational training as education, which is far from the case.

Cost-Benefit Analysis

Cost-benefit analysis (CBA) involves a systematic evaluation of a proposal's impact with emphasis on valuing the gains and losses in monetary terms (Australian Government, 2007). CBA sums the monetary value of benefits and the costs for a business proposal to determine its feasibility. If the absolute value is positive, then the proposal would provide a benefit that exceeds its cost.

The CBA process involves three steps: (1) identify all direct and indirect consequences of the expenditure; (2) assign monetary value to all costs and benefits resulting from the expenditure; and (3) discount expected future costs and revenues accruing from the expenditure to express those costs and revenues in current monetary values (ASIS International, 2009b, p. C-41). Calculating CBA is not always straightforward, with subjectivity in summing intangible components. It could also be more difficult to calculate benefits of a security system in a monentary value compared to calculating the costs involved to install and operate the same security system. Security benefits are uncertain or at least extremely hard to quantify (Joint Transort Research Centre, 2009, p. 5).

The cost of a security failure can be calculated using two components:

- Primary cost consists of the price of the lost asset. Where goods for resale are involved their purchase price is used, as potential profits are dealt with later.
- Secondary costs are those costs that are associated with the loss of the asset, including potential profit and the cost of temporary replacement. Secondary costs are frequently greater than primary costs. Secondary costs also come into play if the offender is caught

and will include such things as investigation, prosecution, and staff costs. If the offender is a staff member, there will be costs to recruit and train new staff.

The cost of a security failure is the combined cost of the primary and secondary costs. This cost is rarely less than 10 times the primary cost, and with high value capital equipment, may be as much as 20 times. To ensure this calculation considers all costs, the following equation can be used:

$$C = [Cp + Ct + Cr + Ci] - [I - Ip]$$

where:

C = total cost
Cp = cost of permanent replacement of asset
Ct = cost of temporary substitute of asset
Cr = total related costs
Ci = total lost income caused by disruption
I = insurance
Ip = insurance premium

For security to provide cost-effective strategies, security costs in general should be less than the combined primary and secondary costs, including all overheads such as plant, utility costs (apportioned to departments), staff, and hardware costs.

Budget

The security budget process involves planning, preparation, authorization, execution, and, as a control, auditing. A budget is "funds allocated to operate a unit for a fixed period of time" (Lussier, 2009, p. 145). It should be noted that a budget is not always in monetary terms; rather, it is the planned allocation of resources against specific activities. Most often, security management will have to support their expenditure requests with persuasive discussion and documentation due to "power and politics" (Lussier, 2009, p. 459), a skill that the security manager will have to gain to be successful.

SECURITY MANAGEMENT POLICIES AND PROCEDURES

Policy and procedures are an important part of security management. A policy is a formal record on the organizations overall intentions and directions expressed by the board and executive management, whereas a procedure is a specified method of carrying out an activity (ASIS International, 2009c, pp. 47–48). Recognition of the difference between procedures and policy is important.

The responsibility for the policy formulation lies with senior management. The policy is more likely to be heeded if it is seen to be formulated at the highest corporate level. For example, many government policies have in their first pages an address from the relevant government minister or senior public servant to the effect that the policy has the absolute support of the government. The policy will require constant review to ensure that it retains the support of management, is appropriate to the changing needs of the organization, and is complementary to achieving corporate objectives. Any policy that impedes the achievement of corporate objectives will not receive or retain the support of management.

Policy has the following functions within an organization:

- Defines the activities of the organization.
- Guides and educates management and staff to senior management's requirements.
- Has a designated owner and point of contact.
- Assists in formulating decisions within guidelines endorsed by senior management.
- Is documented, implemented, and maintained.
- Endorsed by senior management.
- Provides a basis for developing procedures.

Procedures have the following functions:

- To provide consistency and ensure the standards set by the policy are met.
- Establish best practice and ensure quality assurance is attained and maintained.
- Save time by alleviating the need for each individual to decide a course of action for daily events and encourage management by exception.
- Is documented, implemented, and maintained.
- May provide a defense if duty of care needs to be established.

Types of Procedures

Security procedures can be grouped according to whether they are routine, nonroutine, or a rule.

Routine security procedures include orders, instructions, or standard operating procedures (SOPs) for security and other employees. Examples of specific subjects that could be addressed are:

- General duties of security personnel, for example, access control, key issue, patrols, lost-and-found property, and processing visitors.
- Processing of security incidents, for example, trespass, theft, vandalism, suspect item, sabotage, and assault of personnel.
- Arrest procedures and search procedures.
- Use of firearms and other security equipment.
- Correct handling of information, for example, classified or sensitive information.
- Requests from the media.
- Medical emergency procedures.

Nonroutine security procedures, in general, include procedures within a business contingency management (BCM) process. These are procedures that have a rare or unusual occurrence. Examples of specific subjects that could be addressed are:

- Building evacuation plans, for example, fire, bomb threat, and industrial accidents.
- Establishment and duties of an emergency control team (ECT), for example, call-out lists, roles and responsibilities, and duties.

- Bomb threat strategy.
- Industrial accident.
- Mutual aid program.
- Civil disturbances, for example, riot, demonstrations, picketing, and other industrial actions.

Rules are procedures that state exactly what should or should not be done, which relate to safety, environmental, or industrial issues. For example, no smoking, the wearing of personal safety clothing, and stopping at red lights are rules. Violation of rules should subject a person, either employee or visitor, to serious penalties, depending on the offense and frequency of breach.

Features of a Strong Policy and Procedures

The features of a strong policy and procedures include aspects such as staff involvement, conformity to legislative and regulative requirements, following social values and norms, being comprehensive, well written and structured guidelines, and, finally, educating and raising the awareness of security. Therefore, strong security policy and procedures should be developed with the following considerations:

- *Staff involvement in formulation:* The involvement of staff is effective management practice and accords with the principles of industrial democracy. Staff is more likely to comply with a policy that they have assisted in formulating, as opposed to a policy that has been imposed.
- *Conform to the law:* An essential part of any policy. For example, the decree to place padlocks on any unused access points on a building would be contrary to fire regulations if those access points included fire exits.
- *Conforms to social values:* Policy should align to social norms and expectations. For example, apprehension of a trespasser and the subsequent body search by a security officer would, under most circumstances, be an appropriate action. However, such a search, if conducted by a male security officer and the trespasser is female, is socially unacceptable.
- *Comprehensive:* Ensure that where possible, the policy covers all foreseeable situations.
- *Organized, properly written, and presented guidelines:* Such presentation will command respect and greater acceptance.
- *Wide, but qualified dissemination:* Once the policy has been formulated, approved, and published, it must not be locked away in the security manager's safe. While there will be some sections of the policy that should not be made general knowledge, the document must be released on a "need-to-know" basis.
- *Regular review:* A policy treated as a one-off exercise will gradually become outdated and deficient, unable to present effective management decisions to combat recurrent security problems.
- *Reinforce a cultural approach:* Strong security policy emphasizes that security is the responsibility of all staff.

SECURITY PRINCIPLES

Security management can be considered to have 10 core principles:

1. *Informed:* Security must have current data, information, and intelligence on which to base its actions.
2. *Directed:* Security must have clear direction as to what is required of it.
3. *Independent:* Security must be independent of the line management hierarchy to ensure its independence.
4. *Cooperative:* Security must have the cooperation of other internal and external agencies. These agencies include police, fire, and ambulance services. Cooperation must be obtained for all security operations and coordination must be achieved with neighboring businesses.
5. *Monitored:* Security systems and staff must be monitored to ensure they are providing the level of service an organization requires.
6. *Consistent:* Security operations must be consistent in time, space, and application to all staff.
7. *Unpredictable:* When, how, and where security operations will be conducted must be random. Predictability reduces the effectiveness of security operations.
8. *Concentrated:* Concentration of security increases effectiveness, but must be offset against cost and acceptability of this option.
9. *Appreciated:* Security initiatives must be impressed upon all staff to ensure their significance is embraced. Security operations must be subject to the same management by objectives as other management functions.
10. *Acceptable:* Security must be financially, socially, and ethically acceptable.

The security function should be managed in-line with these 10 core security principles.

SECURITY ETHICS

Business ethics are the standards of conduct and judgment in respect to right and wrong perception (Fay, 2007, p. 9) that lead to behavior. The quality of professional security depends on following strong moral standards in all professional relationships and providing a degree of leadership on ethical behavior. Nevertheless, what constitutes ethical business behavior in one nation-state may differ in another. It is important for international or regional corporations to have clear procedures to support and reinforce ethical behavior.

Awareness of the quality of professional security activity ultimately depends on the willingness of practitioners to observe appropriate standards of conduct and to manifest strong faith in professional relationships. The ASIS International adopted a code of ethics for its security practitioners that states that a member shall:

- Perform professional duties in accordance with the law and the highest moral principles.
- Observe the precepts of truthfulness, honesty, and integrity.
- Be competent, faithful, and diligent in discharging professional responsibilities.

- Safeguard confidential information and exercise due care to prevent its improper disclosure.
- Not maliciously injure the professional reputation or practice of colleagues, clients, or employers (ASIS International, 2009a).

Ethical behavior is worthwhile, with a positive relationship between ethical behavior and effective leadership (Lussier, 2009, p. 67). The ASIS code of ethics can be adopted by any security department as their benchmark to develop and maintain their own code. As Lussier states, "honesty is the best policy and some executives are building truth-telling cultures, as ethics impacts the bottom line" (2009, p. 67).

SECURITY DECAY

Entropic *security decay* is the gradual degradation of security mitigation strategies within the greater security management system, due to internal or external factors (Coole and Brooks, 2011). As Underwood states, "the provision of effective security is paradoxically the first step towards decay, as an effective system will not only repel successful attacks, but also prevent the attacks being made. ... An illusion is then created that the established security is unnecessary suggesting decay will follow until the degree of security falls to the point where an attack will succeed" (1984, pp. 249–250).

Early literature on the concept of security decay suggested that the cause was the attitude of apathy, which led to poor compliance to security procedures (McClure, 1997). Nevertheless, decay is a far broader concept, and has to encompass the whole security system and its interrelated elements. In addition, external factors such as the environment and dynamic threats also affect the security system. Each of these internal and external elements is prone to some degree of decay. For example, if:

- The operator receives many false alarms, therefore, he or she will be unlikely to validate the actual alarm event as he or she does not trust the system.
- A detector fails, physical delay is significantly reduced or eliminated.
- An attacker gains access to firearms, the ability to counter-respond by the guard force is significantly reduced.
- If an event occurs, resources are directed toward that latest breach, which takes the focus from other parts of the security system.

After an attack, the immediate reaction is often to increase the established security resources. However, this reaction is not usually necessary, as all that may be required is the reestablishment of the designed or commissioned level of protection. Security becomes reactive, rather than proactive. Thus, resources are used ineffectively to provide ad-hoc or a piecemeal approach to security mitigation.

Security management is operated within a system and any system is prone to entropic decay. Thus, entropic decay can be defined as a measure of disorder in a system and a process characterized with disintegration, running down, and becoming disordered (Bohm and Peat, 2000, p. 137; Herman, 1999, p. 86). Within a system, as entropy increases capability decreases, as systems rely on order and cohesion.

When you first start pushing a child on a swing, it takes greater effort (energy) to get the child swinging high. From that point on, you only need to give the child a slight push to keep him or her swinging high. If you stop pushing the child, the swinging motion decays and the child comes to a stop. Security systems are no different; to identify, design, and implement a security mitigation strategy takes a significant amount of resources (energy). If left on its own, the system will decay; however, to keep the security strategy operating at its maximum efficacy requires only a minimal input of resources.

If security is not effectively managed as a system—that is, provided the appropriate feedback—the system will decay. Entropic security decay is concerned with managing the natural entropic processes or pressures occurring against commissioned levels of effectiveness within the complex security management interrelationships. To effectively manage a security system requires the design, application, and management of security consistent with a security systems approach. Inputs need to be constant, either maintaining the system or aligning the system to the assessed threat (Coole and Brooks, 2011).

CONCLUSION

The security management plan provides a framework that incorporates all other functions of organizational security. The management plan organizes, staffs, leads, and controls corporate security, informing both internal security staff and external stakeholders such as the board, executives, and other managers of the security methodology. Security management plans are not explicit functions or "how-to" instructions; rather, they are an overarching process that integrates the many and diverse functions of security.

Security management takes a systems approach, which provides defined inputs, transformation in various security functions, and measurable outputs or deliverables. Inputs include tactical and strategic direction, leadership, governance, accountability, ethics, culture, and resilience. Transformations are the many functions of security, such as risk management, business continuity, personnel, physical, and technology security. In addition, functions should also include more general business and management functions, such as finance, budgeting, and performance management, to name a few.

Systems theory provides an underlying methodology for the design and application of a security management plan. Systems theory considers an organization as a whole and its interrelated parts, rather than discrete silo-formed departments that have little interaction. There are many benefits of a systems approach, in particular for security, such as promoting the security plan outside of the security department, common lexicon, integration of common business and management practices, flexibility in operations, a strategic approach, and the effective allocation of resources.

Security management plans can be designed, operated, and managed within four discrete types, depending on an organizational type, culture, and expectation. These four types of methodology take a risk-based, quality assurance, governance, or strategic security framework approach. These frameworks are modular in form and should be designed to meet the organization and its operating environment.

Resilience has become a core concept in security management that security can strive toward. Resilience is a common capacity possessed by individuals, groups, or communities that allow them to prevent, minimize, or prevail in the face of adversity. Nevertheless, the application of resilience is still vague and is better considered a philosophy rather than a plan or framework. However, there are clear characteristics that support organizational resilience. These include the need for a top-down culture with strong and aware leadership, as well as bottom-up functions with devolution of responsibilities, reduced silos, robust financial support, and efficacy in risk management and business continuity.

A security manager is first a business manager, and second a security manager. Therefore, beyond the many security functions, there are other functions that a security manager should practice, such as governance, performance management, corporate risk management, succession planning, education and awareness, cost-benefit analysis, and setting budgets.

Important parts of security management include policy and procedures, ethical behavior for themselves and their staff, understanding the principles of security, and being aware of security decay. Ethics has to be high on the list of a security manager, as ethics lead to positive and effective leadership. Finally, security decay is the understanding that all systems will fail if there is not appropriate and directed feedback to maintain the system at its commissioning level or aligned to dynamic threats.

Websites

Resilient Organizations. Organizations Research Group (ResOrgs), www.resorgs.org.nz/.

References

ASIS International, 2009a. Code of Ethics. ASIS International, Alexandria, VA.
ASIS International, 2009b. International glossary of security terms. Retrieved from http://www.asisonline.org/library/glossary/index.xml.
ASIS International, 2009c. Organizational Resilience: Security Preparedness and Continuity Management Systems—Requirements with Guidance for Use. ASIS International, Alexandria, VA.
Australian Government, 2007. Best Practice Regulation Handbook: Appendix B Cost-benefit Analysis. Australian Government, Canberra.
Bertalanffy, L.V., 1968. General Systems Theory: Foundations, Development, Application. George Braziller, Inc, New York.
Bohm, D., Peat, D., 2000. Science, Order and Creativity, second ed. Routledge, New York.
Braes, B.M., Brooks, D.J., 2011. Organizational resilience: Understanding and identifying the essential concepts. In: Guarazio, M., Reniers, G., Brebbia, C.A., Garzia, F. (Eds.), Security and Safety Engineering IV. WIT Press, Southampton, NY, pp. 117–128.
Brooks, D.J., 2012. Corporate security: Using knowledge construction to define a practising body of knowledge. Asian Journal of Criminology, http://dx.doi.org/10.1007/s11417-012-9135-1.
Buczynski, K.K., 2011. Strategic Security Management Systems: A Common Framework for Government and Private Sector Organizations. Masters of Security Management, Edith Cowan University, Perth.
Coole, M., Brooks, D.J., 2011. Mapping the Organizational Relations within Physical Security's Body of Knowledge: A Management Heuristic of Sound Theory and Best Practice. Paper presented at the 4th Australian Security and Intelligence Conference, Perth.
Critical Infrastructure Resilience Branch, 2008. Executive Guide: Resilience—Trusted Information Sharing Network for Critical Infrastructure Protection. Attorney-General's Department, Canberra.
Cubbage, C., Brooks, D.J., 2012. Corporate Security in the Asia Pacific Region: Crisis, Crime, Fraud and Misconduct. Taylor and Francis, Boca Raton, FL.
Dalton, D.R., 1995. Security Management: Business Strategies for Success. Butterworth-Heinemann, Boston.
Fay, J., 2006. Contemporary Security Management. Butterworth-Heinemann, Boston.

Fay, J., 2007. Encyclopedia of Security Management. Butterworth-Heinemann, Boston.

Garcia, M.L., 2001. The Design and Evaluation of Physical Protection Systems. Butterworth-Heinemann, Boston.

Hamel, G., Valikangas, L., 2003. The quest for resilience. Harv Bus Rev. 81 (9), 52–63.

Herman, M., 1999. Entropy based warfare: Modelling the revolution in military affairs. Retrieved April 18, 2010, from http://209.85.173.132/search?q=cache:7Rigu4CTvaAJ:www.au.af.mil/au/awc/awcgate/jfq/1620.pdf+herman+entropy+based+warfare&cd=1&hl=en&ct=clnk&gl=au.

IBM, 2008. Global Innovation Outlook: Security & Society. International Business Machines Corporation, Armonk, NY.

International Organization for Standardization, 2007. ISO 28000:2007 Specification for Security Management Systems for the Supply Chain. Author International Organization for Standardization, Geneva.

Jaquith, A., 2007. Security Metrics: Replacing Fear, Uncertainity and Doubt. Addison-Wesley, Reading, MA.

Joint Transort Research Centre, 2009. Security Risk Perception and Cost-benefit Analysis. Joint Transort Research Centre, Paris.

Lengnick-Hall, M.L., Beck, T.E., 2005. Adaptive fit versus robust transformation: How organizations respond to environmental change. Journal of Management 31 (5), 738–757.

Lussier, R.N., 2009. Management Fundamentals: Concepts, Applications, Skills Development, fourth ed. South-Western Cengage Learning, Mason, OH.

Luthar, S.S., Cicchetti, D., Becker, B., 2000. The construct of resilience: A critical evaluation and guidelines for future work. Child Dev. 71, 543–562.

McClure, S.A., 1997. Security Decay: The Erosion of Effective Security. Edith Cowan University, Perth.

Robertson, A., 2006. Issues in security management. In: Gill, M. (Ed.), Handbook of Security. Palgrave Macmillan, Basingstoke, UK, pp. 561–562.

Stephenson, A., Seville, E., Vargo, J., Roger, D., 2010. Benchmark Resilience: A Study of the Resilience of Organizations in the Auckland Region. Resilient Organizations Research Group (ResOrgs), Auckland.

Talbot, J., Jakeman, M., 2008. SRMBOK: Security Risk Management Body of Knowledge. Risk Management Institution of Australasia Ltd, Carlton South.

Underwood, G., 1984. The Security of Buildings. Butterworths, London.

3

Security Risk Management

OBJECTIVES

- Understand and apply the principles of risk, security risk, and security risk management.

- Discuss the various concepts that form risk and risk management, such as probability, likelihood, consequence, and gaming.

- Apply the international framework of risk management, describing each stage.

- Reconstruct the framework of security risk management, describing each stage and the informing processes of threat assessment, criticality register, and vulnerability assessment.

- Critique the concepts that make security risk management unique from risk management.

- Contrast the social and cultural theories and how these aid or divert the risk management process.

- Be able to evaluate the theories that underlie decision-making within security risk management.

- Be aware of contemporary risk management models.

- Apply theoretical principles and concepts within a professional security risk management environment.

INTRODUCTION

Everyone in their daily lives is exposed to risk and, whether consciously or subconsciously, applies some degree of risk management. It can be argued that this has been the case since humans first made a conscious decision. Today, risk management is often thought of as a formal process in decision-making, considering the chance of being successful and its uncertainties. Such a process may modify your decision to undertake an activity; however, such decision-making can be complicated with multiple and diverse factors, from analytical assessments to human intuition.

Risk can and is applied in all aspects of our daily lives, but within a commercial environment society expects a more formal approach. People are generally less acceptable of risk if it is imposed by external factors over which they have little control. Where risk is seen to be manageable, exposure becomes socially unacceptable. Therefore, risk management is a subjective matter prone to social and cultural bias.

Risk management is becoming a well-established discipline, with its own body of knowledge and domain practitioners. Nation-states worldwide now have their own risk management standards, and in many of these nations, it is the organization's senior executives responsibility to ensure that *reasonable* risk management practices meet internal and external compliance requirements. A subdomain of risk management is security risk management, which is unique from more generic approaches to risk management. Many of these generic risk management models lack key concepts and processes necessary for effective design, application, and mitigation of security risks.

The intent of this chapter is to introduce the wider discipline of risk management and its many considerations, focusing on a specific framework more suitable to the unique process of security risk management. Thus, there are a number of significant points to consider about security risk management, such as:

- Risk takes place in a social context.
- Risk is uncertain exposure to perceived harm.
- To define risk requires an environmental context.
- Security risk management is a unique subdomain of risk management.
- Security risk management integrates threat assessment, criticality assessment, and vulnerability.
- Understanding and articulating threat is central to security risk management.
- Security risk management requires a structured and transparent process.
- Security risk management can only estimate likely outcomes, it cannot predict the future.
- To be effective, security risk management requires a consensual outcome.
- Risk management is not solely a science, but rather science and artistry.

THE CONCEPT OF RISK

The history of the human species is a chronology of exposure to misfortune, adversity, and efforts to deal with risk. Primitive humankind faced risks, such as exposure to inclement weather, hunger, and being hunted by wild animals that threatened their existence (Vaughan, 1997, p. 2). In our modern society, human beings are still subjected to risks. Risk may range from physical risk, such as health, safety, and security, to broader societal risk, such as technology, environment, and the economy. Risk is everywhere, and with such a multifaceted nature, there is "a bewildering array of terminology, usage and definitions of risk" (Duffey, 2008, p. xxi).

Risk as a concept originates from the 17th-century probability theory (Hacking, 1975). For example, Dake (1992) defines risk as "the probability of an event occurring, combined with an accounting for the losses and gains that the event would represent if it came to pass" (p. 22). Another definition is that risk is the possibility of incurring misfortune or loss. Nevertheless, more emphasis has been placed on mitigating the potential losses associated with risk, rather than the potential gains (Dake, 1992, p. 22). The traditional concept of risk was as a wager, where individuals hope to gain something substantial; however, this view has almost disappeared as risk is conceived as a danger. The original speculative term of *risk* has now been transformed to mean a pure or bad risk, becoming "a decorative flourish on the word danger" (Douglas, 1992, p. 40). The nature of risk has changed from a speculative form to a pure form.

Many have proposed variations on the new definition of risk, attempting to revive the idea of *good* risks (Adams, 1995, p. 30). Ballard recommends a more quantitative definition of risk, where a risk is equal to probability multiplied by harm or consequence, where "events which happen often must have a low consequence, or events involving serious consequences must be rare" (1992, p. 100). However, such reference to low or serious consequences is characteristic of the pure risk mindset. Despite risk being inherently speculative, the move toward the pure definition of risk that considers risk as a dire consequence has infused the language of security risk management.

Beck (1992) put forward the idea of the risk society to emphasize that there is no class distinction or immunity from risk and that industrialized society is producing risks that may result in the "self-destruction of all life on earth" (p. 21). Nevertheless, demands for ever-greater reductions in risk exposure, from cultural, social, community, corporate, and an individual basis, can drive risk beyond the point of a benefit and be counterproductive. Risk management and mitigation strategies must be cost effective, unless imposed by law in which compliance is required. Today, there is a drive to make our built environment risk free. The actions taken to reduce one risk can increase the exposure to other, more serious, risks. For example, fitting a vehicle immobilizer to reduce car theft and joy-riding increased car-jacking and assault, as perpetrators and victims came face to face.

DEFINING RISK

Risk, as with security, is difficult to define unless there is context. As Breakwell (2007) suggests, risk is now a promiscuous term that is used to mean many things in many contexts. Nevertheless, risk has to be defined if we are to carry out risk management and, in particular, the subjective process of security risk. Therefore, risk management has driven the need to better define risk, producing many definitions in the process.

The following statements provide a number of risk definitions:

1. Uncertainty of financial loss, with variations between actual and expected results or the probability that a loss has occurred or will occur.
2. Loss potential that can be estimated by an analysis of threat and vulnerability. Reducing either will reduce risk.
3. The effect of uncertainty on objectives, either positive or negative.

Both definitions 1 and 2 examine risk as the potential for loss, which can be considered *pure* risk. In contrast, definition 3 (Standards Australia, 2009, p. 1) considers *speculative* risk, being a loss or gain of likely impacts. Such a view is a more appropriate definition in today's organizational environment.

The concept of risk, in simplistic terms, can be considered the sum of:

$$\text{Risk} = \text{Probability} \times \text{Consequence}$$

THE CONCEPTS OF PROBABILITY TO LIKELIHOOD

Risk management uses probability to better understand uncertainty in risk assessment and to support decision-making. As Fischer and Green state, "probability is a mathematical statement concerning the possibility of an event occurring" (2004, p. 139). For example, probability allows risk estimation through probability trees, where various alternative decisions can be displayed with their relative probability. The end point of a probability tree equals the product of all probabilities in the selected path.

Probability is a form of mathematics and may be considered an analysis of random phenomena. Such an analytical view is the oldest and most common definition of probability (Howell, 2008). Central objects of probability theory are random variables, stochastic processes, and events, where abstractions of nondeterministic events or measured quantities may evolve over time in an apparently random fashion. For example, the coin flip is a random event; if repeated n times the sequence of random events will exhibit certain patterns. Nevertheless, there are many issues with using probability within risk management, in particular, the more subjective security risk. Probability theory considers this issue within the concept of *subjective probability*, being the person's belief in the likelihood of an event.

Uncertainty has influenced human life since the beginning of time. During the Italian Renaissance, merchants insured themselves against trading uncertainties. Many organizations strive to provide protection against risk, and an important component of this is the ability to calculate probability. Probability modeling attempts to define uncertainty within risk assessment; however, probability models are still subjective. For example, in the simple environment of a coin flip such outcomes are relatively defined probabilities. But reality does not provide such simple environments. *Objective uncertainty* arises because of randomness, which is inherent in nature. *Subjective uncertainty* arises because of a lack of information, which can be biased due to differing opinions. Reality tends to combine both types of uncertainty.

Probability in Risk Assessment

Probability refers to the chance that an event will be realized, expressed as a percentage, or an absolute between 0 and 1. Such use of probability is the basis in risk assessment, often referred to as a rational and objective process rather than a product of "mental and social creations, despite even the most ardent realist's exhortations on behalf of objectivity and rationality" (Smithson, 1989, p. 41). There is the inherent impossibility of calculating the probability of a single event such as a terrorism incident. In the most part, risk probability is subjective and defined by degrees of belief, with the role of individuals and their cultural values as part of the risk equation. Thus, the concept of objective risk is strongly influenced by our perceptions.

In Bayes theory, the prior and posterior independent probability can be used to calculate the probability of an event. Prior probability considers such aspects as the base data, historical data, existing probability, or current state of affairs; whereas, posterior probability considers new data, combined in series with prior data. However, people take less account of base rate information that leads to incorrect estimates of probability. Bayes theory is based on the science of probability, so why is this less effective than it should be? In general, people are reluctant to accept an outcome if they do not want it, have already committed to the alterative outcome, or do not understand or want to understand the math. Many take a more heuristic view on assessment, going on how they feel and their subjective probability.

Probability provides a quantitative approach to risk assessment, which for certain data sets may be suitable. However, security risks usually lack historical data sets. In addition, security risks are attempting to deal with intelligent humans who are trying to defeat risk mitigations strategies. For example, the probability of a terrorist event is almost impossible to calculate. Therefore, the use of probability for some security risk assessment tasks is inappropriate and will lead to a number of issues, such as:

- Unreliable input data, leading to unreliable output data.
- Poor validity in the risk assessment output.
- Overreliance and inappropriate belief in the output data.
- A belief that the risk assessment is based on scientific methodology.

Therefore, in security risk management, likelihood should be used over probability. Likelihood still refers to the chance that an event may occur, expressed as a percentage or an absolute between 0 and 1. However, likelihood does not imply as explicitly as probability that the risk assessment is a mathematical methodology. Such an approach far better suits security risk management.

IMPORTANCE OF CONSEQUENCE

Consequence may be defined as the degree of damage that may occur if likelihood is realized. Consequence may also be defined as the criticality of loss, perceived loss, and intangible loss, categorized from unimportant to catastrophic (Standards Australia, 2006, p. 73). Nevertheless, the level of consequence is context-dependent, defined by the individual or group. For example, a five million dollar monetary loss may be a catastrophic consequence to a smaller company, but may be only a moderate consequence to a larger company with strong financial resilience.

When determining the consequence that may be incurred the relevant person or group should be consulted. For example, company operations would best understand the impact on their part of the organization to the realized consequence. However, when consulting it is necessary to ensure that a person's fear or indifference does not cloud his or her judgment. For a variety of reasons, people will make their decision based on the dread of a particular event, rather than based on the actual harm that may be inflicted. For this reason and from a business perspective, it is useful to consider consequence implications in terms of costs. Cost goes beyond just financial issues and should consider the following areas:

- *Financial costs:* Monies lost through having to replace people or equipment, recover from a realized threat, or that may have been stolen.
- *Physical costs:* Lost lives, injuries, lost production, or labor hours.
- *Intellectual costs:* Lost credibility or goodwill. Many of these costs are intangible and are difficult to determine, therefore, their assessment is subjective.
- *Perceptual costs:* The belief that loss will be more or less significant than it could be.

- *Implicit costs:* Most will clearly understand financial and asset loss, but *value* may not be monetary. For example, your mother's wedding ring may be irreplaceable due to a sentimental reason. A company's reputation and loss of trust may have long-term effects that can take years to regain.

When assessing consequence, the parochial nature of people and groups must be considered. For example, the marketing department will believe that only issues related to marketing are important; however, in reality the manufacturing department may be far more important. For this reason, the impact on the total organization is best gained at a more strategic viewpoint. In addition, the ability as a group to gain consensus in consequence could be considered a key necessity in achieving effective risk management. From there, risk may be inferred from the interaction between consequence and likelihood using a risk matrix.

SOURCE OF RISK

The realization of risk will result in many consequences, some expected and others not. The ability of managers to take ownership of risk consequences is important, but in some cases the many resulting consequences become overwhelming. This issue leads to managers reacting to the consequence they feel best able to deal with, rather than addressing the source of the risk. A manager may procrastinate in dealing with the most significant outcome of risk, its consequences. Understanding the source of the risk (Figure 3.1) is important in the risk management process.

The source of risk can be expanded beyond what is considered the responsibility of an organization, rather than back to nation-state governments and society in general (Figure 3.2). Nevertheless, how far back risks can truly be managed will be dependent on the organization, its resources, and the social context.

RISK MANAGEMENT

One of the earliest references of risk management appeared in the 1956 *Harvard Business Review*, with the aim to "outline the most important principles of a workable program for 'risk management'—for so it must be conceived" (Gallagher cited by Vaughan, 1997, p. 27). Like

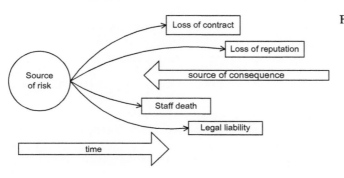

FIGURE 3.1   Source of risk.

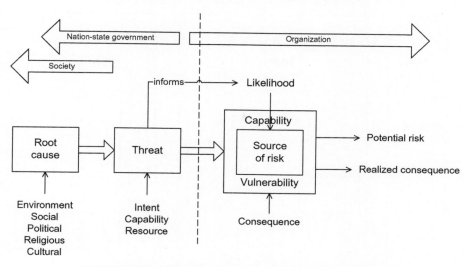

FIGURE 3.2 The upstream and downstream of risk source.

many managerial functions, risk management has predecessor functions and one of the most influential was insurance. The discovery that insurance was unable to meet specific organizational needs and that internal activities could control the impact of risk cumulated in the view that "people are no longer prepared to accept disasters as 'Acts of God,' instead perceiving them as management failures" (Borodzicz, 2005, p. 155). Such views led to the growth of risk management into a specific domain of practice.

The other significant development in risk management was the change of view from loss-only outcomes to a holistic approach that included a range of outcomes, from gains to losses (Skipper, 1998, p. 7)—in other words, *speculative* risk. Organizations realized that such an integrated approach exposed all their risks with greater efficacy.

The importance of risk management in the security context is summed up by Fischer and Green, who stated that "if security is not to be one-dimensional, piecemeal, reactive, or pre-packaged, it must be based on analysis of the total risk potential" (2004, p. 129). Security and risk management are, therefore, intertwined concepts. If the original speculative definition of risk is retained and concepts of organizational culture recognized, then the nexus of security and risk can be defined as "the culture, processes and structures that are directed towards maximising benefits and minimising adverse benefits in security, consistent with achieving business objectives" (Standards Australia, 2006, p. 11).

AN INTERNATIONAL APPROACH TO RISK MANAGEMENT

International Standards Organization (ISO) propagates the ISO 31000:2009 Risk Management standard, which puts forward a risk philosophy, process, and framework. ISO 31000 aims to provide a generic framework for the identification, analysis, evaluation, treatment, monitoring, and communication of risk. The standard does not aim to enforce uniformity

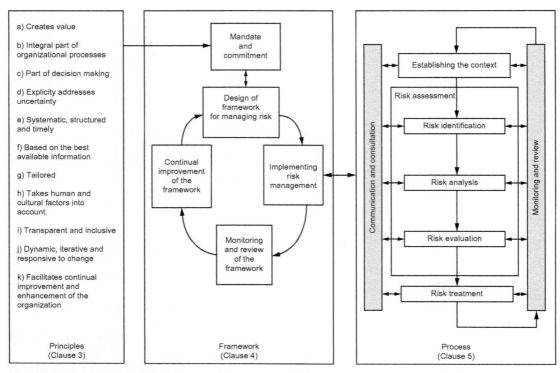

FIGURE 3.3   ISO 31000 Risk Management principles, framework, and process. *(Used with permission from SAI Global, Standards Australia, 2009, p. iv.)*

of risk management systems, rather to specify the risk management process in any given industry, including security. Design and implementation of a risk management system will depend on an organization's environment, legal obligations, social expectations, needs, objectives, products, services, processes, and practices.

ISO 31000 provides a relatively uncomplicated approach to risk management, which identifies generic stages required in a risk management program (Figure 3.3). While in most nation-states these standards are not legally binding, they may be considered persuasive. For this reason, any risk management system and therefore security risk management system should comply with ISO 31000 as its overarching structure.

The ISO 31000 Risk Management process is made up of three distinct stages, commencing with establishing the context, followed by risk assessment, and concluding with risk treatment. Concurrently, communication and monitoring is undertaken.

The Context

Establishing the context is perhaps the most important part in risk management, as it is the definition and planning stage that keeps the risk management task within required boundaries and supports an organization's primary objectives. This stage defines the basic parameters within which risks are to be identified, assessed, and mitigated, including identifying the stakeholders and communications methods? Context should include the organization's

TABLE 3.1 SWOT Context Assessment

Environment		
Internal	External	Outcome
Strength +	Opportunity	= Exploit
Strength +	Threat	= Confront
Weakness +	Opportunity	= Search
Weakness +	Threat	= Avoid

internal and external environment, organizational objectives, stakeholder identification, and assessment criteria.

The internal and external environment may also need to consider strategic documents, practices, and corporate position, taking a strength, weakness, opportunity, and threat (SWOT) analysis approach (Table 3.1). For example, if an organization has an internal strength and an external opportunity, the risk should be exploited; however, if the organization has an internal weakness and an external threat, the risk should be avoided.

Stakeholder identification needs to address who may have responsibility, has some ownership, and may or perceive to be affected. Stakeholders may range from company shareholders to government regulators, from unions to community groups. A stakeholder review allows decision-makers to better understand the many stakeholders, support an appropriate degree of engagement, and to better ensure that the risk management outcome is accepted, even with an adverse decision.

Finally, the assessment criterion defines how risk is to be measured, what model is to be used, and what drives a risk to mitigation. For example, will consequence be measured by a three- or five-ranked table, and will only extreme-ranked risk be taken to mitigation? Full details do not have to be provided at this early stage, but defining the context should provide transparency in the process.

Risk Assessment

The risk assessment stage combines risk identification, risk analysis, and risk evaluation. Risk identification is the first step in the risk assessment process and focuses on identifying the source of risk and potential events that could impact an organization's objectives. Risk identification also provides insight in the interaction between risk and threat. Such insight is an important process as each organization has a unique context and, therefore, needs to focus on different risks (Fischer et al., 2008).

At this stage all risk should be considered, as those not identified here may not be considered later. To extract all risks, there are many techniques such as brainstorming, workshops, scenario development, or group experience, but whatever method is used should promote open and frank discussion. Thus, the outcome is to produce a comprehensive list of risks that can be clustered into common types (Table 3.2).

Risk analysis considers the previously identified risks and analyzes them through the study of their proxies, namely consequence (Table 3.3), likelihood (Table 3.4), and degree

TABLE 3.2 Typical Risk Clustering Groups

Risk Clusters	
Financial	**Environmental**
Health and Safety	Political
Security	Regulatory
Social/Cultural	Community
Reputation	Shareholders

TABLE 3.3 Consequence Scale

Scale	Rank	Descriptor
Catastrophic	A	Organization will cease to function if harm is realized
Very high	B	Major impact on organization's ability to function and may lead to a prolonged period of nonfunction; a major change in operations will be required
High	C	Significant effect on organization's operations and activities
Medium	D	Impact on organization's ability to function, but recoverable with little effort
Low	E	Covered by usual allowances
Unknown	U	Consequence of harm being realized is unknown

TABLE 3.4 Likelihood Scale

Scale	Rank	Descriptor
Certain	1	The event will be realized
Very high	2	Highly probable
High	3	Moderately probable
Medium	4	Probable
Low	5	Improbable
Unknown	6	Likelihood of event unknown

of existing control. It is important to note that such measurements of proxies will only serve to provide an estimation of the risk and the relationship between them cannot be assumed to be absolute nor linear.

There are many techniques to populate these scales, although the most effective is to take a consensual group approach (Beard and Brooks, 2009). A consensual approach brings the relevant people together who have some degree of ownership of the risk, and as a group they agree on where the various risks locate on the two scales.

Existing controls need to be considered, as these controls could reduce either the consequence or likelihood of an event. Controls may be physical, procedural, or technology factors.

Once all risks have been annotated with a consequence and likelihood measure, the sums of these measures need to be ranked. One of the most effective methods is to use a risk matrix (Table 3.5), which should be weighted to consequence for the majority of assessment. Such weighting allows for some degree of social expectations, dread of the event, and people better understand outcomes (consequences).

The outcome of the risk matrix should be a list that commences with the most extreme assessed risk and scales down to the lowest.

Risk evaluation allows the decision-makers to make an informed decision, based on the outcome of the risk analysis section. The risks—in particular, the extreme and high-ranked risks—should be aligned and checked with the initial risk management context. In addition, decision such as whether the risk needs to be treated and its priority, what activity is to take place, and should the risk be reviewed need to be considered?

In reality, there is generally an arbitrary line drawn just below extreme and high risks, which ensures further action of these risks are undertaken (Table 3.6).

TABLE 3.5 Risk Matrix

	Consequence				
Likelihood	Low	Medium	High	Very High	Catastrophic
Certain	High	High	Very high	Extreme	Extreme
Very high	Moderate	High	High	Very high	Extreme
High	Moderate	Moderate	High	Very high	Very high
Medium	Low	Moderate	Moderate	High	Very high
Low	Low	Low	Moderate	High	High

TABLE 3.6 Risk Rating Descriptor

Risk Rating		Corresponding Action
Low	1	Acceptable level of risk, no monitoring required
Medium	2	Tolerable level of risk, with yearly monitoring
High	3	Tolerable level of risk, with regular monitoring
Very high	4	Intolerable level of risk, senior managerial attention with planning for resource allocation within four weeks
Extreme	5	Treatment of risk required with allocation of resources, planning, and monitoring within one week

Risk Treatment

Risk treatment involves the identification and assessment (cost-benefit or compliance analysis) options of the treatment plans. There are five traditional methods for treating risks:

- *Reduce the risk:* Reduce the likelihood or consequence of the risk being realized. Appropriate security policies, procedures, and practices, coupled with situational and social crime prevention strategies, can be used.
- *Transfer the risk:* Outsource the function exposing the organization to the risk. For example, a bank may outsource cash transportation. Insurance is one of the better known methods of transferring some of the risk to a third party.
- *Avoid the risk:* Eliminate the activity causing the risk exposure. For example, paying employees via electronic banking rather than cash reduces the opportunity for armed robbery.
- *Redistribute the risk:* Where possible, distribute functions that expose the organization to risk over a range of locations or time. For example, place the IT department back-up server data at a remote site or have executives travel separately to high-risk areas.
- *Accept the risk:* Sometimes there is no option but to accept a risk, as this is part of both living and doing business. Banks can limit the risk of armed robberies, but they have to accept a level of risk if they are to continue trading.

After risk treatment, remaining risk can be considered *residual* risk. It is not possible to totally transfer or redistribute risks, as there is always some residue.

SECURITY RISK MANAGEMENT

"Security risk management provides a means of better understanding the nature of security threats and their interaction at an individual, organizational, or community level" (Standards Australia, 2006, p. 6). Generically, the risk management process can be applied in the security risk management context. Indeed, the risk management process advocated in ISO 31000 should be used as the foundation to risk management in the greater organization; however, security risk management has a number of unique processes that other forms of risk management do not consider.

The core of security risk management still remains identical to what has been discussed, with the addition of informing assessments, such as the threat assessment, criticality register, and vulnerability assessment. The relationship between risk management and these assessments provides what is considered security risk management (Figure 3.4).

In the process of establishing the context for security risk management, it must be stressed that for the success of the security program the process has to be in-line with the key objectives of the organization, considering the strategic and organizational context. In addition, the outcomes have to been presented from a business perspective, rather than solely as security mitigation strategies.

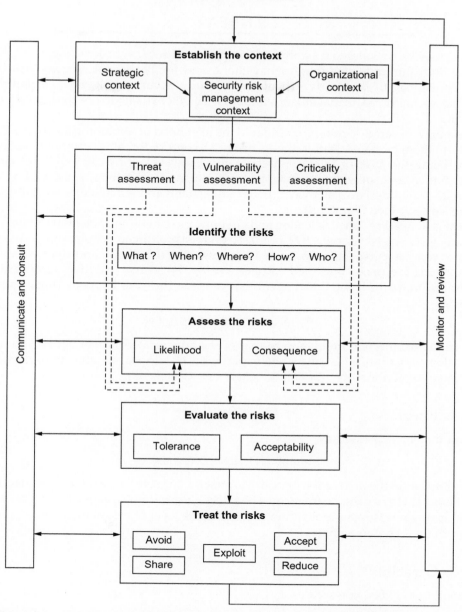

FIGURE 3.4 Security risk management process. *(Used with permission from SAI Global, Standards Australia, 2006, p. 14.)*

THREAT

Threat may be considered a significant component of security risk management, a central theme within the understanding, management, and application of security risk (Brooks, 2011). Threat has to be clearly articulated within a security risk management process. Nevertheless, many risk management standards (e.g., ISO 31000) do not consider the concept of threat.

Threat may, to some degree, be considered the likelihood of something that may affect people, information, or assets. Within the security risk context, threat is better defined as an adversary, being the sum of intent and capability. However, threat is a difficult and often misunderstood concept within a corporate environment, in particular, when dealing with security risks. An underlying method to better understand and articulate threat is through the intelligence cycle (see Chapter 9).

Threat is defined as "any indication and circumstances, with the potential to cause the loss of or damage to assets" (Roper, 1999, p. 13). To understand threat "requires an understanding of the adversaries perspective, in terms of intentions and motives, and their capabilities in compromising the assets concerned" (Roper, 1999, p. 44). Threat and their agents are inextricably linked in that it is the threat agent that causes a threat to happen. Threat can also be defined as:

$$\text{Threat} = \text{Intent} \times \text{Capability}$$

Intent and capability are in relation to that of the adversary or threat agent "to undertake actions that will result in harm or the expectation of harm to another individual, group, organisation or community" (Standards Australia, 2006, p. 49).

What Is Intent?

Intent may be expressed as:

$$\text{Intent} = \text{Desire} \times \text{Expectance}$$

Intention lies in the motivation or desire to attack a target to cause damage or loss (Haimes, 2006). For intent to be present, there must be a desire to perform an activity and an expectation of success or gain. Human motivation requires some level of expectation that a person will succeed in their chosen activity.

What Is Capability?

Capability may be expressed as:

$$\text{Capability} = \text{Resources} \times \text{Knowledge}$$

To be capable of performing the activity, there must be resources available and knowledge of how, when, and where to perform the activity with the available resources. Knowledge includes that of the target organization, personnel, use of equipment, or technical ability, while resources include money, personnel, and equipment.

The sum of intent and capability form to define threat (Figure 3.5).

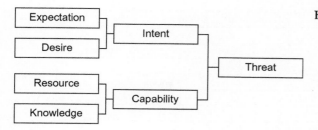

FIGURE 3.5 Elements of threat.

What is a Threat Assessment?

A *threat assessment* is the evaluation and assessment of the intentions of people who could pose a threat to an organization, how they might cause harm, and their ability and motivation to carry out the task. To understand the nature of threat is to also identify the source of threat, which includes "mother nature and mankind" (Landoll, 2006, pp. 30–31). Therefore, threat can be categorized in clusters as shown in Table 3.7.

The threat assessment needs to be able to annotate identified threats, using the elements of intent and capability, comprising of resource, knowledge, and desire (Figure 3.6). In addition, some degree of reliability and validity of the assessment need to be made, considering the confidence of the information. Confidence can also be assessed using the admiralty scale, which was developed for national intelligence services to reflect on the validity and veracity of intelligence information.

TABLE 3.7 Threat Clusters

Threat Cluster	Description
Criminal	Theft, fraud, robbery, burglary, assault, vandalism, arson, workplace violence, outlawed motorcycle gangs, etc.
Commercial	Industrial espionage, sabotage, subversion, sponsor by a competitor, or foreign government
Natural disaster	Fire (not arson), flood, earthquake, tsunami, storm damage, cyclone, etc.
Foreign intelligence	Once national state intelligence services, but now more involved in gaining economic and technical intelligence
Issue-motivated group	Extreme left or right political groups, extreme religious groups, environmental groups, or any other groups with extreme ideas.
Terrorist group	Hijacking, assassination, kidnapping, extortion, blackmail, theft, politically motivated violence, bombings, etc.
Media	Media coverage can become a threat to the security of an organization particularly during a crisis and when unplanned
Internal threat	May incorporate any (exempt natural disaster) of the above, but threat comes from within rather than external

Threat Actor			Threat Actor Motivation	
Resources	Knowledge		Desire	Confidence
Capability			Intent	
Threat Level				

FIGURE 3.6   Threat assessment template.

TABLE 3.8   Threat Level Ranking

	Intent		
Capability	**Low**	**Expressed**	**Determined**
Extensive	Medium	Very high	Extreme
Moderate	Low	High	Very high
Low	Low	Medium	High

Source: Used with permission from SAI Global, adapted from Standards Australia, 2006, p. 57.

Once the threat template has been populated, the threat level can be defined using a matrix (Table 3.8), similar to the risk ranking matrix. The matrix uses the combination of capability and intent of the threat, allowing a priori threat level assessment.

CRITICALITY

What does the organization need to maintain its primary objectives to continue to trade, whether people, information, or assets? Is there a person, a piece of information, or an asset that is critical to the organization's primary objectives? For example, there may be a piece of equipment within your production line that if unavailable for an extended period of time has a significant effect on the ability of the organization to maintain operations. An organization that sells spare parts may believe that their headquarters is the most important part of their business, but in reality the online ordering system is how most suppliers place and receive their orders, with goods dispatched from this system via delivery contractors.

Criticality should be assessed and documented to aid both the security risk management process and inform business continuity management. Both functions can benefit from a comprehensive and organizational wide criticality register (Figure 3.7). Noncritical items need little consideration, if criticality is well understood.

Asset	Location	Owner	Risk scenario	Criticality description	Criticality rating	Rating

FIGURE 3.7   Criticality register sample.

TABLE 3.9 Criticality Rating Schema

Criticality		Impact on Organization	Impact on Group
Extreme	5	Complete cessation of all functions. No short-term recovery capability. Serious prolonged reputational loss (over many months). Extreme financial loss.	Severe prolonged loss of amenity (over many months). Severe community outrage at loss of service. Extreme financial loss.
Very high	4	Complete cessation of one or more key functions. No short-term recovery capability. Serious prolonged reputational loss (from weeks to months). High financial loss.	Severe prolonged loss of amenity (over weeks). Community outrage at loss of service. Very high financial loss.
High	3	Cessation of one or more key functions. Limited short-term recovery capability. Reputational loss (weeks). Significant financial loss.	Loss of amenity (weeks). Community upset at loss of service. Significant financial loss.
Moderate	2	Reduced effectiveness of one or more key functions. Short-term recovery capability is possible. Reputational loss (from days to weeks). Moderate financial loss.	Temporary loss of amenity (days). Community disquiet at loss of service. Moderate financial loss.
Low	1	Little impact on functions. Immediate recovery possible. Little reputational loss. Low financial loss.	Minor loss of amenity. Little negative reaction from loss of service. Minor financial loss.

Some form of criticality rating needs to be assigned, based on the impact to an organization or group (Table 3.9). When assessing criticality, an organization should consider people, information, and assets, as well as internal and external stakeholders. Finally, there may be a need for a third column, considering individuals such as employees, visitors, and VIPs. Consideration should also be made of the interrelationship and independency, in particular, in complex systems such as supply chains, technical facilities, and international organizations.

VULNERABILITY

Vulnerability is exposure to physical or emotional hurt, being open to attack, or lacking resilience. Security risk management should be completed in the *present*, with a clear understanding of current vulnerabilities. As Ezell states, "vulnerability highlights the notion of susceptibility to a scenario, whereas risk focuses on the severity of consequences within the context of a scenario" (2007, p. 571). Thus, vulnerability assessments are not the same as risk assessments.

Now that a list of critical assets has been identified and an understanding of the threats against the organization has been achieved, an assessment of the organization's vulnerabilities can be undertaken. The intent of the vulnerability assessment, or site survey, is to identify and characterize the limitations in the present security strategies. The output of the vulnerability assessment is to provide a better understanding of the potential interaction between the critical asset and the threat.

There are a number of different methods (Table 3.10) for completing a vulnerability assessment, such as a site survey, red-teaming, community vulnerability analysis from Sandia National Laboratories, target analysis, and the U.S. military CARVER model. What method is best used is again based on the context of the assessment.

Whatever method of assessment is used, as with threat and criticality rating, some form of ranking has to be made. A vulnerability matrix (Table 3.11) can be used by the assessor to

TABLE 3.10   Vulnerability Models

Vulnerability Model	Description
Site survey	An outward-in or inward-out comprehensive survey on the facility location, physical security, and procedural controls
Red-teaming	A team attacks the facility, acting like an aggressor
Community vulnerability analysis	Consider issues associated with critical infrastructure
Target analysis	Consider the target attractiveness and controls for just protecting the target
CARVER	Criticality, accessibility, recuperability, vulnerability, effect, and recognizability

TABLE 3.11   Vulnerability Matrix

Vulnerability Rating		Descriptor
Extreme	5	Controls are nonexistent. Controls will be breached. Recent evidence of widespread control failure. No business continuity in place.
Very high	4	Controls are largely ineffective. High likelihood that controls will be breached. Some recent evidence of control failure. Limited business continuity in place.
High	3	Majority of controls are effective. Moderate likelihood that controls will be breached. Some evidence of control failure. Majority of business continuity in place.
Moderate	2	Controls are effective. Low likelihood that controls will be breached. Limited evidence of control failure. Business continuity in place.
Low	1	Controls are effective. Very unlikely that controls will be breached. No evidence of control failure. Business continuity in place and practiced.

Vulnerability description	Rating	Ranking

FIGURE 3.8 Extension to the criticality register for vulnerability.

annotate what he or she believes are the efficacy of the existing control, including physical and procedural outcomes.

An extension of the criticality register (Figure 3.7) can be made, inserting vulnerability and a final overall ranking (Figure 3.8).

THREAT, CRITICALITY, AND VULNERABILITY

The importance of an asset—being a person, information, or physical asset—can be seen as the degree of potential consequence that a threat may cause. Thus, vulnerability serves as a modifier, affecting the level of exploitation that threat can use. The relationship of the three constructs, namely threat, consequence, and vulnerability, is a key component in the identification of security risk (Figure 3.9).

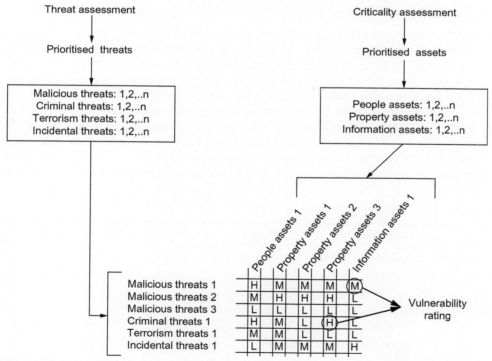

FIGURE 3.9 Mapping threat, criticality, and vulnerability. *(Used with permission from SAI Global, Standards Australia, 2006, p. 67.)*

RISK MODELS AND MODELING

The ability of the computer to process a large quantity of data has enhanced the ability to model risk. Many decisions can be tested in an attempt to achieve the most effective outcome. There are many risk simulation packages on the market. These packages are beneficial in aiding the decision-making process, but should not be seen as a panacea. As Koller stated, "validation of models can [only] be done only over time" (2000, p. 3), and the best that can be applied is a subjective aid within the decision-making process.

A model can be defined as an ideal representation of structure and process; however, a model is only a simplified approximation that attempts to capture and maintain essential elements of the real event. Risk modeling can only simulate reality, not match reality. Nevertheless, security risk management can use a number of different models (Table 3.12), ranging from one-dimensional, to two-dimensional, to multidimensional models that are layered and risk-ranked (Cameron and Raman, 2005, pp. 71–91).

The majority of risk management models are two dimensional, although a full security risk managmenet model with threat and criticaility could be consider multidimensional. What model is used will be dependent on the complexity and scope of the risk task at hand.

GAMING RISK

The risk management process must produce as reliable and valid an outcome as possible, cognizant of its subjective nature. A risk model may be designed at a corporate level, but applied at the divisional level. A typical example may be an internal company's move into a new product, where diverse and geographically spread divisions use a corporate risk model to assess the variability of proposed projects. Regional projects are given the approval to proceed at a corporate level, with one criteria being the risk assessment outcome.

After the risk process has been used for some time, it does not take the user long to begin to understand what he or she needs to achieve from the risk process to reach an outcome that he or she requires, whether positive or negative. Due to the subjective nature of many inputs, the user begins to game the system, using inputs that produce the desired outcome. Users quickly

TABLE 3.12 Risk Models

Model	Description	Security-related Components
One-dimensional	A simple linear model using one measure	Threat, vulnerability, consequence
Two-dimensional	Risk has two components that produce the measure	Consequence × likelihood; harm × threat
Multidimensional	Risk has many compoenents, such as the full seciurty risk managmenet process	Consequence × likelihood × dread; threat × criticality × consequence × likelihood
Layered	Hierarchy of control measures	Defense in depth approach
Risk-ranked	Qualitative ranking of risks, as proposed by ISO 31000	Consequence × likelihood; harm × threat

learn what significant inputs have the greatest impact on the outcome, gaming their required risk result.

A solution to reduce gaming may be to lock the risk model. A better approach is to educate the users in the importance of risk assessment and the benefits to them. Nevertheless, both these methods can still be gamed. Koller (1999, pp. 32–33) suggests that the only effective solution to this problem is to use *risk police*, a group of experts who:

• Review the effectiveness and appropriateness of inputs.
• Come to a consensus as to the validity of input values.
• Become an historical reference.
• Enforce consistency in the risk assessment process across all projects.

The review board members should:

• Be experts in their field.
• Be impartial.
• Have tenure on the panel for an appropriate period.
• Have a high level of interpersonal skills.
• Be empowered.

It would be hoped that those who propagate and use risk management to make a decision, do so with an unbiased and open approach. Otherwise, the ability of risk management to aid the decision-makers is significantly reduced and in some cases could become fraudulent.

DECISION-MAKING IN RISK

People appear to fail miserably when it comes to rational decision-making (Breakwell, 2007, p. 79) and research has, until recently, only focused on statistical judgment and decision-making. Nevertheless, this has changed as greater understanding on why people make certain judgments and decisions has increased. Using a statistical approach may not fully realize the perceptual risk decisions of humans. As Eysenck and Keane (2002, pp. 475–476) discuss, people often:

• Do not have access to all the information needed to make a statistical decision.
• Exaggerate the importance of some parts of the available information.
• May be anxious or stressed, reducing their analytical ability to make an optimal decision.

Decision-making is choosing one option among many possible options, generally biased with personal significance. Affecting factors are many (Table 3.13), ranging from bias to conflicting signals.

Early decision-making research focused on utility theory, which proposed that people will try to maximize their (subjective) value of an outcome. But in real-world decisions, unless simplistic, people do not use utility theory. We are prone to many factors that affect our decision-making process:

• *Loss aversion:* A phenomenon where people are averse to taking risks, with a tendency to be more sensitive to possible loss as opposed to possible gain.

TABLE 3.13   Decision-making Factors

Factors Affecting Decision-making	
Data limited	Exaggeration
Data nonexistent	Stress or anxious
Ambiguous	Complex environment
Uncertain	Conflicting signals
Skewed	Lack of trust
Bias	No ownership

- *Sunk-cost effect:* Sunk-cost effect resembles loss aversion, but becomes apparent when additional resources are committed to justify previous commitment.
- *Framing:* Irrelevant aspects affect the decision-maker. Tversky and Kahnemann (1987) completed a number of significant studies demonstrating aspects of framing, which is particularly prone to social context and psychological factors.
- *Perceived justification:* People feel that they have to justify a decision to themselves or other people.
- *Anticipated regret:* People make decisions that are perceived to provide a desirable outcome, over those that produce anticipated regret.
- *Omission bias:* Follows anticipated regret, where inaction is the preferred decision and action may perceive to increase responsibility if realized.
- *Self-esteem:* Those with high self-esteem are more likely to take a risk in their decision-making. People with low self-esteem are more self-protective and concerned with negative or threatening events (Eysenck and Keane, 2002).

Decision-making and Judgment

It is important to understand the difference between decision-making and judgment, as within cognitive psychology these are two distinct areas of research (Eysenck and Keane, 2002, p. 475):

- Judgment "is concerned with the processes used in drawing a conclusion from knowledge and evidence."
- Decision-making is "choosing among options, and can involve choices of personal significance."

In general, people have a reasonable understanding of risk even when they are not an area expert. People tend to judge risks not on facts, but on what they think and how they feel, thus, allowing people to make quick and relatively effective risk decisions with limited data, a survival technique from our ancestors. This decision-making technique is referred to as *heuristics*, which attempts to account for why certain risks cause more concern for society than others.

Heuristics

Heuristics is a "rule of thumb technique for solving a problem, which does not guarantee the solution of the problem but is highly likely to solve the problem" (Eysenck and Keane, 2002, p. 532). Heuristics can be divided into a number of primary models:

- Representativeness heuristics.
- Availability heuristics.
- Support theory.

Representativeness heuristics is the assumption that a typical or stereotype event fits or belongs to a category. Similar objectives or events will be clustered together and perceived to have a similar likelihood. Such an approach leads to serious errors, such as insensitivity of a prior event, information size, the nature of chance, and not statistically valid (Breakwell, 2007, pp. 79–80).

Availability heuristics is the assumption that memory can accurately assess the frequency of an event, based on long-term memory recall. In other words, the likelihood of an event is based on how easy it is for the person to remember a similar event. But recall could be caused by exposure to events, personal experience, and dread and familiarity of events. Therefore, people estimate the frequency of events and define the likelihood with these frequencies.

Support theory considers that the more descriptive an event, the higher the likelihood of that event occurring. An example may be the likelihood of you dying during your drive home from work, which may be assessed as very low. However, presented in a more descriptive way this could increase the *perceived* likelihood. Therefore, the likelihood of you dying during your drive home from a major car accident, heart attack, losing concentration, or falling asleep would generally be assessed higher. According to Eysenck and Keane, a "key insight lying behind this theory is that any given event may seem more or less likely depending on the way in which it is described" (2002, p. 481). Support theory has proven to be relatively robust and not only appropriate for lay people, but also experts.

PERCEPTION AND CULTURE

"The paradox of those who study risk perception is that, as people have become healthier and safer on average, they have become more—rather than less—concerned about risk, and they feel more and more vulnerable to the risks of modern life" *(Slovic, 1997, p. 233).*

Whether the concept of risk is an objective reality, a social construct, or a subjective individual perception has been a matter of debate for many years (Lupton, 1999, p. 22). As Ewald (1991) states, "nothing is a risk in itself; there is no risk in reality. But on the other hand, anything can be a risk" (p. 199). Such a view is supported by Slovic (1999), who suggests that risk has no external existence "independent of our minds and cultures" (p. 690), but risk is a useful construct invented to aid survival. Objective assessments of risk are subjective and assumption-laden, driven by judgment.

One of the key themes of modern psychology is the subjectivity of perception (Weiten, 2005, p. 19); however, treating perception as a dependent variable "ignores prior issues"

(Clarke and Short, 1993, p. 379). Such a view does not suggest that there is no *real danger*, rather that "there is no such thing as 'real risk' or 'objective risk'" (Slovic, 1999, p. 690).

There are two broad approaches to risk perception, namely psychometric theory of risk and cultural theory of risk. The psychometric theory of risk "uses psychophysical scaling and multivariate analysis techniques to produce quantitative representations ... of risk attitudes and perceptions" (Slovic, 1997, p. 237), whereas, the cultural theory of risk originates from the work of Douglas, M., & Wildavsky, A. (1982) clustering competing cultural worldviews.

Psychometric Risk Perception

The psychometric risk perception model is essentially a cognitive map of social risk perception, broken into axes of *dread risk* and *familiar to risk*. The origin of the psychometric risk is the expressed preferences approach (Starr, 1969), weighting technological risks against social benefits. Dread risk is a gradation of measurement along the horizontal axis, which "reflects the degree to which a risk is understood and the degree to which it evokes a feeling of dread" (Slovic, 1992, p. 121). Risks further to the right of the scale have a higher degree of dread than those to the left of the scale.

Familiar risks are represented along the vertical axis of the risk map and indicate public knowledge. Therefore, familiar risks such as motorcycle riding and elevators are found on the lower part of the axis and, as a result, gain a lower societal risk perception. Whereas unfamiliar risks, such as lead paint and medical X-rays exposure, appear higher up the axis, indicating that people perceive these activities or technologies as posing a higher degree of risk to their health and safety (Slovic, 1997, p. 235).

Nevertheless, perhaps some of the most important aspects to come out of psychometric research are the importance of dread, control, and trust. These concepts play a significant role in defining societal views on risks, biasing the risk management process and making some risk treatment almost impossible.

Cultural Theory of Risk

The cultural theory of risk features four worldviews, known variously as solidarities, myths of nature, or ways of life, defined by their position within the grid and group typology (Douglas and Wildavsky, 1982, p. 138). The characteristics of the worldviews are defined by their positions in the grid/group typology, being high or low group (indicating degrees of binding to social groups) and high or low grid (indicating degrees of socially defined circumscription). The four worldviews that emerge from the grid/group typology are labeled *hierarchical, individualist, egalitarian,* and *fatalist.*

Group refers to the extent to which an individual is bound by a group ethos or is morally coerced by a social unit to accept a group's goals, aspirations, beliefs, or other internal prescriptions. Mars and Frosdick (1997) suggest that a weak group measure would indicate that members of a social group tend to work toward individual goals and negotiate their interactions on an individual level. The grid is the extent to which social classification, regulation, or other external prescriptions are imposed on the members.

Perceptual and cultural issues consider the level of risk an organization or, more correctly, its members are willing to accept. For example, the introduction of an access control system may restrict the movement and flow of people and goods throughout the working environment. If such a system does not fit into the culture of the organization, it will be quickly circumvented, will decay, and the purpose of the system will be lost, as with the capital funding and any proposed risk mitigation strategy.

Gender and Risk

Risk perception and gender are two areas that have progressed as mainstream fields in risk research over recent decades. While the studies conducted into the field of risk have typically focused on technology and statistics, they have since moved into the social and behavioral science domains (Gustafson, 1998). Research has demonstrated that gender has an impact on how risks are perceived and therefore need to be treated. Women perceive more threat in the environment than men, there is a greater perceived risk of crime among women (Breakwell, 2007, p. 65), and women have a higher level of psychometric dread. It has been widely accepted by risk researchers that men and women have different perception levels of risk (Davidson and Freudenburg, 1997), but it is still not entirely clear what the underlying reasons are for the differences.

Nevertheless, Finucane et al. (2000) suggest that one traditional example to explain the differences in risk perception revolves around the differences in rationality and education. The notion is that if people are better educated about a particular risk, then they would be able to comprehend the risk in a more informed way; however, often the findings from studies are contradictory and it is difficult to ascertain common themes. Factors such as ethnicity, race, culture, socio-demographic, groups, and individuals all play a part.

TRUST

Failures of risk communication are not only influenced by the message content and the risks, but also by *trust* in those responsible for providing information (Lofstedt, 2003). The importance of trust—in whether a risk is accepted or opposed—has been well known, and is supported by much research from the individual to the societal level (Breakwell, 2007, p. 140). The Cambridge dictionary (2008) defines trust as belief, confidence, goodness, and skill or safety of a person or organization; however, it is important to distinguish at least three levels of trust, namely public trust, institutional trust, and specific trust (Breakwell, 2007, p. 140):

- *Public trust:* Societal communal feeling of confidence toward institutions and public leaders.
- *Institutional trust:* Feeling of confidence toward a particular organization.
- *Specific trust:* Feeling of confidence toward a particular organization over a particular issue.

Trust relates to public perception of risk, as perception is based on what is really happening, the cause of the events, the affected and estimated value, and who informs us of the risks.

As Australian Standard (2006, p. 19) states, "trust in itself will depend upon the organization's or community's abilities to communicate with clarity and without conflicting messages being received." Trust is a key element in risk communication, which Giffin describes as "reliance upon the communication behaviour of another person in order to achieve a desired but uncertain objective in a risky situation" (1967, p. 105).

Trust has often been claimed to be an important factor of perceived risk, which has important consequences for risk communication. Therefore, trust is of interest for its consequences (Earle, 2010) and why it is essential for successful communication plans. Nevertheless, the understanding of trust in risk management and risk communication is still rudimentary, which does not provide a predictive model or practical strategies (Breakwell, 2007, p. 146)

Trust the Information

Source credibility supports the idea that personal trust is based on a listener's perceptions of a speaker's expertness, reliability, intentions, activeness, personal attractiveness, and the majority opinion of the listener's associates (Giffin, 1967). Trust effects decisions of risks and benefits, which may lead to cooperation and, ultimately, acceptance. Risk information from a reliable source is incorporated by the receiver and this contributes to the way that an individual perceives and responds to a specific risk.

There are a number of aspects that will raise the profile of a risk, turning it into a public and media issue. These include questions such as who is to blame, whether the perpetrators tried to cover up the event, or who was really at fault. Furthermore, human interests that effect children, those who cannot protect themselves, or the underprivileged, and links to high-profile issues, personalities, and sex will raise the profile of the risk. Finally, pictures or video increases the signal value, making the media more interested.

To support trust requires effective risk communication, integrating (adjusted from Breakwell, 2007, pp. 155–156):

- A planned process that identifies key stakeholders and their views.
- Anticipated "fright factors," which may raise social concern, such as harm to children and minority groups.
- Recognized media triggers that gain the interest of the media and make risk newsworthy.
- Secondary effects that change the nature and consequence of the risk.
- A clear message that is understood by decision-makers.
- A nonexpert format presentation without jargon.
- An interactive process engaging to maintain and build trust.
- An acknowledgment of uncertainties with transparency in process.
- Fairness.

Trust in risk management is important and as Slovic (1993, p. 675) states, "recognizing the importance of trust and understanding the 'dynamics of the system' that destroys trust has vast implications for how we approach risk management in the future." Constant exchange of information between risk managers and the stakeholders is fundamental to the risk management process. Also, decisions that are made with the participation of the stakeholders are more effective and resilient.

GAINING CONSENSUS

The primary purpose of security risk management is to gain a consensus among decision-makers. Many who carry out security risk management rarely consider this fundamental aspect. Some carry out the risk management process as an administration burden or perhaps for compliance. However, if security risk management is done in isolation, it is likely to fail.

There is a need to gain common understanding of risk within a group. Such common understanding should not only include decision-makers (often seen as the corporate executive), but also other stakeholders who may be affected by the risk activity.

Security risk management is increasingly used to direct limited resources in the mitigation of threat; however, risk management can result in these limited resources being directed in an inappropriate or less effective manner. It is at the assessment stage that many factors may result in the process being less than effective, including the individuals' perceptions of risk, parochial attitudes, invested interests, undefined risks, bias, or a limited understanding of a risk. To overcome these issues, some form of group consensus should be achieved.

An individual approach to risk assessment produces unreliable risk results. While this outcome would be expected-due to an individual's attitudes and perceptions—there are few patterns in the difference between individuals that can be extrapolated to departments. People will, without conferring, identify the top 20% of the most significant risks within their organization (Beard and Brooks, 2009), but is the risks that are just below this that become wildly unreliable. Thus, many of these unreliable risks are mitigated, resulting in a significant resource implication to the organization.

There is a need to gain common understanding or clear definitions of risk within a group. For example, what is considered a serious assault will vary between a single group based on aspects such as gender, experience, and knowledge. An individual's assessment is driven by

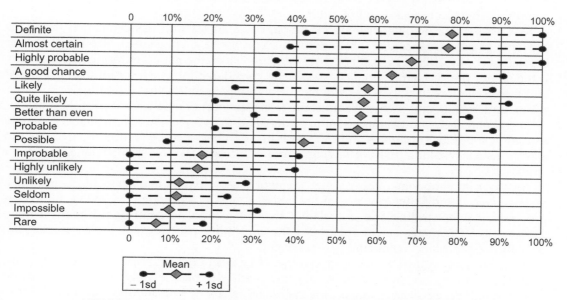

FIGURE 3.10   Range of estimated probability. *(From Hillson and Hullet, 2005.)*

his or her own perceptions, with more common risks (high likelihood) having a broader range of views than those less common risks (low likelihood).

Another issue, among many, is semantics of risk terms. For example, the effect of words and their meaning were studied (Hillson and Hullet, 2005) with the result that some commonly used words within risk management produced quite different views of an event (Figure 3.10). The widest deviation was observed among the higher probabilities, whereas the lowest deviation was among the unlikely events such as rare to improbable.

Risk management's ability to achieve consensus is driven by many factors, but one that can be most effective is to carry out risk assessment as a collaborative group, using group interviews, the Delphi method, and nominal group techniques. Thus, the results gathered from such group approaches can be used to ascertain accuracy and, importantly, can confidently be used to allocate limited resources.

CONCLUSION

Risk could be considered uncertain exposure to a perceived harm, within an environmental context. Risk management takes place in a social context, but requires a structured and transparent process for decision-making that considers the chance of being successful and provides an understanding of uncertainties. However, any form of risk management can only estimate likely outcomes, it cannot predict the future.

The International Standards Organization ISO 31000:2009 provides generic risk management principles, a framework, and a process. The standard should be the default process for all risk management tasks within an organization, adjusted to suit the simplicity or complexity of the project or task. Most risk management processes should follow defined stages, such as establishing the context, risk assessment, and risk treatment, along with risk communication and review and monitor.

Risk assessment involves risk identification, risk analysis, and risk evaluation, using the concepts of consequence and likelihood. In security risk management, likelihood should be used over probability, as likelihood does not imply a mathematical outcome. Consequence is the other primary element in risk assessment, considered more significant than likelihood and therefore more heavily weighted. Such weighting considers that individuals can better relate, understand, and picture an outcome (consequence) of an event.

In risk management it is important to understand the source of a risk, which is generally caused by a number of threats and can result in a number of consequences. Source risk can cluster many resulting risks, allowing a more focused risk assessment and treatment approach.

A unique and subdomain of risk management is security risk management. Security risk management retains the process of ISO 31000, but is supported by other informing processes. Understanding and articulating threat is central to security risk management; so, security risk management integrates the informing processes of threat assessment, criticality register, and vulnerability assessment.

Perception and culture theories are significant factors in risk and risk management. Thus, these theories provide some insight into how and why people view risks, the ability to carry out unbiased risk assessments, the degree of risk treatment, and the acceptance of risk.

The psychometric risk theory highlights the importance of dread, control, and trust in risk management, whereas cultural risk theory provides some degree of social group understanding.

Due to the subjective nature of risk management inputs, in particular with security risk management, there needs to be an awareness of risk gaming. Gaming is where users play the risk management process to produce their desired outcome, defeating the purpose of risk management. It is important that users understand and gain a benefit when using risk management, and it is not just an administrative burden or compliance process.

The importance of trust supports whether a risk is accepted or opposed, supported by research at the individual and societal levels. Trust can be distinguished at three levels: public trust, institutional trust, and specific trust. Finally, there should be an understanding that risk management is not wholly a science, but rather part science and artistry. However, to achieve effective security risk management, there needs to be a consensual outcome.

Further Reading

International Standards Organization, 2009. AS/NZS ISO31000:2009 Risk Management—Principles and Guidelines. International Standards Organization, Geneva.

References

Adams, J., 1995. Risk. UCL Press, London.

Ballard, G.M., 1992. Industrial risk: Safety by design. In: Ansell, J., Wharton, F. (Eds.), Risk: Analysis. Assessment and Management. John Wiley & Sons, Chichester, pp. 95–104.

Beard, B., Brooks, D.J., 2009. Consensual Security Risk Assessment: Overcoming Bias, Conflicting Interests and Parochialism. Paper presented at the Proceedings of the 2nd Australian Security and Intelligence Conference, Perth.

Beck, U., 1992. Risk Society: Towards a New Modernity. Sage, London.

Borodzicz, E.P., 2005. Risk, crisis and security management. John Wiley & Sons Ltd, Chippenham, Wilkshire.

Breakwell, G.M., 2007. The Psychology of Risk. Cambridge University Press, Cambridge.

Brooks, D.J., 2011. Security risk management: A psychometric map of expert knowledge structure. Risk Management: An International Journal 13 (1/2), 17–41.

Cambridge Dictionary, 2008. Cambridge Advanced Learner's Dictionary. Cambridge University Press, Cambridge.

Cameron, I., Raman, R., 2005. Process Systems Risk Management. Elsevier, Amsterdam.

Clarke, L., Short, J.F., 1993. Social organization and risk: Some current controversies. Annual Review of Sociology 19 (1), 375.

Dake, K., 1992. Myths of nature: Culture and the social construction of risk. The Journal of Social Issues 48 (4), 21.

Davidson, D.J., Freudenburg, W.R., 1997. Gender and environmental concerns: A review and analysis of available research. Environmental Behaviour 28, 302–339.

Douglas, M., 1992. Risk and blame: Essays in cultural theory. Routledge, London.

Douglas, M., Wildavsky, A., 1982. Risk and Culture: An Essay on the Selection of Technical and Environmental Dangers. University of California Press, Berkeley.

Duffey, R.B., 2008. Managing Risk: The Human Element. John Wiley & Sons, New York.

Earle, T.C., 2010. Trust in risk management: A model-based review of empirical research. Risk Anal. 30 (4), 541–574.

Ewald, F., 1991. Insurance and risks. In: Burchell, G., Gordong, C., Miller, P. (Eds.), The Foucalt Effect: Studies in Governmentality. Harvester/Wheatsheaf, London, pp. 197–210.

Eysenck, M.W., Keane, M.T., 2002. Cognitive Psychology: A Student's Handbook, fourth ed. Psychology Press Ltd, New York.

Ezell, B.C., 2007. Infrastructure vulnerability assessment model (I VAM). Risk Anal. 27 (3), 571–583.

Finucane, M.L., Slovic, P., Mertz, C.K., Flynn, J., Satterfield, T.A., 2000. Gender, race and perceived risk: The "white male" effect. Health, Risk and Society 2 (2), 159–172.

Fischer, R.J., Green, G., 2004. Introduction to Security, seventh ed. Butterworth-Heinemann, Boston.

Fischer, R.J., Halibozek, E., Green, G., 2008. Introduction to Security, eighth ed. Butterworth-Heinemann, Boston.

Giffin, K.I.M., 1967. The contribution of studies of source credibility to a theory of interpersonal trust in the communication process. Psychol. Bull. 68 (2), 104–120.

Gustafson, P.E., 1998. Gender differences in risk perception: Theoretical and methodological perspectives. Risk Anal. 18 (6), 805–811.

Hacking, I., 1975. The Emergence of Probability: A Philosophical Study of Early Ideas about Probability, Induction and Statistical Inference. Cambridge University Press, Cambridge.

Haimes, Y.Y., 2006. On the definition of vulnerabilities in measuring risks to infrastructures. Risk Anal. 26 (2), 293–296.

Hillson, D., Hullet, D., 2005. Assessing risk probability: Alternative approaches. In: Proceedings of PMI Global Congress 2005 EMEA. Prague, Czech Republic.

Howell, D.C., 2008. Fundamental Statistics for Behaviorial Science, sixth ed. Thomson, Belmont, CA.

Koller, G., 1999. Risk Assessment and Decision Making in Business and Industry: A Practical Guide. CRC Press, Boca Raton, FL.

Koller, G., 2000. Risk Modeling for Determining Value and Decision Making. Chapman and Hall/CRC Press, Boca Raton, FL.

Landoll, D.J., 2006. The Security Risk Assessment Handbook: A Complete Guide for Performing Security Risk Assessment. Auerbach Publications, Boca Raton, FL.

Lofstedt, R., 2003. Risk communication: Pitfalls and promises. European Review 11 (3), 417–435.

Lupton, D., 1999. Risk. Routledge, New York.

Mars, G., Frosdick, M., 1997. Operationalising the theory of cultural complexity: A practical approach to risk perceptions and workplace behaviours. International Journal of Risk Security and Crime Prevention 2 (2), 115–129.

Roper, C.A., 1999. Risk Management for Security Professionals. Butterworth-Heinemann, Boston.

Skipper, H.D., 1998. International Risk and Insurance: An Environmental Managerial Approach. Irwin McGraw-Hill, Boston.

Slovic, P., 1992. Perception of risk: Reflections on the psychometric paradigm. In: Krimsky, S., Golding, D. (Eds.), Social Theories of Risk. Praeger, Westport, CT.

Slovic, P., 1993. Perceived risk, trust and democracy. Risk Anal. 13 (6), 675–682.

Slovic, P., 1997. Risk perception and trust. In: Molack, V. (Ed.), Fundamentals of Risk Analysis and Risk Management. CRC Press, Boca Raton, FL, pp. 233–245.

Slovic, P., 1999. Trust, emotion, sex, politics, and science: Surveying the risk-assessment battlefield. Risk Anal. 19 (4), 689–701.

Smithson, M., 1989. Ignorance and Uncertainty: Emerging Paradigms. Springer-Verlag, New York.

Standards Australia, 2006. HB 167:2006 Security Risk Management. Standards Australia, Sydney.

Standards Australia, 2009. AS/NZS ISO31000:2009 Risk Management—Principles and Guidelines. Standards Australia International Ltd, Sydney.

Starr, C., 1969. Social benefits versus technological risks. Science 165 (3899), 1232–1238.

Tversky, A., Kahnemann, D., 1987. Rational choice and the framing of decisions. In: Hogarth, R., Reder, M. (Eds.), Rational Choice: The Contrast Between Economics and Psychology. University of Chicago Press, Chicago.

Vaughan, E.J., 1997. Risk Management. John Wiley & Sons, New York.

Weiten, W., 2005. Psychology: Themes and Variations, sixth ed. Wadsworth/Thomson Learning, Belmont, CA.

4

Built Environment

OBJECTIVES

- Characterize the term *built environment*.
- Explain the interrelationship between the built environment and security.
- Compare and contrast security strategies that may be used to improve the built environment, considering such techniques as physical measures, CPTED, lighting, and landscape.
- Describe the primary roles and responsibilities of a facility manager.
- Distinguish the interrelationships of the facility manager and security manager.

- Describe a typical facility's plant and equipment.
- Identify the likely vulnerabilities of a typical facility's plant and equipment.
- Formulate strategies to mitigate likely vulnerabilities of a typical facility's plant and equipment.
- Appraise the security requirements for an intelligent building system (IBS) used in a national critical infrastructure facility.
- Develop a strategy to protect an IBS used in a national critical infrastructure facility.

INTRODUCTION

Both security and facility managers operate within the human-constructed built environment that supports human activities, such as towns, cities, factories, parks, and transport systems. Much of our interaction to this built environment is through our buildings and facilities, which are managed by facility managers. But the type and quality of the built environment has a direct impact on security, therefore security should have input into its design, development, and operation.

Facility management can be defined as the practice of coordinating the physical workplace to maintain and develop facility services that support and improve an organization's primary objectives. Like security management, facility management is a developing discipline that has an undefined and broad body of knowledge, is a support function for the operations of the facility, and is often not given the importance that it may deserve.

Facility managers, although well aware of security, tend to consider security as a supporting service (Langston and Lauge-Kristensen, 2002). Many facility managers believe security is their responsibility (Cotts et al., 2010, p. 309), an appropriate view when ensuring that occupants and their visitors are safe. However, providing a safe environment is quite different to providing organizational security and there needs to be clear demarcation.

This chapter introduces the concept of the built environment, facility management, and the facility manager. The built environment can use a number of security strategies, such as crime prevention through environmental design (CPTED), the effect of lighting, and landscaping to achieve the desired outcomes of the process. As a consequence, these strategies provide a healthier built environment.

The development, definition, and function of a facility manager and his or her department are discussed. Thus, leading to the importance of the relationship between the facility manager and security, and through discussion of the facility plant rooms and equipment, vulnerabilities can be identified and how security can treat these risks. Security managers and facility managers need to operate in tandem, and such an approach will benefit both departments. It is difficult to totally divorce one manager from the other, as they both have independencies and interrelationships.

BUILT ENVIRONMENT

The *built environment* is the establishment and formation of our external surroundings, which influences our development and behavior. The built environment refers to all human-made structures in our towns and cities that provide and support human activities, ranging in scale from private homes to city megastructures. Furthermore, the built environment includes the landscape that we have modeled to better suit our purpose, for activities such as agriculture, transport, and entertainment. The built environment is a material, spatial, and cultural product developed by people for living, working, and leisure.

The built environment is the sum of a number of elements that combine the use of land space, urban design of space, and transport systems (Figure 4.1). Land space considers how the environment is used and what activities are undertaken. For example, is the land zoned for residential, commercial, entertainment, or light/heavy industrial use? Urban design is the design of cities and towns, including their physical elements, arrangement, appearance, function, and appeal. Finally, transport systems include infrastructure to allow us to move about our environment, such as roads, paths, bridges, trains, and airports

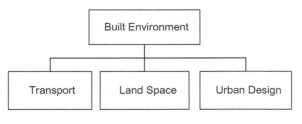

FIGURE 4.1 Elements to define the built environment.

(Handy et al., 2002, pp. 64–65). The integration of these three elements with the patterns of human activities define the built environment.

The built environment may be considered an interdisciplinary field that incorporates the design, construction, management, and use of the human-made surroundings as an interrelated system. It also considers the relationship of human activities over time to their surroundings. Planning the built environment should address the needs of humans to function in these artificial surroundings, considering the consumption of resources, disposal of wastes, and the facilitation of productive enterprise. The impact on the health of the population will be affected by the built environment, with the *feeling of safety* being crucial. Integrating the built environment and the management of security has the ability to improve safety and ensure people feel safer.

SECURITY AND THE BUILT ENVIRONMENT

The built environment has a direct effect not only on our feelings of safety, but also on how we may develop, behave, and respond. Therefore, both the built environment and security have a strong interrelationship. However, the level of understanding of this relationship is still limited, due to the complex nature of the problem. For example, why do some people grow up in very difficult environments, but lead model lives, whereas others follow a path of crime? There are a number of theories that security and the urban designers can use to improve the built environment, including the controlled use of physical barriers, CPTED, lighting, and managed greenery, which all lead to a physically healthier environment for all.

Physical Reinforcement

Physical reinforcement provides a safer and more secure environment, but does not necessarily provide a greater feeling of safety. In some instances the presence of physical security will negatively affect the legitimate users' perception of the environment, leading to an increasing sense of insecurity and not wishing to return. Therefore, the design and application of physical security measures in mitigating risks, such as fencing, bars, grills, security doors, and the like, should be considered within the environment.

Crime Prevention through Environmental Design

CPTED strategy fosters social interaction to reduce both the opportunity for potential offenders and the fear of crime by legitimate users. CPTED involves overlapping principles in the design of the built environment:

- Natural access control to prevent access to an area, increasing an offender's perception of detection and effort when entering. For example, natural access control includes clearly marked borders, single restricted entry points, and statements like gate pillars to define transitional zones, which also act as a psychological deterrence barrier.
- Natural surveillance has the purpose of keeping potential intruders under observation by legitimate users and, again, raises the perception of intruders being seen. Surveillance

creates a perception of increased safety and security for legitimate users. For example, facing office windows and desks toward entry points and staff car parks provides natural surveillance.

- Territorial reinforcement develops a sense of ownership and therefore control. This approach is achieved by structurally defining public and private spaces to reduce ambiguity of ownership. For example, building private spaces to reduce the possibility of illegal entry.
- Quality management ensures continued use of the space for its intended purpose and maintains the legitimate users feeling of safety. Proper lighting, facility maintenance, the removal of crime indicators, and vegetation management creates a perception of care. For example, rapid removal of graffiti is a successful strategy.

By designing areas according to these strategies, the crime level in the built environment can be reduced. CPTED, as a security principle, provides a robust approach to the design and maintenance of the built environment.

Lighting Effect

Organizations demand a high level of productivity and effectiveness in the workplace. In general, such space is designed for maximum productivity and requires an environment aligned to the ergonomic needs of the workforce. Architects and facility managers, in particular lighting designers, recognize the psychological and physiological affect that lighting has on the performance of people in the workplace.

The work environment, whether it is an office, workshop, or other space, requires the design of the lighting systems to provide the visual comfort necessary to enable workers to perform their tasks safely, effectively, and comfortably. Therefore, lighting is a major element of most facilities. The effort placed in designing quality lighting systems is more than recouped by greater worker productivity and personnel well-being. Nevertheless, facility managers tend to consider lighting from a productivity and ergonomic perspective, rather than lighting as a security tool.

Lighting has long been known to have an impact on the crime level in the built environment, but there was limited research to support cause and effect. It was not until the late 1980s that the effectiveness of lighting to influence the crime level and perception of safety was demonstrated (IESNA, 2003). Painter (1994) found a marked reduction in the incidence of crime and fear on lighted streets, such as theft, vandalism, vehicle theft, personal crime, and the level of delinquency (IESNA, 2003, pp. 1–2). Such results demonstrated that lighting has a significant part to play in crime prevention and therefore security.

Lighting as a security tool is considered effective through two factors. First, lighting supports surveillance, both formal from authorities such as police and security, and informal through natural surveillance from legitimate users. Second, lighting and its investment provide an improved built environment, which supports and builds the confidence and social control of legitimate users.

Greener Environments

In an urban environment, vegetation needs to be trimmed to maintain clear *lines of sight* and support natural surveillance to reduce actual and perceived fear of crime. Such an approach extends back to medieval times, when kings demanded that lords clear the kings' highways to a width of 200 feet on either side to remove cover for malefactors. Nevertheless, we live in a very different environment that is far more urban than in the past. Removing vegetation to reduce crime may be effective if the greenery is dense and unmaintained where antisocial behavior is prominent. However, the true benefit of vegetation is becoming better understood and the view that greenery is a negative factor is not the case. For example, Kuo and Sullivan state that those "living in greener surroundings have lower levels of fear, suffer fewer incivilities, and less aggressive and violent behaviors" (2001, p. 343). They also found that the greener the facility's surrounds, the fewer crimes are reported. Greenery still needs to maintain line of sight, but the use of high canopy trees and green grass areas work to deter crime and improve wellness.

FACILITY MANAGEMENT

Facility management can be defined as the practice of coordinating the physical workplace using business administration, behavioral sciences, and engineering. Furthermore, facility management is the "integration of processes within an organisation to maintain and develop the agreed services which support and improve the effectiveness of its primary activities" (British Standards, 2006). Within a single management responsibility, facility management integrates many of those job functions that have traditionally been handled in an uncoordinated fashion by separate and discrete departments.

As with other management roles, the facility manager plans, organizes, staffs, leads, and controls the facilities of an organization to provide a productive work environment. In addition to the practical aspects of cost and efficiencies, the facility manager has much to do with the quality of life within the working environment. This responsibility has emerged as organizations—large, small, private, or government—realize the capital involved in their offices, factories, workshops, warehouses, and plant rooms and equipment associated with facilities.

Importance of Facility Management

There is a cost to the business when owning or using a facility, and that cost has to be managed effectively, as should any other business function. For example, to leave rooms empty is poor space management and ineffective use of limited resources. For the average organization, staff account for up to 80% to 90% of its total expenditure and are a major cost for consideration (Langston and Lauge-Kristensen, 2002, p. xiv). Thus, not to provide appropriate facilities for staff will result in a significant burden to business. For example, if the heating, ventilation, and air conditioning (HVAC) system is not performing effectively and the inside temperature is either too hot or too cold, the workers will be uncomfortable and their performance will reduce. In addition and less tolerant, IT equipment may overheat and fail, significantly reducing the ability of staff to work.

Purpose of Facilities

Facilities must provide three core factors to achieve their objectives (Figure 4.2), namely provide a positive influence, be aligned to productivity, and finally be fit for purpose

FIGURE 4.2   Core factors for a facility to achieve productivity.

(Langston and Lauge-Kristensen, 2002, p. xvi). For example, when installing access control to a door, it will fail if staff has to move packages back and forward all day through that access control point. This action will adversely affect productivity and not be fit for purpose, resulting in the supervisor blocking the door open. To ensure a positive influence, the facility has to meet expectations such as providing a safe and secure environment, use natural light where possible, and have bathrooms and kitchen facilities.

WHO IS THE FACILITY MANAGER?

Facility managers coordinate the operational, tactical, and strategic management of facilities in a broad range of organizations across all property sectors, industries, utilities, and facilities. Their roles and responsibilities range from making decisions to the board, contributing to tactical and strategic planning, to those involved with the day-to-day management, operations, and maintenance of facilities. They often manage the capital and maintenance budget in these areas, and are responsible for the delivery of performance outcomes (fmedge, 2011).

The primary role of a facility manager is to provide a safe environment, followed by legality, costs, and customer service. Customers can include those who are external to the organization as well as other departments and staff who require fit-for-purpose facilities. Therefore, to achieve their primary role, facility management needs to provide two core outcomes: maintain the integrity of the facility services and maximize the return on investment for the facility owners.

Emergence of the Facility Manager

Prior to the 1970s, management of a facility was often divided between a number of individuals such as the building engineer, house officer, furniture officer, and building superintendent. In many cases, facility management was a secondary function that someone inherited or was assigned—there was limited communication, rudimentary air conditioning and elevator services, and fire life safety systems consisted of a hose reel on each floor of the facility.

With the advent of taller facilities containing modern services of air conditioning, high-rise elevators, building codes that demanded increased fire protection systems, and security systems, it became necessary to manage a facility and commensurate with the standards of services within the facility; as a result, the position of facility manager began to evolve. In many ways facility management has paralleled security management; where previously individuals were unlucky enough to inherit the position, now it is a full-time professional occupation and professional qualifications are becoming the norm.

Functions of a Facility Manager

Facility management is a complex function that requires a diverse set of skills and knowledge across many parts of an organization, as well as an appropriate understanding of business. A facility manager, much like a security manager, has to operate at many levels within an organization. For example, during a normal working day he or she may have to discuss technical problems and likely solutions with a refrigeration technician, as well as brief senior management on strategic facility matters.

Nevertheless, facility management is expected to provide effective financial management as a core activity (Langston and Lauge-Kristensen, 2002, p. 141). Thus, facility management is a business task, with facilities and their operations being a direct business overhead. Facility management has to add value to the function and facilities, ensuring that they provide a return on investment.

Functional Management Structures of Facilities

The functional structure of most organizations will vary, depending on their locality, size, industry, and other factors. Nevertheless, Cotts et al. (2010, pp. 35–47) suggest that there are five general facility management structures as shown in Table 4.1.

In general, facility management follows a relatively typical structure (Figure 4.3), from the facility owner through to the facility manager and onto their supporting staff. The building owner may be a bank, an investment company, a corporation, or an individual. A managing agent could be a local or international property management agency. At the facility manager's level, there is a tendency to focus on the facility and its occupants. Finally, the facility manager's supporting staff may include administration, liaison, and technical personnel.

TABLE 4.1 Facility Management Structures

Model	Characteristics
Office manager	Single facility dependent on a landlord, with consultants, contractors, and limited in-house facility staffing
One location, one site	Simplest approach providing full in-house facility services, with limited staff
One location, many sites	Headquarters approach providing in-house facility services, but reliant on consultants and specialists to meet demand
Public works	Complex or unique environments with strategic services at central and remote sites having full in-house facility services
International model	Large facility group where central acts as overseer and resource allocator, with national offices using various models

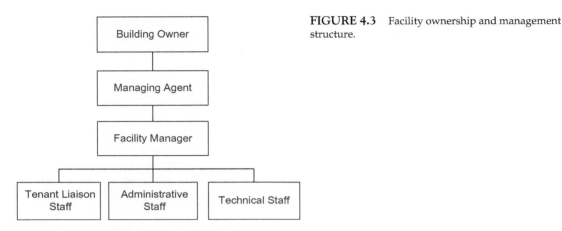

FIGURE 4.3   Facility ownership and management structure.

The tenant liaison staff falls into four broad categories, namely tenant liaison, staff liaison, internal refurbishments, and contractor management. A tenant liaison provides services such as moving tenants into the building, car parking, mail services, and public relations. A staff liaison provides concierge services, an elevator for moving goods, a fitness center, and other such services. Internal refurbishment provides new and existing tenants with upgraded fixtures and fittings. Finally, contractor management is the selection, hiring, and management of outsourced contractors, such as security services, technical contractors, mail services, cleaning and rubbish removal, and the like.

The administration staff includes tasks such as audits, financial management, estate management, lease administration, project management and coordination, reporting, insurance, and risk management. Finally, the technical services staff falls into three categories: electrical, mechanical, and hydraulic services (Figure 4.4).

Sustainability

Over two decades ago, energy usage was coming to the attention of facility managers and in particular their organizations. There are considerable financial savings in energy usage, as most facilities can reduce energy consumption by 25–50% (Langston and Lauge-Kristensen, 2002, p. 70). In addition to the direct financial savings, there was the need to be seen as a socially responsible corporation.

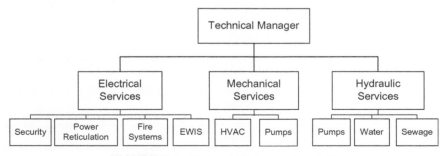

FIGURE 4.4   Typical technical services staff.

TABLE 4.2 Changing Focus from Energy to Sustainability

Decade	Changing Focus on Usage
1960s	Greater use of facility-wide systems with little focus on energy use
1970s	World oil crisis with increased focus on oil-generated energy use
1980s	Automation rare but increasing as microprocessing became more common
1990s	Automation common with focus on energy reduction
2000s	Integrated automation with other subsystems such as lighting and elevators
2010s	Fully integrated automation to all facility's plant rooms with whole of facility sustainability becoming more important
2020s	Fully integrated intelligent automation to all subsystems and plant, and their components with greater self-generation and whole of facility recycling

Today, the drive toward energy management has now extended to sustainability (Table 4.2). Sustainability considers not only the consumption of power, but also the reduction in water usage, recycling of gray water, waste reduction, and the increased recycling of materials that contribute to the sustainability of an organization.

Becoming a sustainable facility requires an organization to balance the impact it has on the environment, with the social well-being of customers, employees, and the local community in a way that is financially viable.

Future Issues of Facility Management

Facility management is a distinct function with its own challenges and future issues. Thus, there are many challenges facing the facility manager. The future challenges for facility managers (Cotts et al., 2010, p. 19) range from outsourcing of functions to that of the validity of their own profession (Table 4.3).

TABLE 4.3 Future Challenges of Facility Managers

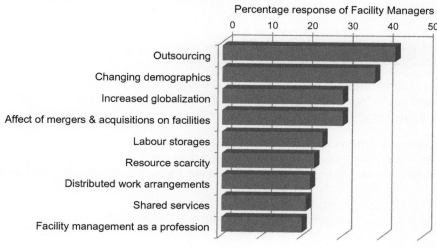

FACILITY MANAGEMENT AND SECURITY

Security integrates, interacts, and has interdependencies within the built environment and therefore with facility management. Facility management may view security as "one of the more universal services that must be provided" (Langston and Lauge-Kristensen, 2002, p. 134); however, both operate in discrete practicing domains. Thus, there has to be a clear understanding of each other's roles and responsibilities, which allows both supporting management functions to achieve the maximum gain from such an interrelationship.

The degree in which these two management functions interoperate will depend on the organization, its size and structure, geographical location, resources, regulatory requirements, and the type of work the organization performs. There is no single model for facility management. Nevertheless, as Brooks (2012a) proposed, facility management is an integral knowledge domain that supports security management (Figure 4.5).

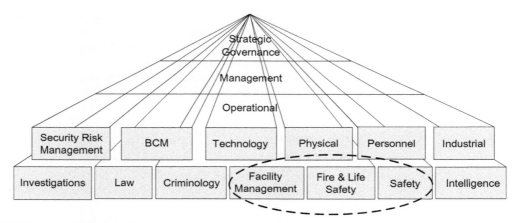

FIGURE 4.5   Integrated science of security framework. *(Adapted from Brooks, 2012a, with permission from Springer Science.)*

BUILDING MANAGEMENT SYSTEMS

Security operates in the built environment with a particular focus on facilities. Although many of the plant and equipment located in a facility are managed and operated by facility management, security needs to understand these aspects because of factors such as:

- Plant and equipment contain security vulnerabilities.
- Facility management do not always "think or act" about security.
- Security, if involved during the design phase, can reduce the vulnerabilities of plant and equipment.
- Security can use many plant functions, for example, elevator recall.
- Failure of plant will affect an organization and therefore security.

Security management should have a reasonable understanding of their facility's various plant and equipment, such as:

- HVAC, including heat and smoke extraction.
- Fire and life safety systems, including fire detectors, fire control, suppression, fire doors, and fire compartments.
- Elevators.
- Emergency warning and intercommunications system (EWIS).
- Lighting systems, including emergency, standby, and general lighting.
- Building codes, regulations, standards, and guides.

The level of threat to a facility's plant and equipment will be related to an organization's threats. Thus, equipment risks are contextual, defined by the threat to the organization and its operating environment. Understanding what function equipment performs allows an assessment of the criticality of such equipment and therefore what degree of security may be required.

Heating, Ventilation, and Air Conditioning

The environment within the buildings in which humans live and work is critical to our performance. In any facility, air is the prime heat-transfer medium, as it can be effectively conducted throughout the facility to absorb and dissipate energy. Energy is transferred with the principle of thermodynamics. As material is heated the distance between molecules expand and energy in the form of heat is added. For example, a compressor will compress a gas that is heated and can be used to warm the air. Thus, by managing the physical properties and distribution of air, it is possible to create a physical environment suitable for the purpose of the facility. This environmental management is achieved through HVAC systems.

HVAC is the term applied to the processes to clean, heat, cool, treat, and handle airflow in a facility to provide an environment that is fit for purpose. The HVAC controls the facility's internal climate to maintain a comfortable environment for occupants. In addition, HVAC provides a suitable environment for other purposes, such as server rooms, cool rooms, and clean rooms. HVAC is important to occupants' health, because a well-regulated and maintained system will keep the environment free from external pollutants such as dust, pollen, and environmental contaminates.

HVAC can also provide a critical fire and life safety function, through heat and smoke control. In a fire, the HVAC would normally draw in smoke and heat from the fire zone and spread these by-products of fire around the facility. Therefore, HVAC needs to sense fire in a facility and close down air functions in those areas to reduce the spread of fire products. In multistorey HVAC control, the system restricts the spread of heat and smoke, maintains fire-resistive integrity, and permits smoke control.

An HVAC is the integration of many parts, including heating (boilers), cooling (chillers), humidifiers, fans, ductwork, and vents (Table 4.4). These many parts are controlled by an automated controller that monitors the environment and adjusts the HVAC to meet a predefined need.

TABLE 4.4 HVAC Equipment and Components

Equipment	Description
Cooling elements	Chillers for refrigeration and heat exchangers for evaporation
Heating elements	Boilers, heaters, and convection
Humidifiers/dehumidifiers	Moisture injection, steam, and spray
Air distribution	Fans for supply, pressure, and exhaust; ductwork for distribution
Filters	Media of various sizes to remove particulates of contamination from air
Control elements	Dampers, valves, fan control, pump control, and equipment control
Control systems	Manual or automatic
Passive elements	Insulation, window treatments, facility structure, and facility orientation

HVAC Security Issues

Considering the many plant and equipment within most facilities, HVAC poses the most significant vulnerabilities.

HVAC Supporting a Critical Function

HVAC provides cooling and heating to all parts of a facility, with some sections supporting critical business objectives. For example, computer ITC servers produce significant heat and will quickly overheat and fail if cooling is lost. Such an outcome could have a significant effect on the ability of an organization to continue to function.

TREATMENT

Provide a secondary cooling source, such as a split-refrigerated system, mobile air conditioning unit, or similar system as a redundancy measure. Or alternatively, provide an uninterruptable power supply to those critical HVAC sections.

HVAC Air Intakes Prone to Contaminates

HVAC air intakes may be on street level or in easily assessable areas, resulting in vulnerability to noxious gas, smoke, and other contaminates. The HVAC filters are designed to reduce particle concentrations, but usually not to nano-size particles. An accidental or planned injection of some readily available gases such as pepper-spray is quickly spread throughout the facility.

TREATMENT

Reengineer intake vents by locating them well above head height. The installation of sloping vents will reduce the likelihood of items being thrown and remaining on the intake vents. It is necessary to develop procedures to respond to such an event, such as event identification and emergency evacuation. The protocols should allow the security control room or other responders to have the authority to switch the HVAC system into a predefined function, such as a dormant "off" state. After identification of the substance, the HVAC can be set to spill air, removing contaminates from the facility.

Loss of Power

HVAC may provide cooling and heating to critical systems that if lost for an extended period of time, will have a significant impact of business objectives. HVAC has a reliance on utility power, which if lost will result in the loss of HVAC.

TREATMENT

Provide a secondary power source to primary or secondary HVAC systems, such as a generator or uninterruptable power supply.

External HVAC Plant and Equipment

HVAC components are diverse and spread across all parts of a facility or site. For example, air intake ducts may be on the side of the facility, just adjacent to the plant room that houses the boilers and chillers. Most HVAC designers do not consider the security implications when locating such plant. Heat exchangers, due to their physical requirements, are generally located on the roof, which offers a natural barrier; however, many other HVAC components are located in more exposed positions.

TREATMENT

During the design phase of a facility, ensure that relevant HVAC components are offered a commensurate degree of protection based on the criticality of their function. For example, if the HVAC system is providing cooling to general office space, little protection may be required; however, if the HVAC is cooling a major server node, then a higher degree of physical and electronic protection should be provided.

Physical Access via Ducting

Depending on the size of the facility, the HVAC system requires a large intake of outside ambient air through external intake ducts. These external intake ducts can be large openings with only a limited physical barrier and filter, which can be breached to allow access to the plant room.

TREATMENT

Install intruder-resistant bars across the external air intakes and internally in the ducts. Re-engineer intake vents, similar to that for contamination treatment; however, these options will require an HVAC engineer to review the physical effects such barriers will have on air flow.

Industrial Espionage

HVAC delivers processed air throughout a facility, achieved via a broad network of ducts, fans, and baffles (Figure 4.6). Most HVAC systems will have a plant room on each floor, where a major supply duct will transverse that floor. Smaller spur ducts will branch from this supply duct, feeding air into the various zones. There is also a return duct (not shown in the figure), extracting "used" air back from each zone. These ducts provide an ideal method to gain access to other parts of the facility, in particular for industrial espionage such as audio or video

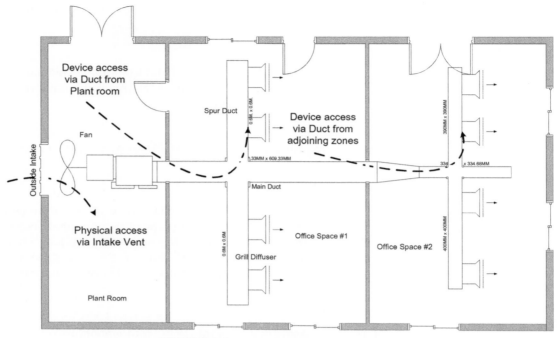

FIGURE 4.6   Internal layout of HVAC ducting.

listening devices. As shown in Figure 4.6, it would be quite simple to insert listening or video devices into the HVAC ducts from either the plant room or office space #1 into adjacent spaces.

TREATMENT

Create an audio secure room or install acoustic attenuators in the ducts. Alternatively, use splint air conditioning systems that do not use air ducts, but rather transfer liquid and gas for heating and cooling from the external heat exchanger.

Fire and Life Safety

Fire and life safety systems take precedence over security requirements. For example, if a door is an assigned fire exit, only free handle or a single sweeping motion egress can be used. Presenting a security card reader to unlock a door handle for egress will not meet most fire egress codes.

The consequence of fire and life safety determines that such equipment should be treated as vital systems. Recent statistics indicate the cost of fire damage in the United States alone is $331 billion or 2.3% of gross domestic product (Fire Analysis and Research Division, n.d.). Such cost of fire includes human loss (lives, medical treatment), economic loss (property damage, business interruption), and prevention and response to fire (fire departments, insurance, fire protection equipment, construction).

Fire and life safety is a generic term used to describe the overall level of fire safety provided to facilities and their occupants, which includes both passive and active systems. Fire safety engineering is multidisciplinary, having substantial relationships with building services (mechanical, hydraulic, and electrical), chemical and structural engineering, and an understanding of human behavior (National Engineering Registration Board, n.d.). The principle of fire safety includes a broad range of design, technology, and process solutions, with most facilities using a combination of all three.

There are many reasons for fire safety systems, apart from the protection of human life and property. Fire and life safety systems are designed, installed, and maintained to meet codes and standards for compliance. Design and construction can take a novel approach, if an appropriate fire solution is applied. Many modern high-rise facilities would not meet past fire safety expectations if they relied solely on a physical fire protection (passive) approach. Operational, local, and specialist site conditions can be satisfied by the application of novel solutions, such as water deluge and early warning fire detectors. Finally, fire safety systems support community relations inasmuch as people feel safe entering high-rise facilities or sleeping in a hotel—that is, they maintain social confidence.

There are a number of key elements in the understanding of fire and life safety, such as fire chemistry, design and construction, passive and active protection, and human behavior (Table 4.5).

The fire management cycle (Figure 4.7) applies elements in the management of fire and life safety. For example, the types of detectors are defined by the expected fire that is the result of the facility's fuel load. Fire control applies preplanned action, commencing suppression, and alerting the occupants. The fire and its by-products are contained within the fire compartment, allowing people to escape and response to occur. Concurrently, the suppression system will attack the fire by breaking one side of the fire triangle, such as water to cool (remove heat) or gas to suppress (reduce oxygen), therefore extinguishing the fire.

TABLE 4.5   Key Elements in Understanding Fire and Life Safety

Element	Description
Fire chemistry	Chemistry of combustion, better known as fire, for a scientific appreciation of the phenomenon and its effects; the fire triangle states that all three elements of heat, material, and oxygen must be present for combustion
Design and construction	Design, construction, and the use of the facility must consider appropriate building materials, their resilience to heat and smoke, expected fuel loading, building layouts, occupancy rates, and means of egress
Passive protection	Methods such as fire compartments, fire routes, fire doors and curtains, and their resistance to heat and smoke
Active protection	Methods such as automatic fire detection, fire suppression, heat and smoke venting, and emergency and exit lighting
Active management	Methods such as emergency warning and intercommunication system, elevator recall, and directional lighting
Human behavior	Reaction and action of people to fire, methods for estimating occupant response in a fire emergency, evacuation plans, fire plans, and other emergency response

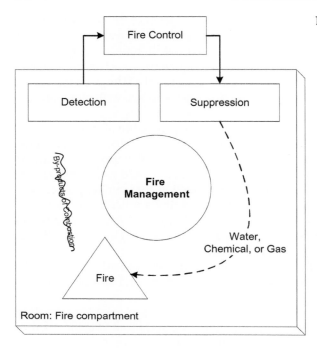

FIGURE 4.7   Fire management cycle in life safety.

The type of fire and life safety system installed in a facility is generally determined by the fire engineer during the design or major refit phase, in consultation with architects and structural engineers. Security will rarely be involved in this process; nevertheless, they need an understanding of fire safety systems due to their many security vulnerabilities.

Fire and Life Safety Security Issues

Security should have a basic knowledge of the operation of various types of fire and life safety systems to have an understanding of their benefits, limitations, and vulnerabilities. Fire and life safety systems will have some degree of impact on the operations of the facility and will be a concern of security.

Maintaining a Means of Egress

Fire and life safety egress routes are mandated by legislation in most jurisdictions. These egress routes are designed to allow facility occupants to escape the building in a timely manner, considering factors such as the likely fire type, number of occupants, means of escape routes, width of corridors and doorways, and minimum illumination.

Fire safety egress routes must be maintained at their commissioned level according to defined protocols. In addition, if the facility or a part of the facility changes its occupancy, then egress design may also have to be reengineered. For example, if parts of the facility change from office space to a short-term accommodation, greater fire and life safety would be required.

TREATMENT

Ensure that security has an appropriate understanding of fire safety systems from at least an operational level. Furthermore, understand what equipment is inclusive to the facility's fire and life safety, including both passive and active systems. Such a level of understanding should enable security to ask the fire and life safety questions, before making changes that may affect these systems. Security should be trained to provide clear and well-executed reporting procedures for such issues as broken fire doors and blocked egress routes.

Access Control and Fire Egress

Fire safety egress routes allow occupants to escape in a timely manner during an incident and these requirements are mandated in legislation. When there is an access problem in a facility, an option for security is to install an access control reader with an electric lock. If such work is carried out on a designated fire door, this modification could destroy the integrity of that fire door and the compartment that the fire door supports.

TREATMENT

Fire egress doors should not have additional locks installed, be locked, or have fastening devices, and should never be behind a room that is locked.

It is necessary for security to have an appropriate understanding of fire and life safety systems, and the equipment that forms a life safety system. This equipment includes passive methods such as curtains, fire doors, and fire screens, while active systems include detectors, fire panels, suppression, HVAC heat and smoke extraction, lighting, EWIS, and elevators with fire recall.

Fire and Life Safety Plant and Equipment

Fire and life safety equipment is distributed across all parts of the facility. For example, the entry foyer in most multistory facilities is likely to contain a fire indication panel, with an integrated EWIS. These control panels are designed to be in a prominent position to allow fire and emergency personnel rapid access. In addition, control systems, fire pumps, detectors, and the like are located throughout the facility. Thus, such distribution of fire equipment exposes the fire safety system to many types of attacks, ranging from casual vandalism such as turning off external water supply valves, to premediated use of fire alarm evacuation to remove people from certain areas.

TREATMENT

During the design phase, ensure that relevant fire safety equipment is provided a commensurate degree of protection based on the criticality of their function. For example, the water supply shut-off valve should be located in a secured zone or padlocked open with a fire department–issued keyed lock.

Elevators

An aim in facility design, in particular for a multistory facility, is the transportation of persons and materials efficiently and economically through reduced traveling times, reduced energy usage, increased productivity, and enhanced investment values. Elevators have been indispensable in the development of multistory facilities, as without elevators high-rise buildings would not be able to function.

There are three primary types of elevator drive mechanisms: hydraulic, geared-traction, and gearless-traction drives.

- Hydraulic elevators use a hydraulic ram to lift the car and its occupants to a travel limit of 60–65ft (18–20m). Its energy needs are higher than a traction elevator of equal duty; however, it will continue to be cost relevant for lower-rise facilities where it can raise greater loads over shorter distances at slow speeds. For example, typical facilities using this type of drive are industrial sites, hospitals, and storage facilities.
- Geared-traction elevators use a hoist cable that is attached to the top of the car and wrapped around a grooved drive pulley, sited at the top of the facility. The other end is attached to a counterweight that slides up and down the shaft on its own rails. With this weight and driven traction, lifting power is gained by the pressure of the cable on the grooved drive pulley. Geared traction elevators are designed for low- to medium-height facilities and vary in speed from 1.6–6.5ft (0.5–2m) per second, considered the upper limit for mechanical efficiency, hoisting wear factors, and noise emission. Drive options range from single- and two-speed AC drives for industrial and commercial use, to the more sophisticated, variable-voltage AC and DC drives for high-rise buildings.
- Gearless-traction elevators use the same hoist rope principle as the geared-traction elevators, but are normally found in medium- to high-rise facilities over 12 floors. These gearless elevators are used where short waiting intervals and high handling capacity are desirable. Typical speeds of the elevators are from 8–26ft (2.5–8m) per second. Gearless elevators are seldom installed as single units, and are typically found in banks of three or more. They use efficient DC direct-drive gears or variable-frequency AC drives.

Whatever drive mechanism an elevator has, they are provided with a number of standard fire and life safety devices. In general, these include such functions as fire recall to park the elevator on the ground floor, firefighter key override operation, EWIS for occupants during breakdown, and some may be fitted with emergency power.

Elevator Security Issues

Although elevators have the lowest level of equipment vulnerabilities than any other component in a facility, security will still be involved with elevators from an operational perspective.

Security Control of Elevators

Elevators are a primary route for people and goods into and out of a multistorey facility. If effective elevator security can be achieved, greater control of the facility can be gained. Thus, other routes within the facility, such as fire escape stairways, can be monitored to reduce illegitimate security avoidance use.

TREATMENT

Many building management systems allow a software-driven elevator control panel to be integrated into the security center, allowing more effective security control. Also the development of procedures for a planned response to various incidents is necessary; for example, it is possible to lock down all elevators to and from a floor from the security control system. Alternatively, all elevators can be directed to "home" on a predetermined floor, where occupants can be met by security.

Access Control Readers to Elevators

Card readers are often placed into elevator cars, as these can provide an effective method to control access to and from various floors. Nevertheless, there are a number of considerations with this strategy such as the physical installation of card readers, the delivery of goods, and visitor access and visitor movement.

Older elevators use trailing multicore cables that after a period of time suffer broken cable cores. Such breakage leads to limited spare cores, restricting the ability to install card readers or requiring an expensive cable replacement. However, modern elevators use digital data transfer for the transfer of data and communication with and between elevator cars. Jurisdictions require elevator maintenance and interfacing access control equipment to be performed by an accredited technician.

TREATMENT

When considering the installation of card readers into elevators, ensure that full technical understanding is gained on what is achievable and what the full cost of the interface is. In addition, perform an activity flow process that maps likely and unlikely events to consider how these events can be dealt with before the work is carried out. For example, write a procedure before the event occurs or inform the facility tenants on access limitations.

Elevator Plant and Equipment

Elevator equipment, unlike fire safety equipment, is generally located in a single plant room above the elevator shafts. Access to this room has to be controlled from both a physical perspective to protect equipment and a regulatory need, as only accredited technicians can maintain elevator equipment.

TREATMENT

Ensure that the elevator plant room has appropriate access control measures.

Intelligent Building Systems

Intelligent building systems (IBSs) or building management systems (BMSs) are facility-wide control systems that connect, control, and monitor a facility's equipment. These facility-wide systems are being installed and operated in many different types of buildings, from critical infrastructure such as airports to residential smart homes. IBSs allow the occupants to have a better experience in their home or workplace. For example, when a person arrives at work and presents his or her credential to the card reader to enter, the IBS will call the elevator to the foyer, allow access to the employee's designated floor, and activate the relevant office lights and HVAC zones. The IBS maintains the operation of the lights and HVAC while it detects movement in the office and adjacent areas, and deactivates these services when that person leaves the building.

In the last decade, IBSs have become a significant factor in the design, build, operation, and maintenance of commercial facilities. Such systems have become popular, driven by the need to save energy, provide more reactive and safer facilities, and reduce operational costs. IBSs integrate and enable connectivity within a facility's plant and equipment subsystems, including HVAC, lighting, fire and life safety, elevators, power, and security systems. The integrated security systems not only include access control, but also intruder detection and CCTV.

The ability of IBSs to integrate such diverse systems is achieved through common and open data communication protocols and hardware. Nevertheless, such an open architecture leave facilities vulnerable to external and internal threats and risks. Depending on a facility's threat environment, vulnerabilities can be diverse and extended throughout many parts of the IBS (Brooks, 2012b). IBSs are still at an early stage of development; thus, understanding the feasibility of such technological solutions should be considered from the onset as privacy, information control, and security, which are often neglected (Gadzheva, 2008, p. 6). Many of these systems are designed and installed by building engineers, and owned and operated by facility managers, with both groups generally having limited security awareness.

IBS Architecture

IBS architecture comprises of three levels of both software and hardware, namely management, automation, and field levels (Figure 4.8). At the field level, many types of sensors and actuators transmit and receive data from the automation level controllers. The automation level controllers provide the interface between the many subsystems and their field devices of the facility. This interface allows these subsystems to interact and respond to each other to maintain the performance of the environment. The human interface is located at the management level, supporting system programming, monitoring of activities, and reporting of events.

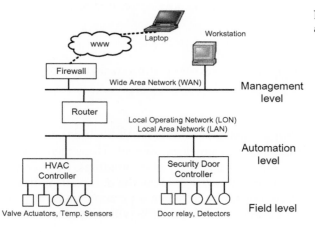

FIGURE 4.8 Intelligent building system architecture.

IBS Security Issues

IBSs suffer from generic vulnerabilities, with their levels of exposure commensurate to the organization and their facilities. A facility that is exposed to a greater threat level will result in equal exposure of the IBS. For example, critical infrastructure will have a significantly higher threat profile than a corporate office. As a result, vulnerabilities of IBS include:

- Physical access to the IBS workstations and its operating software, which results in compromise of the management level including the greater organizational IT network and BMS programming.
- Compromise of the management and automation level networks (Ethernet) through physical network wiretapping, where the network cables are stripped back and an external connection made, allowing the network data to be monitored, data injected, or other devices connected.
- Insertion of a foreign workstation and/or controller into the network; for example, a rogue device that takes commands away from the authorized system. Insertion of a rogue device can be achieved through access to any part of the automation level network.
- Embedded system memory and functionality modification, in particular embedded wireless connectivity. Many controllers are generic devices that may have wireless capability, but are sold and installed with this function disabled. Reenabling such functionality is relatively simple.
- Compromise of open and standardized operating software, such as LonWorks and BACnet. Many manufacturers build their devices to have plug-and-play capability, allowing equipment to directly connect to a BMS with no interface devices.
- Use of a foreign programmer. Access to any controller located somewhere within the facility will allow access to the automation level, by plugging in a local programmer or laptop. If appropriate controls are not in place, changes to the program can be made. For example, isolating certain intruder detection inputs for predetermined periods of time will allow illegitimate access to the facility.
- Controller enclosures are designed only to provide a cover for their internal electronics. Therefore, these covers are designed as clip-off, not robust and with no form of anti-tamper function.
- Loss of power supply, in general, will result in the IBS failing, along with its monitoring and control functions.

Being able to covertly log into the IBS, in particular the automation network level, will allow a "picture" of the facility to be built. For example, when an employee arrives at the facility and presents his or her card for access, the request and resulting action is propagated onto the network. As a result, it is possible to track that person, as various subsystems activate on or off by sensors such as card readers, elevator controls, and light sensors. Most programming is coded in plain English, so location codes are relatively easy to decipher. When the CEO leaves the office, it becomes a relatively easy monitoring task to track his or her movements. When and where security guards patrol the facility and their current location after hours can also be tracked. Finally, as security devices such as intruder detectors and CCTV are incorporated into IBSs, such inclusion increases the criticality and vulnerabilities of the IBS as a whole.

TREATMENT

Mitigating IBS vulnerabilities require a broad approach that combines the many strategies of security and protection of facility plant and equipment. Generic treatment strategies are presented in the next section.

PROTECTING THE FACILITY

Risks to a facility's plant and equipment are contextual—that is, they align with an organization's threat exposure. If an organization and its facility contain sensitive or highly protected information, the threat can be significantly higher. To protect a facility, there are a number of generic mitigation strategies that can be taken:

- *Security risk management*: A sound, holistic security risk management strategy informed by threat assessments, criticality register, and vulnerability assessments.
- *Information system and communication protection*: Provide some degree of network isolation and partitioning, both internal and external, between the IBS, subsystems, and wider networks.
- *Physical and environmental security*: Control and validate access to the critical plant and equipment, with layered protection measures wherever possible.
- *Personnel security*: Ensure personnel are vetted to use and maintain the facility's systems, including third parties such as vendors and service personnel.
- *Continuity of operations*: Provide a degree of emergency power and redundant networks to the more critical plant and equipment functions and devices, directed by the criticality register.
- *Security awareness*: Increase awareness of risk and threats to the facility's plant and equipment. In addition, ensure greater integration of the various stove-piped departments such as ITC, physical security, personnel security, and facility management functions.

CONCLUSION

The built environment is our human-constructed surroundings that provide and support human activities. This environment includes all human-made structures and landscapes such as buildings, transport systems, and, to some degree, the countryside. The type and quality of the built environment has a direct impact on security; therefore, security should have some degree of input into its design, development, and operation. The built environment is typically used to describe the interdisciplinary field that incorporates the design, construction, management, and use of human-made surroundings as an interrelated system and its effect and behavior on people using the environment.

This chapter introduced the concept of the built environment, facility management, and the facility manager. The built environment can use a number of security strategies, such as CPTED, the lighting effect, and landscaping. These strategies lead to not only an improved feeling of safety, but also a healthier environment.

Organizational security integrates, interacts, and has interdependencies within the built environment, in particular, with facilities that are managed by facility managers. Although facility management operates in a discrete practicing domain from security, there should be a clear understanding of each other's roles and responsibilities. From a security perspective, such understanding leads to improved security outcomes.

Much of equipment located in a facility is owned and operated by the facility manager. Security management needs to understand this equipment, as they do contain security vulnerabilities and facility management does not always consider security. In addition, understanding facility equipment allows security to better use these items in an operational, tactical, and strategic context.

Security management should have a reasonable understanding of equipment, including intelligent building systems, HVAC, fire and life safety systems, elevators, passive fire methods, emergency warning and intercommunications systems, and lighting, and their related codes and regulations. The level of threat to a facility and its equipment will be commensurate with the organization and its environmental threats, something that security should understand, articulate, and address.

Further Reading

Craighead, G., 2009. High-rise Security and Fire Life Safety, third ed. Butterworth-Heinemann, Boston.

Websites

European Facilities Management Network (EuroFM), www.eurofm.org.
International Facility Management Association (IFMA), www.ifma.org/about/.
National Fire Protection Association, http://www.nfpa.org/.

References

British Standards, 2006. BS EN 15221-1:2006. Facilty Management. Terms and Definitions. Bristish Standards, London.
Brooks, D.J., 2012a. Corporate security: Using knowledge construction to define a practising body of knowledge. Asian Journal of Criminology, http://dx.doi.org/10.1007/s11417-012-9135-1.
Brooks, D.J., 2012b. Security threats and risks of intelligent building systems: Protecting facilities from current and emerging vulnerabilities. In: Laing, C., Badii, A. (Eds.), Securing Critical Infrastructures and Industrial Control Systems: Approaches for Threat Protection. IGI Global, Hershey, PA.
Cotts, D.G., Roper, K.O., Payant, R.P., 2010. The Facility Management Handbook, third ed. Amacom, New York.
Fire Analysis and Research Division. (n.d.). The total cost of fire in 2009. Retrieved March 30, 2012, from http://www.nfpa.org/assets/files/PDF/TotalCostFactSheet.pdf.
fmedge, 2011. What is facility management? Retrieved March 20, 2012, from http://www.fmedge.com.au/index.php?option=com_content&view=article&id=27&Itemid=28.
Gadzheva, M., 2008. Legal issues in wireless building automation: An EU perspective. International Journal of Law and Information Technology 16 (2), 159–175.
Handy, S.L., Boarnet, M.G., Ewing, R., Killingsworth, R.E., 2002. How the built environment affects physical activity views from urban planning. Am. J. Prev. Med. 23 (2S), 64–73.
IESNA, 2003. Guideline for Security Lighting for People, Property and Public Space IESNA G-1-03. Illuminating Engineering Society of North America, New York.
Kuo, F.E., Sullivan, W.C., 2001. Environment and crime in the inner city: Does vegetation reduce crime? Environment and Behavior 33 (3), 343–367.
Langston, C., Lauge-Kristensen, R., 2002. Strategic Management of Built Facilities. Butterworth-Heinemann, Boston.
National Engineering Registration Board. (n.d.). Fire safety engineering. Retrieved March 30, 2012, from http://www.engineersaustralia.org.au/nerb/fire-safety-engineering.
Painter, K., 1994. The impact of street lighting on crime, fear and pedestrian street use. Security Journal 5, 116–124.

5

Physical Security

OBJECTIVES

- Realize the need for physical security for the protection of assets.
- Understand the security principle of defense-in-depth for the protection of assets.
- Know the functions of barriers in a defense-in-depth approach to physical security.
- Understand the concepts involved in crime prevention through an environmental design approach to the effective use of the built environment.

- Be able to apply the routine activity theory to the protection of assets through defense-in-depth and crime prevention through an environmental design.
- Be aware of the modes of attack for the penetration of a perimeter and internal barriers to gain unauthorized access.
- Know the methodology for assessing glazing barriers against ballistic attack.

INTRODUCTION

Physical security is a term used to define the integration of humans, procedures, and equipment for asset protection against threats and risks. Fischer et al. (2008) define physical security as the means by which a given facility protects itself against theft, vandalism, sabotage, and unauthorized access. Smith (2006) indicates that physical security decribes the physical measures designed to safeguard people, to prevent unauthorized access to property, and to protect assets against sabotage, damage, and theft. The physical security of an organization prevents access for unauthorized people to premises, areas, buildings, rooms, vaults, and car parks. This form of security relies, in part, on the *strength of materials* to prevent access by force.

Physical security components provide target hardening and contribute to the deterrent effect of a complete security protection plan. Effective and well-designed physical security measures, in conjunction with an appropriate security plan, will deter an opportunist intruder. However, in the case of a determined intruder, these physical security components and measures will only serve as detection, delay, and response layers, as it is considered that with sufficient time and resources any barrier can be breached. The protection of assets by physical security is achieved through layers of physical protective measures (physical controls), and is considered to be the most fundamental aspect of physical protection (Fennelly, 2004, p. 101).

Arrington (2006, p. 34) states that opportunity reduction is the key element in crime prevention, where crime opportunity is defined as a measure of how easy it is for a threat agent to commit a crime (Cox and Ricci, 1990, p. 326). It can be stated that opportunity reduction can be achieved through manufacturing unwanted events or circumstances to be more difficult, risky, and less rewarding to a threat agent.

This chapter discusses two major principles of crime reduction through the applications of physical security to the protection of assets: defense-in-depth (DiD) and crime prevention through environmental design (CPTED). Furthermore, components of physical security and methods of attack in the context of organizational security are discussed.

ROUTINE ACTIVITY THEORY

The routine activity theory has evolved from the rational choice theory, which seeks the most cost-effective means to achieve a specific goal without reflecting on the worthiness of the goal. It is a main theoretical approach in the paradigm of microeconomics, and is a proponent of human decision-making in the behavior of individuals in microeconomic models and analysis. Because the rational choice theory has a deficiency in the understanding of consumer motivation, some economic researchers restrict its application to understanding business behavior where goals are well stated. The theory assumes that humans make decisions in a rational manner, which implies that their behavior can be modeled, and so predictions can be made on future activities.

The routine activity theory was developed by Cohen and Felson (1979) from the criminological application of rational choice, and focuses on the characteristics of crime rather than the characteristics of the offender. Thus, the environment has a role in the occurrence of crime and the routine activity theory can be considered an aspect of crime prevention theory. The characteristics of the routine activity theory are that three elements must be present at the same time:

1. An available and suitable target.
2. A motivated offender.
3. No presence of an authority figure to prevent a crime from occurring.

An available and suitable target, a motivated offender, and the absence of an authority figure can result in a crime being committed. The routine activity theory describes how likely offenders come to commit a crime partly based on their normal everyday activities. Routine travel and activities can bring a motivated offender into contact with a desirable though vulnerable asset without appropriate guardianship. The simultaneous concurrence of the three elements of the routine activity theory will witness the possible occurrence of a crime.

DEFENSE-IN-DEPTH

The DiD strategy is a robust fundamental principle that is applied in a range of situations in the physical asset protection of an organization (Smith, 2003, p. 8). It is noted that the DiD strategy has been applied by armies and tribes for many centuries by enclosing an asset with a succession of barriers. The purpose of physical security is to delay the progress of a *determined* intruder toward an asset for sufficient duration until a response team arrives to apprehend the trespasser. It has been found, initially through experience, that a series of barriers rather than a single strong barrier will best delay the progress of the intrusion. The principle of DiD imposes a succession of barriers, which require controlled access, between the public and the asset to be protected.

The DiD is a classic protection strategy from ancient military principles that presents a series of physical barriers or layers that deter and delay an intrusion until such time as an appropriate response is mounted.

Using the DiD model, Figure 5.1 shows the valuable asset to be protected, surrounded by a succession of barriers. These barriers have the function of preventing access by an intruder or detecting the presence of an intruder. The strategy is designed by reviewing the security threats and risks to these areas to allow for future preventative measures to be deployed. Current DiD strategies, also referred to as elastic defense, seek to delay rather than prevent the advance of an attacker, and were originally developed as a military strategy to "buy" time by a defending army by yielding space. This strategy is now used by modern-day security professionals to control access to their facilities and protect their assets.

The current functions of the barriers in the DiD principle are *deterrence, detection, delay,* and *response* (D^3R). Further refinement to D^3R is the additional inclusion of *recovery* to the model: thus, the D^3R^2 model has become a modification of the DiD strategy.

- *Deterrence* is achieved when the implementation of physical security measures are sufficiently strong that potential intruders perceive the breaching of a barrier to be too difficult to defeat. Therefore, deterrence is achieved either by the psychological effect of the

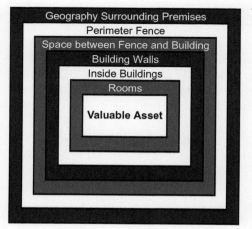

FIGURE 5.1   Principle of DiD applied to a warehouse facility.

Geography Surrounding Premises
Perimeter Fence
Space between Fence and Building
Building Walls
Inside Buildings
Rooms
Valuable Asset

detection, delay, and response layers, or physically by the presence of the response team. Psychological deterrence is also achieved by proper signage, lighting, and definition of boundaries. The efficacy of deterrence has to be questioned as it is difficult to measure and, in some ways, conflicts with routine activity theory; nevertheless, this component has merit and, if supported through a threat assessment, provides value.

- *Detection* of an overt or covert intruder must be accomplished to prevent an attack on the assets being protected, and can be achieved through a variety of sensors including personnel, electronic detection, and CCTV. The detection function activates an alarm that initiates a response to apprehend intruders. Thus, detection is a critical function of the DiD strategy, as without detection, it is only a matter of time before an intruder penetrates the facility and reaches the assets. Early detection of an intruder is required to facilitate apprehension and deterrence. Intruder apprehension and deterrence is dependent on the critical detection point (CDP), which is dependent on the readiness and rapidness of the response force.
- *Delay* of the progress of an intruder attacking a facility is achieved through the strength of materials in physical barriers, presence of personnel, aggressive barriers such as razor wire, and difficult environmental factors such as water, mud, and dense undergrowth. Delay is achieved by installing a series of physical barriers such as fences, walls, doors, and locks, all of which must be successively defeated to reach the assets of an organization.
- *Response* is a necessary function of a DiD strategy to prevent success from an intrusion and the protection of assets. The response action may be performed by a response team, whose force matches the attacker and who will attend the location of the detection. The ability to match or exceed the attackers' likely force can be informed by the threat assessment (see Chapter 2); for example, an armed intruder needs to be countered by an armed responder. The response time must be less than the delay time for the barrier(s), or else the intruders will have completed their mission before the attendance of the response function. Response is the deployment of a deterrent system that either apprehends or drives away an intrusion. An effective delay layer must provide sufficient and substantial barriers to allow the response team to attend the facility and prevent the intrusion. It could be stated that these functions truly define the DiD strategy (Smith, 2003, p. 9).
- *Recovery* is the resilience of an organization to rebound from an incident or crisis, achieved through appropriate and preplanned business continuity management strategies (see Chapter 9).

The routine activity theory requires the presence of an authority figure to prevent the occurrence of an opportunistic crime. However, the function of response in the DiD strategy provides the appropriate authority within the context of the model. Also, the deterrence function of the DiD strategy provides a demotivator for an opportunistic and motivated offender in the prevention of a crime.

The DiD principle employs barriers in its design to realize the D^3R functions of physical security. The design of the barriers of the DiD strategy must be able to deter, detect, delay, and respond to the presence of an intruder in an attack on assets. The classes of barriers that provide these functions are:

- *Psychological barriers* provide deterrence through signage, security lighting, low fences on boundaries, and CCTV.

- *Physical barriers* such as fences and walls, shutters, locks of all forms and types, and safes and security cabinets through strength of materials provide a delay function against penetration.
- *Electronic barriers* detect the presence of intruders in restricted areas so that an appropriate response can occur to prevent the loss of an asset. These technological barriers include optical and infrared beams, intelligent CCTV, volumetric detection systems such as passive infrared and microwave systems, linear detection systems such as microphonic cable and laser infrared beams, and point detection systems such as break glass and magnetic reed detectors.
- *Procedural barriers* in security management through procedures can place barriers to impede the progress of an intruder into a facility. Such management procedures can include key management systems, static and mobile guards, and identification badges.

The number of layers of barriers, and the classes of barriers, according to the DiD principle for the protection of an asset will be determined by the perceived level of threat, the criticality of the asset, and the value of the asset. Thus, the selection of appropriate barriers for the DiD strategy will depend on the assets to be protected and the strategic importance of the facility. Effective layers of barriers provide sufficient and substantial obstacles to allow the response team to attend the facility and prevent the intrusion. It could be stated that these functions truly define the DiD strategy (Smith, 2003, p. 9). The application of security technology, through layers of protection, is an essential component in the protection of assets according to the DiD principle. The selection of appropriate technology will be determined by the *threat, criticality,* and *risk* of an attack on a facility under protection (Smith, 2006, p. 613).

A DiD strategy can be planned and designed using a flowchart model to show that barriers can be employed to protect the assets of an organization. Figure 5.2 shows the progression of an attack on a facility with a hypothetical DiD strategy with single barriers of deterrence, detection, delay, and response, with apprehension as the final outcome. If any one of the electronic, physical, or procedural barriers fails, then the attack has been a success; however, if all barriers fulfill their functions, then the DiD strategy has been successful. It is interesting to note that the psychological barrier can/will fail, yet the strategy can apprehend the intruders. If the response is too slow, then the attack has been successful. Again, apprehension of the intruders is required, and some security management plans require conviction of the intruders for a successful DiD strategy.

Again, Figure 5.2 shows a flowchart for the planning of a series of barriers of a facility such as a computing center. The strategy should use appropriate functional barriers for psychological, electronic or technological, physical, and procedural barriers to protect the assets of the computing center. Figure 5.2 shows the intrusion path will progress from top to bottom, where the initial psychological barriers of signage, CCTV, and cleared ground outside the perimeter fence are located. If the potential intruder is deterred from the attack, then the presence of the potential intruder is ignored. However, if the intruder attacks the physical barrier in the form of a chain-mesh fence and this barrier fails, then the intruder has penetrated the precinct of the computer center.

In progressing through the grounds of the facility toward the buildings of the computing center, electronic or technological barriers are encountered. These barriers include security lighting, intelligent CCTV, fence-mounted sensors, and microwave detection. If the intruder

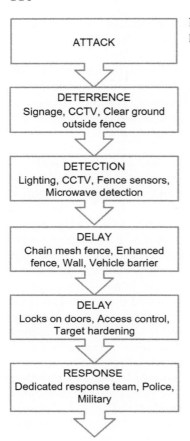

FIGURE 5.2 A flowchart of the DiD strategy applied to the design of physical protection of a computer center.

is able to bypass these detection systems undetected, then these detection systems have either failed or were defeated. For example, bypass may be achieved through defeating or spoofing the technology, or the technology has failed due to environmental factors, lack of maintenance, or an inappropriate design and application.

The final set of barriers at the buildings of the facility can include further physical barriers such as the walls of the buildings, the physical locks on the access ways, an access control system, and target hardening of the windows. Success of these physical barriers will result in apprehension of the intruder by a response team as a procedural barrier. However, failure of these barriers will have the consequence of loss of assets.

Figure 5.2 is a generic design for the DiD strategy for the protection of a computing center. It can be seen that the psychological, physical, electronic or technological, and procedural barriers can be placed in different orders and repeated in placement as needed to defend the facility, although Garcia (2001, p. 7) argues that delay before detection is primarily a deterrent. Nevertheless, in a facility that has restricted space (reduced ability to insert multiple barriers) or a need for greater security, detection before delay may be more appropriate.

How much physical security is needed to protect the assets of an organization is dependent on the value, both tangible and intangible, and importance of the assets. Government organizations and companies conduct a range of differing activities, and have assets of greatly different values and importance. As a result, it is not necessary for all installations to have the same amount of physical security to protect the assets of an organization. The degree of protection warranted in any particular facility can be predicted by analysis of the *threat*, *criticality*, and the *vulnerability* functions of the assets.

- *Threat:* the capability and intent of the attacker.
- *Criticality:* an asset is critical if the organization has a reduced function when it is stolen or destroyed.
- *Vulnerability:* an asset is vulnerable if it is at risk of being stolen or vandalized.

As a result, facilities can have the following ratings on the factors affecting the level of physical security to be installed:

- High criticality only.
- High vulnerability only.
- High criticality and high vulnerability.
- High threat.

If a facility is both *highly critical* and *highly vulnerable* with an anticipated *high threat*, then an extensive physical security program is necessary. However, it is neither economically possible nor necessary to provide a high level of physical security for all facets of the facility. Because of the costs involved in physical security measures, many security managers will choose not to achieve maximum protection for the entire installation or activity within the organization.

To best use resources available for asset protection, the anticipated threat and specific criticality and vulnerability of the various areas within a facility must be determined. Then prioritization will determine which areas of the facility will be designated for enhanced physical security (see Chapter 2). Special protection will be provided for the most critical and vulnerable areas that have the greatest threat, while areas of lesser susceptibility are subjected to lesser amounts of physical protection. The term *target hardening* is used for the enhancement of physical security for a highly critical and highly vulnerable area in an organization.

CRIME PREVENTION THROUGH ENVIRONMENTAL DESIGN

An extension of the routine activity theory is the development of a crime prevention strategy to reduce the environmental factors to reduce crime. Thus, the factors of the routine activity can be manipulated by environmental design to reduce the opportunity for potential offenders to engage in criminal activities. The development of CPTED by Crowe (2000) has presented a model for crime reduction through the intelligent design of urban space.

CPTED is a principle of security to reduce the occurrence of crime in urban locations. CPTED is described as a proactive strategy that calls for the proper design and effective use of the built environment (CPTED Ontario, 2002). The CPTED strategy fosters social interaction to reduce crime opportunity for potential perpetrators and reduce the fear of crime by legitimate space uses (New Zealand Ministry of Justice, 2005, p. 5). Crime prevention strategists are currently involved in the design of urban, commercial, residential, institutional, and transportation structures and areas for business and recreation.

Over the past two to three decades there have been many mistakes in urban planning, community development, and architectural design with regard to the well-being, safety, and security of a community. Many of the failures in community design that have led to deterioration in environmental conditions can now be overcome through the application of technology. This outcome has resulted in a failure of designers to carefully examine the relationship between human behavior and the urban environment so as to improve the living surroundings for a community.

The renewed interest in adopting CPTED practices has enabled planners to redefine design strategies and concepts that have been neglected over the years through conflicting views and beliefs about planning and design. The CPTED principle has been proposed by Crowe (2000) as "the proper design and effective use of the built environment [that] can lead to a reduction in the fear of crime and the incidence of crime, and to an improvement in the quality of life."

Environmental design is an approach to preventing crime in an area, region, or community. Its objective is to improve security in residential and commercial areas by limiting criminal opportunity through the use of natural barriers and natural surveillance.

The CPTED Principle

It is important to acknowledge that the concept of CPTED is not intended to describe how to design buildings or facilities to provide better security. Rather, its purpose is to create the working environment that enables professions engaged in the tasks of planning and design to better relate to the task of designing for people. The concept of CPTED seeks to encourage participants in the design process to pursue the purpose of the design in a particular area by seeking responses to previously unaddressed problems, and most importantly to examine the environment of a planned facility in the CPTED model of safety and protection.

Urban and local planners should understand the basic concepts of CPTED and are encouraged to:

- Comprehend and understand the terminology, objectives, and language of other professions collaborating with them.
- Question all conventions and practices in current design and planning applications and seek responses to issues raised. As the concept of CPTED gains greater acceptance, the planning industry will need to assimilate these ideas into the standard approach of planning.
- Planning professionals will need to consider the environment of the area to be developed from a perspective that will emphasize the planning and design components according to CPTED principles.

A facility or event designed according to CPTED principles involves the design of physical space in the context of the needs of genuine users of the space. This design feature has been termed *defensible space* and incorporates an area or region in and around the facility that can be adequately protected to render it crime-free, increase its perceived perception of safety, and encourage legitimate users.

A facility that has been planned according to CPTED principles takes into account a range of needs of legitimate users:

- The physical requirements of the occupants to perform the functions of the organization.
- The social attributes of the facility should enhance the objectives of the organization and encourage individuals to perform at a superior level.
- The psychological needs of the facility may include natural lighting, open-space design, and covert security systems.

The design of the facility must meet all requirements of legitimate users for the normal and expected use of the space. Thus, the planning phase must consider the predictable behavior of both legitimate users of the space and offenders in the area. Armitage and Monchuk (2011, p. 327) have discussed the factors impacting crime by physical security, surveillance, and territoriality with subsequent reductions in crime.

The emphasis of design of CPTED differs from the traditional target-hardening principles used in a DiD approach. Target hardening is aimed at denying or limiting access to a potential crime target through the use of physical barriers such as fences, gates, locks, alarms, and walls. A limitation of a target-hardening approach is that it leads to a reduction in pleasure derived from use of an area, and results in its use being limited and the users losing the perception of ownership, territorialism, or safety. Nevertheless, "there is much disagreement concerning whether or not target hardening should be considered as a component of CPTED" (Cozens et al., 2005, p. 338), although target hardening does go hand-in-hand with CPTED.

The traditional approach tends to overlook the opportunities available for natural access control and natural surveillance. Normal and routine use of surroundings and environment has been considered as a natural approach to access control and surveillance. It is possible to adapt natural uses of surroundings to achieve the same outcomes of physical security target hardening. Also, CPTED can apply target-hardening strategies to facilities when the application supports them and not impair the effective use of the environment.

The CPTED strategy shown in Figure 5.3 involves overlapping strategies for design principles of urban space:

- *Natural access control* prevents access to an area and creates the perception of risk of detection by an offender if entering an area, and also increased effort required by an offender to bypass the natural barriers. Access management is described by the Western Australian Planning Commission (2005, p. 10) as the use of design features that deny target access to offenders and minimize escape opportunities, yet guide legitimate users through the space. Access management includes methods of using the built environment to clearly mark borders and transitional zones, which also acts as a psychological deterrence barrier.
- Crowe (2000, p. 36) has indicated that certain strategies sometimes achieve both access management and surveillance objectives in CPTED. Understanding the difference in both is critical in performing analysis and design. Access management methods work to minimize crime opportunity through denial of access to perpetrators and create a perception of risk to offenders. Whereas, natural surveillance is a design concept that keeps

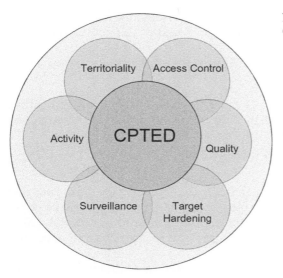

FIGURE 5.3 The CPTED principle. *(Adjusted from Cozens et al., 2005, p. 340.)*

intruders under observation, surveillance has an effect over access management as it could keep intruders out because of the increased perception of risk.

- *Natural surveillance* in open design has the purpose of keeping potential intruders under observation by legitimate users of a space, and ensures a higher perception of risk to the potential intruders. The purpose of surveillance is to create a perception of increased safety and security for legitimate users of a space and also to create a perception of increased risk of detection for perpetrators. The deliberate placing of people and activities in visible areas discourages crime, as criminals do not usually want to be observed. The key element in surveillance is to place less safe activities in safe areas and to place safe activities in the lesser safer areas (Western Australian Planning Commission, 2005, p. 9).
- *Territorial reinforcement* of an area is an outcome of CPTED design that develops a sense of territoriality, or ownership, by users of an area that produces a perceived risk of detection to a potential intruder. The Western Australian Planning Commission (2005, p. 10) state that the territorial reinforcement principle in CPTED designs of physical features of the built environment should be applied to express ownership and control. This approach is achieved by structurally defining public and private spaces to reduce ambiguity of space ownership. Structurally defining private space reduces the possibility of nonoffenders entering and gives credibility of anyone crossing the well-defined space as being an offender, which reduces crime opportunity and eventually minimizes crime.
- *Quality management* is taking adequate measures to ensure the continued use of the space for its intended purpose and maintain the safety feeling for users (Western Australian Planning Commission, 2005, p. 11). It proposes that proper lighting, painting, maintenance, the removal of crime indicators, and vegetation management create a perception of care that can reduce the fear of crime and induce legitimate behavior.

These four overlaying CPTED principles provide the foundation upon which environmental crime prevention is founded. By designing areas according to these strategies, the level of crime can be reduced. The routine activity theory supports the four overlaying CPTED principles through denying the opportunity for a motivated offender, and lessening the availability of a suitable target.

Activities of Space

Assessment of space in which people are employed and recreate can provide an indication of the effectiveness of the design principles for crime deterrence. The appropriateness of how a particular space has been designed and used can be determined by assessing the three functions or dimensions of human space:

- All human space has some *designated* purpose, where the designation focuses the purpose and intention of the structure or space.
- All human space has social, cultural, or physical *definitions* that prescribe the desired and acceptable behaviors. Definition aims to indicate ownership and boundaries of space, and resolves conflicts with designation.
- All human space is *designed* to support and control the desirable behaviors. Design is the understanding and ensuring that the physical structure or area is suitable for its original intended function and supports the productive use of the space.

The four strategies of CPTED of territorial reinforcement, natural access control, natural surveillance, and quality control are inherent in the activity of space or CPTED functions of designation, definition, and design. When bearing in mind the CPTED functions for a particular human space, the practical considerations should be addressed:

- Does the space clearly belong to someone or some group?
- Is the intended use of the space clearly defined?
- Does the physical design match the intended use?
- Does the design provide means for normal users to naturally control the activities, to control access, and to provide surveillance?

That is, the design of the space must ensure that the intended activity can function appropriately, as well as directly support the control of behavior to reduce the opportunity for crime.

Although this form of CPTED has been shown to be effective, it is considered to be outmoded and is termed traditional or first-generation CPTED. Researchers have refocused on Oscar Newman's theory of territoriality (Newman, 1972), where the principles have led to a modification of CPTED termed second-generation CPTED. Secondgeneration CPTED extends beyond the physical design of a space, and focuses on social issues in a community as well as situational factors. This approach to CPTED uses risk assessments and socio-economic and demographic profiling to ensure security and safety of a community. The approach attempts to consider *tipping points* by which behaviors are triggered, and includes active community participation. A consistent criticism of defensible space and CPTED has been a lack of consideration for socioeconomic variables and demographic variables, and how these variables may affect offender motivations, victim behavior, and guardianship from residents and passers-by. In addition, such aspects as irrational offenders, crime displacement, and insufficient community participation add to CPTED criticisms (Cozens et al., 2005, p. 342).

Studies that consider the correlation between the strength of territoriality and the fear of crime have vindicated the second-generation CPTED approach (Cozens et al., 2003; Painter, 1994). Brassard (2003) showed that there is a strengthening of community ties by conducting public events in a local park, increasing the feeling of ownership and territoriality within a community. Saville and Cleveland (2002) supported this approach by stating that "second-generation CPTED offers the promise of greatly enhanced and more realistic prevention strategies." While second-generation CPTED has its applications, it is largely limited to those communities that are enthusiastic about maintaining it.

Examples of CPTED Design Applications

To reinforce the concepts of CPTED involving a fresh perception of people and their activities, the strategies of CPTED of territorial reinforcement, natural access control, and natural surveillance have been applied in situations to reduce the incidence of crime. Some examples of CPTED strategies in practice can include:

- Provide clear definition of controlled space with boundaries, borders, markings, roped areas, and signage.
- Provide clearly marked transitional zones that indicate movement from public space to semi-public space to private space.
- Relocate gathering areas to locations with natural surveillance and natural access control. For example, bus shelters should be in an open area for natural surveillance.

CPTED techniques can be applied to most residential, industrial, and commercial facilities to provide this crime prevention approach to design and planning, and could include:

- Entrances, driveways, gardens, and exterior windows that overlook adjacent spaces to enhance that opportunity for natural surveillance.
- Garden landscape planning with low bushes and hedges, and relatively level ground increases natural vision and removes potential concealment for intruders.
- The internal design of buildings that include lobbies, halls, elevators, and stairwell exits are locations of high crime rate in facilities. The crime rate can be reduced by locating these vulnerable areas where natural surveillance can be implemented. That is, a reception desk or guard station can be located in a central position in the building.

The principles of CPTED are available for us to observe all around: these principles have been designed into areas, spaces, and public facilities as a matter of *commonsense*, but can be justified by the CPTED principles. The application of color on walls and through lighting can either sooth patrons, or discourage the presence of crowds in an area. The tactile feel of types of flooring or paving can discourage the presence of people: gently sloping floors and rippled surfaces on pavement will ensure that people will move away from the area. The selection of music being broadcast on public address systems may encourage or discourage certain groups of people. The extent of the innovativeness of CPTED principles to ensure security and safety is considerable, and can be observed in residential, industrial, and commercial precincts both for working conditions and for leisure pursuits. Furthermore, combining the CPTED principle with DiD target hardening provides security managers with effective threat and risk mitigation strategies.

PHYSICAL BARRIERS

The defense-in-depth principle uses layers of barriers in a physical security design to restrict access to the major assets of an organization. A barrier can be a natural or constructed obstacle to movement and may define the boundaries of a facility. The purpose of a barrier is to prevent the penetration of an area by intruders. However, as most barriers can be defeated with sufficient time and resources, then the purpose of a barrier is to delay the progress of the intrusion sufficiently for a response team to intercede and apprehend the intruders. Barriers are used for the protection or control of a diversity of assets including people, physical assets, sensitive data and information, and other materials.

Intrusion into a facility through the barriers for the protection of assets can occur by accident, force, and stealth. Accidental penetration of an area can be prevented by prominent signage about trespassing. Penetration by force may be caused by terrorists and fanatics who use vehicles or explosives to breach a barrier to gain access to an area. However, of the three types of intrusion, penetration by stealth is the most serious attack upon the assets of an organization, as there is no indication that an attack on the facility is or has occurred. Access by stealth leaves no obvious trace of entry, so that there is no knowledge that assets have been tampered with or removed. It is the role of the security manager that when designing the physical security for the protection of assets, intruders are forced into modifying the environment to achieve access to the assets. Such strategies could include physical or optical trip wires, a sterile zone of raked sand within a fence line so that footprints can be observed, and, for a large facility, perhaps dogs or geese that will alert a response team. Intrusion by stealth is an important attack method to be protected against for both exterior and interior barriers.

Barriers can be grouped into the two general categories: natural barriers and structural barriers. Natural barriers can include lakes and bodies of water, mountains, deserts, and other difficult-to-traverse terrain. Facilities can be located on islands so that the water forms the initial barrier. Structural barriers such as fences and walls are constructed to provide physical and psychological deterrence to unauthorized access. Appropriate physical barriers will depend on:

- The type and location.
- The area available to construct the barrier.
- The type of response available when intruders have been detected in a restricted area.
- The time delay that the barrier can reasonably delay the progress of an intruder.
- The technology to support the barrier.

It is not possible to construct a barrier that cannot be compromised. Any structural barrier can be penetrated if sufficient time, finance, personnel, planning, and imagination are applied to the assignment. It has been found that rather than build a single barrier of superior quality, it is preferable to construct a series of barriers each of which must be penetrated before assets can be violated.

Perimeter Protection

Perimeter protection is effectively the first line of defense in a physical security plan for a facility. However, an examination of the threat assessment of the facility together with the risk management strategy will determine the role of the perimeter in the security management plan. Perimeter security can vary from such items as a white line painted on the ground, to sophisticated high-level perimeter configurations involving multiple barriers with numerous detection systems, permanent surveillance, and continuous patrols. Physical barriers will discourage an undetermined intruder, but will only delay a determined person. Thus, physical barriers must be combined with other security controls for an integrated security solution.

Fences are the usual form of perimeter barrier used to protect the assets of an organization. Fences are relatively cheap and rapid to build, surveillance can be conducted through the barrier, and fences can follow the barrier and be configured into different shapes, and may be enhanced with barbed wire, razor wire, or topped with anti-climbing devices (Figure 5.4).

However, fences are not flawless as physical barriers as they will not usually stop vehicle penetration. They are also susceptible to cutting, the nature of their construction assists scaling, and they can be tunneled under unless additional barriers such as plinths can be provided. Fences require a high level of maintenance and usually have a finite life depending on the environment.

FIGURE 5.4 A perimeter fence enhanced with razor wire to resist climbing. *(Copyright: Centre of Applied Science and Technology of the Home Office, United Kingdom. This material is reproduced by permission.)*

Barbed wire can be installed over a chain-link fence by holding it on extension arms installed over the fence. Single-barbed wire can be installed outwards of the perimeter being protected, whereas double-barbed wire is installed on V-shaped extension arms. Barbed wire is installed to provide added difficulty for anyone attempting to scale a fence. For the same reason as barbed wire, concertina or spiral sharp edge wire is also installed on fence extension arms.

Evaluation of penetration times of chain-link fencing have been conducted by the U.S. Army Mobility Equipment Research and Development Command. Chain-link fences with extension poles installed have been subjected to climbing attacks by fit young men to estimate the effectiveness of fences as barriers against penetration. The 2.8ft (2.6m) fence with pole has been penetrated by a man with another man assisting without the use of aids in 4 seconds and the 2.8ft (2.6m) fence with 2.5ft (2.3m) pole was climbed by a man with three men assisting in 2.5 seconds; using carpet as an aid the fastest time was 7 seconds.

Again, a 2.2ft (2m) fence was climbed unassisted and without the use of aids in a time of 3 seconds, and with one man assisting without the use of aids was 1.5 seconds. Finally, a 2.5ft (2.3m) fence was penetrated by a man with one man assisting without the use of aids in 2 seconds. The fastest penetration time with one man assisting using canvas as an aid was 6 seconds (Knoke, 2004).

Chain-link fences with outriggers and barbed wire to increase the level of difficulty for scaling was penetrated with one man assisting without the use of aids in 4 seconds for a 2.5ft (2.3m) fence with barbed wire outrigger, and 5 seconds with one assistant. Also 2.5ft (2.3m) chain-link fences with a collapsible and a double outrigger with one man assisting were 4 seconds (Knoke, 2004).

A chain-link fence is neither crash rated nor intended to stop forcible entry, for example, entry by vehicle or physical cutting. In most cases, a chain-link fence can be easily penetrated by a normal passenger vehicle. As a consequence, target hardening must be installed for facilities where forcible vehicular entry is an issue. A chain-link fence may be enhanced with the aid of crash-rated tension wires threaded through the fence, or with concrete crash structures, or simply by digging a trench around the perimeter of the fence to stop vehicles from reaching the fence.

Perimeter Barrier Access

The defense-in-depth principle ensures that concentric layers of barriers protect the assets of an organization, and that only authorized people have access to the assets. However, access can only be gained to the assets by crossing the barriers in the DiD strategy. Access ways in the barriers are necessary for authorized people to cross these barriers and access the assets. Therefore, the inclusion of gates and doors in barriers are necessary for access to the assets.

There is a wide range of barriers that could be installed as gates allowing vehicle entry ranging from access control barriers in the form of a simple drop arm to a hydraulic crash-rated barrier. The drop arm will only control traffic flow for legitimate users. Therefore, high-security facilities at risk of forcible vehicle entry will need to install crash-rated barriers.

The U.S. Department of State (DOS) standard SD-STD-02.01, Revision A, from March 2003, provides physical testing criteria to certify anti-ram vehicle barriers. This is a performance standard and testing procedure for both active entrance barriers and passive perimeter barriers designated as vehicle impact–rated barriers or anti-ram barriers. The test standard rates the anti-ram barriers within three categories: K12, K8, and K4. The rating of the barrier is

FIGURE 5.5   A selection of cappings for walls to reduce the application of climbing equipment. *(Copyright: Centre of Applied Science and Technology of the Home Office, United Kingdom. This material is reproduced by permission.)*

determined when a 15,000 lb. (6,810 kg) gross-weight vehicle impacts a barrier from a perpendicular direction. A K12 rating is achieved when a vehicle traveling at a nominal speed of 50 mph (80 kph) is successfully arrested by the barrier from the perpendicular direction. A K8 rating is achieved for a nominal speed of 40 mph (65 kph); and, a K4 rating is achieved for a nominal speed of 30 mph (50 kph). To be DOS certified at any rating, the penetration of the cargo bed must not exceed 1 m beyond the pre-impact inside edge of the barrier (U.S. Department of State, 2008).

Also perimeter barriers can take the form of well-constructed walls that present a strong and robust barricade to a potential intruder. The building of walls as barriers in a DiD strategy presents an impenetrable barrier that must be scaled, is an impenetrable barrier to vehicles, has low maintenance, and can be topped with anti-attack devices and detection devices. Figure 5.5 shows a selection of cappings on walls to prevent attacks using climbing equipment.

However, walls are very expensive to build as security barriers and they take long durations to construct; that is, long-term planning is needed for the construction of walls. Unfortunately, walls present a firm visual barrier for surveillance, so that intruders cannot be observed through the wall, and so are effectively not visible.

RELATIONSHIPS BETWEEN DiD FUNCTIONS

The relationships between the functions of DiD as deterrence, detection, delay, and response can be mapped as a time distribution for the entire duration of an attack on a premise. An analysis of the time distribution of an intrusion on a facility can indicate the weaknesses in the DiD design in the protection of assets. Figure 5.6 shows the duration of time for the functions of a DiD design to occur while an attack is progressing on a facility. The progress of time is shown from left to right in a one-dimensional map, where the events associated with the functions of a DiD strategy are plotted.

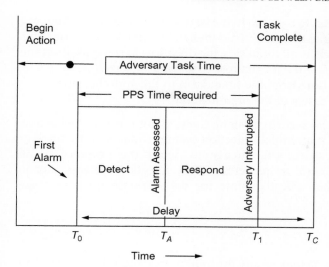

FIGURE 5.6 A flowchart of the DiD strategy applied to the design of physical protection of a computer center.

The commencement of the intrusion event occurs at the beginning of the duration, but this commencement time is not known by the security management system because no detection has been made, and no alarm has been received. The alarm is first received at T_0 when perhaps a fence-mounted detection system is disturbed and sounds an alarm. This alarm signal must be authenticated to establish its veracity, as false alarm rates can be large for highly sensitive detection sensors. The assessment of the alarm will be completed at T_A so that a response to the alarm may commence. Obviously, the time duration from T_0 to T_A must be kept to a minimum, as this time duration is available to the intruder to commence defeating the barrier to gain access to the assets of the organization.

Once the alarm is verified, the response phase of the protection strategy commences with an interruption to the progress of the adversary at T_1, and the time duration of T_0 to T_1 being the time required for the DiD system to respond to the attack on the facility. Apprehension of the intruder occurs at T_C, where T_0 to T_C is the time duration for the delay function of the system. From Figure 5.6 it can be observed that the total time from the initial progress of the intrusion until T_C is the time available to the intruder to gain entry to the facility or damage the property of the organization.

The DiD principle employing the functions of deterrence, detection, delay, and response can be modeled according to Figure 5.6, the time distribution of DiD functions. To achieve best likelihood of apprehension of intruders, the following outcomes should be sought in the design of physical security barrier system:

• The time between the commencements of attack on a facility needs to be minimized. This outcome can be achieved by having detection systems outside of the perimeter barrier, and CCTV directed beyond the perimeter boundary.
• The validation of the alarm from the detection system should be keep to a minimum period of time (T_0 to T_A), so authenticating the alarm signal can initiate the response force to respond to the scene of the intrusion.

- The period of time for the response team to respond to the intrusion should also be kept to a minimum (T_A to T_1), to reduce the time that the intruders have to attack the barrier and create a breach. For large facilities such as oil refineries, the distances to some locations on the perimeter can require considerable time for the response team to travel.
- Therefore, minimizing the period of time from the first alarm to the apprehension of intruders, T_0 to T_C, best protects the assets of the organization.

Because DiD is a multilayered physical security system, many if not most of the barriers can include detection systems. That is, if an initial detection system is defeated by force or stealth, then subsequent detection systems will engage to detect the presence of an unauthorized intrusion. However, it should be recognized that detection systems later in the progress of intrusion will leave less effective time for the response force to make a successful apprehension.

Relative Time to Penetrate Walls

There are several international standards that specify the minimum standard for strength of materials resisting attack against forced entry. These international standards are similar in application and intent and each specifies a level of resistance to forcible attack on domestic dwellings, commercial facilities, public buildings, and institutions (Standards Australia, 1988). The standard for testing and rating building elements for intruder resistance considers the components of walls, floors, ceilings and roofs, doors and windows, and skylights and vents. The standard has defined the tools used in a forcible attack according to the categories of:

- Hand tools such as chisels, hammers, and saws.
- Power tools such as hammer drills, cutting saws, and angle grinders.
- Hydraulic tools such as hydraulic jacks, hydraulic spreaders, and hydraulic drills.
- Cutting tools such as oxygen/gas cutting equipment and a thermal lance.

The categories of attack tools have attempted to indicate the range of tools that can be used to assist intruders to breach barriers and penetrate into facilities. The tools indicated in the categories need to be portable as intruders will progress through a series of barriers to access the assets. It is interesting to note that gas-cutting equipment is available in portable backpacks, where previously they were only available in large gas cylinders that were not as portable in their application.

The levels of attack on a barrier, as specified by the standards, can be classified as:

Level 1: one man with common hand tools.
Level 2: two people with common hand tools.
Level 3: one people with power tools and hand tools.
Level 4: two people with power tools and hand tools.
Level 5: two people with hydraulic tools and hand tools.
Level 6: two people with cutting torch and hand tools.

These designated levels of attack on barriers provide a structure for assessment of the effectiveness of the materials. The resistance to attack or strength of materials in a barrier or surface is a measure of the effectiveness of the construction of the barrier. As it is assumed that the tools will be used to breach the surface of the barrier to gain access, then the time taken to make a standard opening in the barrier will be a measure of the resistance of the barrier to attack. An opening size of 620 cm^2 in size is considered to be sufficiently large to allow a person to pass through. To achieve this opening size, the following opening configurations have been specified:

- Rectangular opening: the smaller side has to be more that 15 cm in length.
- Circular opening: the diameter of the circle should be more than 28 cm.
- Triangular opening: the longest side of the triangle should be more than 50 cm in length.

The standard for testing and rating building elements for intruder resistance considers the duration taken for levels of attack on the surfaces of barriers. The time taken, together with the level of attack, will be a rating for the effectiveness of the strength of materials in the barrier. The rating system applies a time rating for a particular level of attack as either a 10-minute rating or a 5-minute rating. For example, a 10-minute (level 5) rating is more than a 5-minute (level 2) rating for a particular barrier. That is, the first barrier will resist cutting tools for at least 10 minutes, while the second barrier will only resist hand tools for a duration of 5 minutes. Thus, the first barrier is considerably more intruder-resistant than the second barrier.

Bullet-Resistant Glass Panels

Bullet-resistant glass is composed of multiple plies of glass and plastic to produce a panel that will prevent the penetration of ballistic projectiles. The construction of bullet-resistant glass is such that there is spallation from the glass panel after being struck with a ballistic projectile—that is, there are no small pieces of glass flying from the glass panel to cause injury. Spallation occurs from the reverse side of the glass panel that was impacted by the bullet, and is caused by a shock wave being propagated through the glass to blast off small glass fragments.

International standards for the construction and performance of bullet-resistant glass panels describe the classification and performance of glazing panels that resist bullet penetration (Standards Australia, 1983). A standard specifies that a projectile-resistant glazing panel is a complete bullet-resistant unit that is classified according to its resistance to ballistic attack by firearms. A standard may have its classification according to bullet resistance to attack from the following weapons:

Class G0: 9 mm military weapon.
Class G1: 357 magnum.
Class G2: 44 magnum.
Class R1: 5.56 mm rifle.
Class R2: 7.62 mm rifle.
Class S0: 12-gauge shotgun firing shot.
Class S1: 12-gauge shotgun firing a single slug.

The performance of the bullet-resistant glass panel is evaluated by not allowing the projectile to pass through the panel nor allowing any splinters of glass from the panel to perforate the witness card. The performance of the glass panel is tested in a rig similar to that shown in

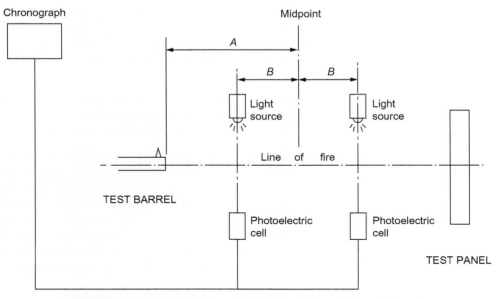

FIGURE 5.7   Test rig for the evaluation of a bullet-resistant glass panel.

Figure 5.7, where a bullet is fired from the test firearm into the glass panel. The projectile passes through two beams of light at a set distance apart to determine the muzzle velocity of the firearm. A witness card is located on the far side of the test glass panel to detect the production of glass slivers as spallation.

The standard for bullet-resistant opaque panels has the same classification as that for glass panels, with performance requirements and test conditions.

Safes and Vaults

Sensitive material or information should only be used or stored in an area that has appropriate protective measures adequate to prevent unauthorized access (Fennelly, 2004, p. 167). *Vaults* are defined by ASIS International (Knoke, 2004) as specially constructed rooms intended to limit access and provide protection to the property secured within. *Safes* are lockable metal containers used for storing valuables, intended to limit access and provide protection to the property secured within.

Both the construction and materials in safes has considerably advanced over the past few decades, with present-day safes have the following features:

- Made from pressed steel or alloy.
- Contemporary safes are welded rather than riveted.
- Safes use tongue-and-groove construction.
- Safes have extensive fire-resistant capabilities.

Safes are rated according to the construction of the doors and walls, where laminated or solid steel is used for the protection of assets. The thickness of the door is measured, excluding the bolt works and locking device.

The standards for the construction and testing of safes that have been adopted are:

- USA Standard Underwriters Laboratory (UL).
- Australian and New Zealand Standard AS/NZS 3810:1998.
- Japan Industrial Standard (JIS).
- European Standard Eurosafe.

The UL have performed systematic testing of fire- and burglary-resistant security containers, safes, and vaults for about the last century. Physical security containers, safes, and vaults that meet specific test requirements can attach a UL rating label to their products. The label indicates the type and rigorousness of test conditions complied with by assessment. However, it is understood that some safes are fire-resistant while others are burglary-resistant. Although safes appear to be physically strong and robust, they may not have both capabilities of fire resistance and burglary resistance; however, it is possible to procure safes with both capabilities. The UL safes classification describes tests for mechanical strength, impact resistance, manufacturing tolerance, product endurance, and the operability after prolonged exposure to adverse conditions. The UL also provides testing procedures for combination locks, which involves evaluation of locks at various combinations and operating within specific tolerances.

Similarly, the Australia/New Zealand Standard AS/NZS 3810:1998 Safes and Strong Rooms provides comprehensive methods for protection of assets in physical containers. The principle of testing is to establish the resistance values (RUs) for complete access or partial access for secure storage units. The tests for the minimum standard of the physical barriers formed by containers are:

- Test for physical attack.
- Test for anchoring strength.
- Test for explosive resistance.

These tests provide a strategy of comparing the resistance values of physical containers for cutting, grinding, hammering, levering, blasting, and thermal cutting to gain access to the assets in the container. A history of attacks on safes shows that most assaults are made to the door and hinges with the intent of opening the door to gain access to the contents. Therefore, most physical protection is concentrated on the door, the bolt work, and the combination locks.

Methods of Attack

The usual method of physical attack on safes used to be the application of explosives; however, this method is much reduced due to the stronger construction of modern safes and the greater difficulty in obtaining explosives. Present-day criminals have access to a considerable range of tools and devices that can be applied to safes to gain access to the contents. Oxygen/gas cutting equipment can severe metal by heating it to the kindling or ignition temperature and rapidly oxidizing it by a regulated jet of oxygen. This thermal cutting equipment is readily available, portable in application, easy to use, and quiet in operation.

An arc/electrode piercing process strikes an arc between a welding electrode and a metal surface creating a very high temperature to melt the metal and pierce the cladding. However, the high current needed by the equipment requires a heavy transformer that restricts the portability of the equipment.

Air/arc/electrode piercing cutting equipment uses the same principle as the arc/electrode piercing system, but has hollow carbon electrodes that emit high-pressure air along the electrode that removes the molten metal.

Thermal lance preheats to ignition the end of a bundle of steel rods, which produces fusion of the rods by oxygen fed through the lance of the rods. This reaction becomes self-sustaining at very high temperatures and melts and disperses the slag from the metal surface. The thermal lance will penetrate almost any material, but there are several disadvantages in its application:

- The thermal lance can only cut holes in the material.
- A breathing apparatus is essential, as a considerable amount of smoke is produced.
- There is a danger of the slag causing fire through the high temperatures.
- The heat generated by the thermal lance would more likely destroy the contents of a safe.

In previous times, large gas bottles were necessary for the thermal lance to operate; however, there are currently portable systems available.

CONCLUSION

The protection of assets of an organization is usually achieved through physical security or appropriate security design for the facility, or a combination of both strategies. The physical security is attained through the defense-in-depth principle, where layers of security barriers are imposed between the intruder and the assets to be protected. The functions of deterrence, detection, delay, and response for these barriers are achieved by employing psychological barriers, electronic or technical barriers, physical barriers, and procedural barriers. Combinations of these forms of barriers according to the security management plan can establish an asset protection system for national, commercial, and industrial facilities. However, urban planning for residences and recreational spaces needs a less intrusive approach to the safety and security of people who work and live in these areas.

The CPTED approach both plans and designs spaces and areas using crime reduction strategies to enhance the quality of living for people. The principles of natural surveillance, natural access control, and territoriality are CPTED approaches to safer urban living and present a methodology that does not have the rigid approach of DiD. The CPTED strategy plans for an area or space to have a *designated* purpose, physical *definitions*, and is *designed* to support the requirements and activities of the attending authorized people.

These two approaches of physical security can be considered as principles for the protection of assets of people, information, facilities, and materials for the nation, organizations, and urban locations. Although security science is an emerging discipline with theories and models of the science still under development, the principles of DiD and CPTED are important as initial approaches to the development of theories for security science.

Applications of DiD and CPTED have been presented in the contexts of the principles of the protection of assets approaches. The importance of DiD barriers and perimeter barriers have been considered according to the functions of these barriers with attack strategies being discussed. Methodologies to defeat barriers have been presented so that security managers can devise and develop strategies to prevent these attempts to defeat the DiD approach for the protection of assets.

Further Reading

Garcia, M.L., 2006. Vulnerability Assessment of Physical Protection Systems. Butterworth-Heinemann, Boston.

Garcia, M.L., 2008. The Design and Evaluation of Physical Protection Systems, second ed. Butterworth-Heinemann, Boston.

Gill, M. (Ed.), 2006. The Handbook of Security. Palgrave Macmillan, Houndmills, Hampshire.

References

Armitage, R., Monchuk, L., 2011. Sustaining the crime reduction impact of designing out crime: Re-evaluating the secured by design scheme 10 years on. Security Journal 24 (4), 320–343.

Arrington, R.L., 2006. Crime Prevention: The Law Enforcement Officer's Practical Guide. Jones and Bartlett Publishers, Richmond, VA.

Brassard, A., 2003. Integrating the planning process and 2nd generation CPTED. The CPTED Journal 2 (1), 46–53.

Cohen, L.E., Felson, M., 1979. Social change and crime rate trends: A routine activity approach. Am. Sociol. Rev. 44, 588–605.

Cox, L.A., Ricci, P.F., 1990. New Risks: Issues and Management. Plenum Press, New York.

Cozens, P.M., Adamson, D., Hillier, D., 2003. Community CPTED: A case study of a housing estate in South Wales. The CPTED Journal 2 (1), 2–15.

Cozens, P.M., Saville, G., Hillier, D., 2005. Crime prevention through environmental design (CPTED): A review and modern bibliography. Property Management 23 (5), 328–356.

CPTED Ontario, 2002. What is CEPTED? Retrieved March 31, 2008, from http://www.cptedontario.ca/index.php.

Crowe, T.D., 2000. Crime Prevention through Environmental Design. Butterworth-Heinemann, Boston.

Fennelly, L.J., 2004. Effective Physical Security, third ed. Butterworth-Heinemann, Boston.

Fischer, R.J., Halibozek, E., Green, D., 2008. Introduction to Security, eighth ed. Burtterworth-Heinemann, Boston.

Garcia, M.L., 2001. The Design and Evaluation of Physical Protection Systems. Butterworth-Heinemann, Boston.

Knoke, M.E. (Ed.), 2004. Protection of Assets: Introduction to Assets Protection. ASIS International, Alexandria, VA.

New Zealand Ministry of Justice, 2005. National Guidelines for Crime Prevention through Environmental Design in New Zealand. Ministry of Justice, Wellington, New Zealand.

Newman, O., 1972. Defensible Space. Macmillan, New York.

Painter, K., 1994. The impact of street lighting on crime, fear and pedestrian street use. Security Journal 5 (3), 116–124.

Saville, G., Cleveland, G., 2002. 2nd generation CPTED: An antidote to the social Y2K virus of urban design. Retrieved October 5, 2011, from http://www.e-doca.eu/content/docs/CPTED_2ndGeneration.pdf.

Smith, C.L., 2003. Understanding concepts in the defensein-depth strategy. Paper presented at Security Technology, 2003. In: Proceedings, IEEE 37th Annual 2003 International Carnaham Conference. Taipei, Taiwan, Republic of China.

Smith, C.L., 2006. Trends in the development of security technology. In: Gill, M. (Ed.), The Handbook of Security. Palgrave Macmillian Ltd, Basingstoke, Great Britain, pp. 610–628.

Standards Australia, 1983. AS/NZS2343:1983, Part 1—Bullet-resistant Panels for Interior Use. Standards Australia International Ltd, Sydney.

Standards Australia, 1988. AS/NZS3555:1988 Building Elements—Testing and Rating for Intruder Resistance. Standards Australia International Ltd, Sydney.

U.S. Department of State, 2008. DS Certified Anti-ram Vehicle Barriers. U.S. Department of State, Washington, DC.

Western Australian Planning Commission, 2005. Designing Out Crime. Western Australian Planning Commission, Perth.

Detection Systems

INTRODUCTION

The security design principles of defense-in-depth (DiD) and crime prevention through environmental design (CPTED) provide strategies for the protection of assets in a facility or community. However, the concept of target hardening through the application of security technology will enhance most approaches to security design and reduce the threat to the assets being protected. Target hardening is aimed at denying or limiting access to a potential crime target through the application of artificial or physical barriers. Target hardening can take a variety of forms that range from strengths of materials (i.e., make the barrier more resistant to penetration) to covert surveillance of perimeters, open ground, and facilities. The purpose of the target hardening through security technology is to assist a security manager to design or support a security management plan that will provide comprehensive protection of the assets of an organization. The relevance of security technology to security design principles will enhance the quality of the protection provided by the security management plan, and therefore present an effective strategy for the protection of assets. Therefore, an understanding of the principles and concepts of the security technologies will allow the appropriate integration of barriers and technologies to prevent intrusion into restricted areas.

A condition of security for a facility or organization can be achieved through the application of the Campbell triangle (Campbell, 2003), which proposes the components of *planning and design*, *the security management plan*, and *the security technology* to support the security strategy. The function of the security technology installed in a facility is an outcome of the security management plan, and it should be recognized that the security management plan determines the extent and application of the technologies (Purpura, 2002). That is, there should be no consideration of reactive decisions to install security technology outside of the security management plan; the plan should be coherent and self-sustaining, and reactive decisions will destroy the integrity of the design of the security management plan.

Security technology is applied in a security protection strategy to prevent damage or removal of assets through unauthorized intrusion. However, it is realized that security technology is not the fundamental component in asset protection, but rather should be considered as a component of the protection strategy with its function to enhance the management of asset protection. The professional skill of the security analyst is to achieve the optimum mix of the components of design and planning, security technology, and security management for a particular risk and threat assessment of a facility or organization. The inclusion of security technology in a security management strategy can be justified in a theoretical context through the application of security asset protection principles applied to a facility or organization (Smith, 2006).

THEORY

To achieve a condition of security for a facility or organization, a security strategy is needed that will consider the components of *security planning and design*, a *security management plan*, and the *security technology* (Campbell, 2003). An element of the security management plan may be the DiD approach to asset protection, where the delay against intrusion by an unauthorized intruder must be a greater time period than the response time by an authorized custodian. Thus, a DiD strategy can be considered as a function of critical path analysis, also through the estimate of adversary sequence interruption (EASI) model for performance presented by Garcia (2006), and the universal element conceptual mapping model presented by Alach and Smith (2006).

Critical Path Analysis

The DiD approach to the protection of assets requires that barriers in a system have the capacity to delay the progress of an intruder at least as long as a response group will take to apprehend the unauthorized person. Thus, the response time must be less than the delay time for the barrier(s), or else the intruders will have completed their mission before the attendance of the response group. The response is the deployment of a deterrent system that either apprehends or discourages an intrusion. An effective delay layer must provide sufficient and substantial barriers to allow the response team to attend the facility and prevent the intrusion. It could be stated that these functions truly define the DiD strategy (Smith, 2003, p. 9).

A study of the resistance to intrusion by the barriers and the time taken for an adequate response can be achieved through the application of *critical path analysis* (CPA) to determine the best attack strategy, or alternatively an assessment of the need for barrier enhancement. Critical path analysis is a project management tool that allows assessment of effective project management through time and activities accomplishments such as:

- Breaks down a large project into smaller individual activities.
- Establishes the order in which these individual activities must be performed.
- Indicates which activities can only commence once other activities have been completed.
- Indicates which activities can be undertaken simultaneously.
- Shows which activities will require special resources or equipment to be satisfactorily completed.

It is important to estimate the required time period for each of the individual activities to be completed in the project. When assessing the time taken to breach barriers in a DiD strategy, barrier force resistance standards might be applied as a minimum for these components for CPA assessment. Then the total time for the intrusion to occur will be that taken from commencement of the attack to the acquiring of the assets.

For example, when CPA is applied to a construction project, then other factors need to be considered:

- The availability of labor and other resources.
- Lead times for delivery of materials and other services.
- Seasonal factors such as dry weather required in a building project.

Thus, the time taken to complete the project will be the time taken to sequentially complete the individual activities. This is the critical path and it represents the minimum time to complete the project. In terms of a DiD strategy, it will represent the time taken to penetrate all barriers and gain the assets.

The technique of CPA is to use symbols to display the logic of the sequence of events or actions of a process to provide analysis of the effectiveness of the process (Lockyer, 1996). Table 6.1 shows the events or actions necessary to bake a cake. While some activities

TABLE 6.1 Activities Required for Baking a Cake

Activity	Preceded by	Elapsed Time (minutes)
A: weigh ingredients	—	1
B: mix ingredients	A	3
C: prepare tins	B	2
D: preheat oven	C	10
E: place ingredients in tins	C	2
F: cooking time	D	40

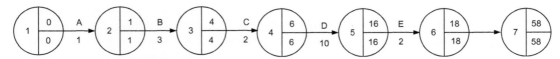

FIGURE 6.1 Critical path for a CPA of a project to bake a cake.

are dependent on others having been undertaken in order, other activities may be performed independently.

The data shown in Table 6.1 have been applied to the critical path shown in Figure 6.1, where the process of baking a cake has been described. Trace the path shown in Figure 6.1 and observe that it describes the process of baking a cake, and that it represents the most efficient way to complete the project. However, the correctness of the completion time for the project depends on the accuracy of the information applied in the assessment.

The application of CPA can provide a tool for security analysts to determine the effectiveness of DiD strategies to protect the assets of an organization. By building a critical path through a series of barriers protecting an asset, it is possible to assess the minimum time taken to breach the security and allow an analyst to recommend enhancements to the design of the security barriers in the plan. The response time to attend the alarm from detection must be less than the minimum time to breach the security for the assets to be protected. It is important that comprehensive testing has taken place on the times taken to penetrate the barriers by cutting through, climbing over, and tunneling under physical barriers in the DiD plan, so that reasonable resistance times against attack can be used in the CPA model.

Security Critical Path Analysis

A number of analytical tools are available for the assessment of the effectiveness of physical protection of critical assets (Garcia, 2008). Among these tools is the analytical model EASI, which is a computer model that evaluates physical security performance along a specific path and under specific conditions of threat and system operation. EASI is a quantitative tool that assesses the effect of changing physical protection parameters of detection, delay, and communications values along a specific path. As only one adversary path can be considered at a time, it is necessary for the EASI model to present appropriate output to achieve a timely and sufficient response. The input for the model requires:

1. Detection and communication data as probabilities that the total function will be successful.
2. Delay and response data as mean times with standard deviations for each component.

The output from the model will be P_I as the probability of intercepting the adversary before gaining access to the assets. However, as EASI analyzes one path at a time, and as protection systems become larger and more complex, more advanced computer models are needed to perform analysis of multiple paths.

The delay time provided by the barriers in the system will be some form of addition of the times required to penetrate each of the barriers by the intruder. However, exact times to traverse the location through the barriers are not able to be predicted, as the skills and resources of the adversary are not fully known. So an error function is attached to the estimated time for the attack, and is usually presented as a standard deviation of the time derived from a reasonable estimate of the variation.

The response time in the EASI model is derived from the difference in time from when the alarm signal is received to the interception of the intruder by the response group (Garcia, 2008). The response time can be considered as being composed of the components of time as:

- Alarm communication time
- Interval of time for assessment of alarm
- Time to communicate alarm to the guards
- Preparation time for guards, such as accessing equipment and vehicles
- Guard travel time
- Time required for guard group to assemble and deploy

Thus, the *response force time* (RFT) is an interval of time to receive, assess, and respond to an alarm, and this time interval must be less than the time to resist the attack on the security system. The *critical detection point* (CDP) is the point on the path where the delay time remaining first exceeds the RFT. That is, it is the point on the adversary path where the remaining delay time still exceeds the response time. The concept of the CDP is important as it provides information to locate additional detection capabilities prior to the CDP, and additional physical barriers after the CDP.

A detailed discussion of the EASI model has been presented by Garcia (2008) where a presentation of the approach to EASI has been considered in the context of DiD protection of assets. The computer model supporting the EASI model is presented and discussed, with consideration given to multiple path analysis of potential attacks on a facility. A discussion on adversary sequence diagrams is presented by Garcia (2008) with multipath and multilayer barriers being considered. Thus, the EASI model accommodates quantitative analysis of a protection system, where the asset requires a high level of protection and performance data are available to support the determination.

Universal Element Conceptual Mapping

Several theories of physical security have been considered by Garcia (2008) where a *physical protection system* (PPS) is defined as a complex configuration of detection, delay, and response elements that can be analyzed to determine system effectiveness. The concepts of *delay, detection,* and *response* are widely accepted across the field of physical security as the functions of DiD and these form the highest level of consideration in risk assessments from a theoretical analysis of physical security.

The position that Garcia (2008, p. 265) proposed in an ordered attempt to explain the theoretical relationship of the functions of DiD is that:

> The goal of an adversary is to complete a path to an asset with the least likelihood of being stopped by the PPS or, conversely, the highest likelihood of successful attack. To achieve this goal, the adversary may attempt to minimize the time required to complete the path. This strategy involves penetrating barriers as quickly as possible with little regard to the probability of being detected. An example of this adversary tactic is a force attack. The adversary is successful if the path is completed before guards can respond. Alternatively, the adversary may attempt to minimize detection with little regard to the time required. This adversary tactic is based on a stealth attack. In this case the adversary is successful upon completion of the path without being detected.

Garcia (2008) recognizes two modes of attack where physical systems may serve to maintain security. Effectiveness measures are considered through *minimum cumulative time delay* and *cumulative probability of detecting* since both are able to assess the overall risk of an attack on physical security defense arrangements. In the former effectiveness measure, Garcia noted that delay without detection is not appropriate since a response force must be alerted to respond and interrupt an adversary. In the latter effectiveness measure, it was noted that no consideration for delay is assessed, which is considered a disadvantage.

Alach and Smith (2006) present a conceptual map identifying risk curves for the terms *delay probability* and *detection probability* in Figure 6.2, where the variables have been established relative to the time scale and probability as a percentage. The intersections of these curves define a set of quadrants where the concept of *probability* is further separated into the two effective regions of *suitable* and *unsuitable*. In a real-world scenario the regions corresponding to each of the quadrants will be influenced by a combination of the defense systems of any facility and also by the total resources of a potential attacker. A mapping of this combination of influences will determine the shape of the curves and therefore determine the total area available for each quadrant.

Delay probability is presented as a concept in the physical security model of Figure 6.2, where the path of an attack through a facility is defined by the relationship of a facility's barrier system to the resources of an attacker. Delay probability effectiveness may be considered as suitable only while the likelihood exists that an attack does not defeat a barrier system. For time increments of $t=0$ (the origin of time) onwards, the curve for delay probability commences at 100% suitable and decreases to 0% suitable after some final increment of time (t_f). In Figure 6.2 it can be seen that quadrants 1 and 2 represent the regions of the conceptual map that contain suitable delay. This region can be defined as the region commencing from

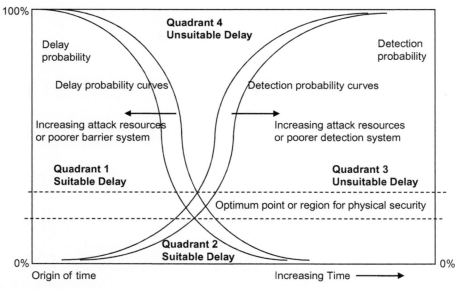

FIGURE 6.2   Conceptual map for delay probability and detection probability. *(Reprinted from Alach and Smith, 2006.)*

$t=0$ bounded in time by the curve representing a delay probability for values along the time axis t. Quadrants 3 and 4 in this situation represent the regions for unsuitable delay.

Detection probability is presented as a concept in the physical security model (Figure 6.2) where a security system is able to determine that a breach of physical security has occurred. The effectiveness of detection probability may be considered as suitable only after a correct response to an attack can be generated. For time increments of $t=0$ onwards, the curve for detection probability commences at 0% suitability and will increase over time during, and potentially after, an attack depending on both the attack resources and the ability of the detection systems in place. Suitability will eventually approach 100% after an elapsed time t_e interval for any attack.

It is assumed that without a detection system there is infinite time available to breach physical security systems, and so penetration to the asset is assured. In Figure 6.2 it can be seen that quadrants 2 and 3 both represent the regions of the conceptual map that contain suitable detection. These regions are bounded by the curve representing detection probability and continue for all larger values of t increasing along the time axis until t_e. Quadrants 1 and 4 in this case represent the regions for unsuitable detection. This region commences at $t=0$ and is bounded by the curve for detection probability.

The major outcome from the interpretation of Figure 6.2 in describing the risk estimate of the overall combined effectiveness of physical security suggests that when a larger region for quadrant 2 exists, the better the overall effectiveness of the physical security. In comparison, when a larger region of quadrant 4 exists, a poorer overall effectiveness for physical security results. Figure 6.2 also identifies an optimum region (or point) of effectiveness for physical security bounded by the intersection of the curves for delay probability and detection probability. Increasing this intersection point in the probability value effectively corresponds to maximizing quadrant 2 and minimizing quadrant 4. Similarly, decreasing this intersection point in the probability value effectively corresponds to minimizing quadrant 2 and maximizing quadrant 4.

Figure 6.3 presents a single case using a delay probability curve and a detection probability curve of a hypothetical facility with a demonstrated optimum point of effectiveness for physical security. Several options can be considered to change the intersection point between the two curves along the axes of probability that suggest different overall effectiveness to the physical security arrangement for the hypothetical facility.

Alach and Smith (2006) present a number of analyses of the model, and produce knowledge matrices of the system to demonstrate the effect of delay probability and detection probability on the physical security of a facility at risk. The model presented is an indicative device for relative comparisons. While the validity of the presented model may be critiqued in its own right, the model's primary purpose is to provide a means of interpretation for the knowledge matrices that are generated.

Garcia (2008, p. 31) considers that the *adversary factor* is the reason behind the dependency in effectiveness measures, so the best effectiveness measure is one that combines all of the considerations of minimum cumulative time delay, cumulative probability of detecting, and response time:

> Adversaries may use combinations of force, stealth, and deceit in order to accomplish their goals. This is why a well-defined design basis threat is so important to system effectiveness. The most successful adversary is assumed to be knowledgeable enough to defeat or bypass detection along the path up to the CDP (critical detection point) and also knows the response force time.

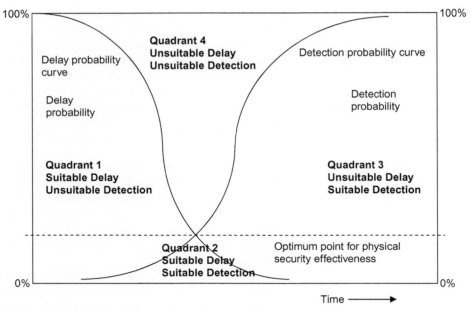

FIGURE 6.3 Conceptual map for delay probability and detection probability for a hypothetical facility. *(Reprinted from Alach and Smith, 2006.)*

In consideration for delay times and detection probabilities, Garcia (2008, p. 269) assumes that with an assessment of a facility the

> analyst must repeat this process for many adversary paths, find the most vulnerable path, and decide whether this is a satisfactory result (when) there are many adversary paths into a facility. The critical path characterizes the effectiveness of the overall protection system in detecting, delaying, and interrupting the adversary.

These theoretical considerations are limiting in suggesting that a protection system needs to identify its critical path, while in reality the critical path is elusive since it is always strongly reliant on the adversary factor. Therefore, effectiveness of the system is somewhat dependent on adversary tactics (Garcia, 2008). Without predetermined adversary tactics, any consideration of risk estimation leads to a circular argument involving the determination of a PPS's path effectiveness.

The effectiveness assessments on elements of physical security such as those reported by Armstrong (2005), Armstrong and Peile (2005), Peck and Trachier (2004), and others in this field who have considered standardizing or modeling the protection of assets, are not able to provide critical time delays or "nondetection" probabilities. This deficiency in critical time delays is because it is not realistically feasible to consider exhaustive physical testing of any delay or detection equipment for a complete range of adversary tactics.

Preliminary analyses of worst- and best-case effectiveness of physical security in a DiD strategy shows the curves for delay probability and detection probability in Figure 6.4. The concept of universal element is that of a continuum of items or actions on a single dimension that will give a family of elements within a DiD strategy. That is, the concept continuum of force attack contains a reference list such as rock, hammer, axe, electric drill, oxy cutting, and explosives, where rock represents the lowest reference value of force and explosive represents the highest reference level of force in a universal element continuum. Thus, the model is built on universal elements that pertain to the DiD strategy.

The model that has been described provides a structure for assessing risk evaluations from real-life scenarios through values contained in knowledge structures. These knowledge structures can be identified in theory and a combination of theoretical approaches can provide the structure and data for a physical security hierarchy using DiD functions, relational descriptors, and concept continuums. These approaches have been identified for their theoretical ability to transform actual physical security elements into universal elements.

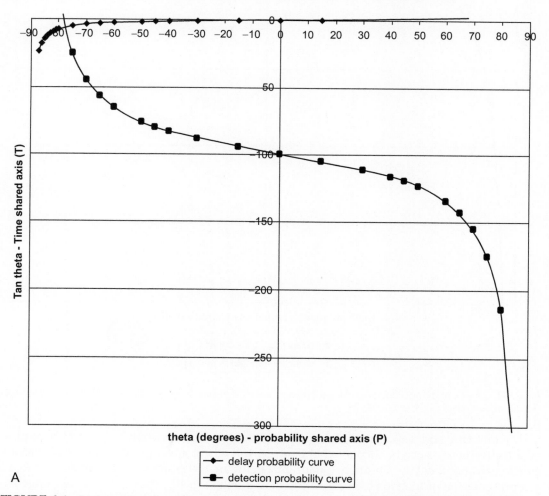

A

FIGURE 6.4 (a) A conceptual map for demonstrating worst-case scenario effectiveness of physical security.

(Continued)

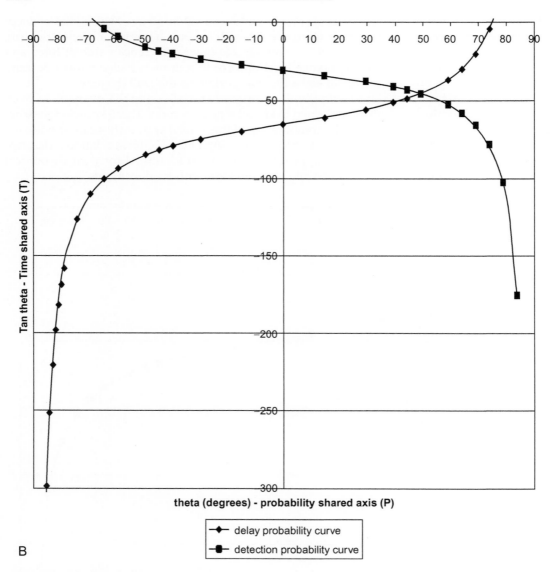

B

FIGURE 6.4—Cont'd (b) A conceptual map for demonstrating best-case scenario effectiveness of physical security. *(Reprinted from Alach and Smith, 2006.)*

A worst-case scenario of poor delay of barriers and poor detection values of physical security effectiveness can be displayed in Figure 6.4(a) where appropriate knowledge matrices can be used to model the situation. Quadrant 2 in Figure 6.4(a) shows a very small area that is a representation of the effectiveness of the model. Figure 6.4(b) shows a best-case effectiveness for the model with appropriate knowledge matrices derived from strong delay from physical barriers and strong detection values from electronic barriers.

The universal elements approach to the assessment of the effectiveness of DiD strategies is still in the development phase where appropriate descriptors of the elements for determination of the knowledge matrices are being considered. Future analyses can include orthogonal dimensions to the delay and detection probabilities as presented. These dimensions can include breaking for attack force against material strength, and the dimension of invading can include a detection system against a stealth attack.

The development of theories for the knowledge domain of security science will provide a better understanding of the concepts and therefore the applications for the protection of assets. These approaches to modeling DiD and its functions are an attempt to provide security analysts with some tools to explore the options for protecting assets and optimizing the effectiveness of the security. The development of knowledge structures within the DiD model for asset protection provides a paradigm for achieving quality security protection of facilities.

FUNCTION OF SECURITY TECHNOLOGY

In the major applications of security technology of access control and intrusion detection, the need for high-performance sensing and detection is required to ensure appropriate identification of authorized persons. Therefore, the function of security technology is to detect the presence or activities of people who provide a threat to the assets of an organization. Thus, with an absence of people or activities there is no security problem, although safety and environmental problems may exist.

The security technology associated with intrusion and access control is concerned with the authorization, identification, and detection of people in circumstances that may provide a threat to an organization. Then the security management plan of the organization is operationalized by the security technology, by detecting the presence or activities of people either from within the organization or as an external threat to the organization. The risk level presented by the threat will determine the degree of sophistication of the security technology to protect the assets (Smith, 2006). The detection of unauthorized people and their activities within an organization pose a major threat to the assets of its people, its information, and its materials. Thus, the detection function is considered a barrier in the DiD strategy and contributes to the effective control of authorized people in an organization through security protocols and polices to reduce the risk to organizations and community groups.

Types of Detectors

The principle of detection relies on sensing technology to discover the presence of a person or object within its field of view. That is, if the purpose of security technology is to detect the presence or activities of people, then the detection methods must be devised to respond to these stimuli. Thus, the detection of the presence or activities of people will require the development of appropriate sensors, and is currently a major applied scientific endeavor for the protection of assets.

A schematic approach to the functional components of security detection for the detection of the presence or activities of people requires the following:

- A signal must be produced by the person or the actions of the person to be sensed by the detector. The signal could be in the form of reflected light (detected by a camera), near-infrared radiation through body heat (detected by a passive infrared [PIR] detector), a sound (detected by a microphone), by movement when touching a fence (detected by a microphonic cable embedded in the fence), or from a molecular vapor from a package of drugs (detected by specific molecular sensors). All of these examples describe a signal for detection.
- The function of a sensor in security detection system responds to a signal for which it is compatible. That is, the sensor is capable of detecting the source that produced the signal, complying with the application of the detector in a DiD strategy. There is a wide range of sensors in security technology systems, including break-glass detectors that are microphones tuned to the frequencies of breaking glass, to X-ray detectors for the presence of explosives. Some other examples of sensors include charge-coupled device (CCD) chips in cameras to detect low levels of light, and the disturbances in magnetic fields produced by the presence of ferromagnetic metals.
- Usually, a low-amplitude signal is received by the sensor in a detector, and so it is necessary to increase the level of signal through an amplifier. The signal-to-noise ratio (SNR) is increased by the amplifier to detect a change in the signal strength from the presence of a person. The effect of the amplifier is to increase the sensitivity of the detection function so that it may detect subtle changes in intrusion within the system's field of view. Depending on the type and style of sensors used in the security technology, the amplifier will possess functions to increase the signal strength. Typically, fiber-optic cable could use laser amplification and opto-electronic solid-state amplifiers can be applied to light intensifiers.
- The function of the analyzer is to decide if a signal has been detected, or if the only noise has been received. Even after amplification, some signals are still weak and need to be discriminated against background noise. Discriminant analysis is often included in the circuitry to determine if the immediate signal shows that a change has occurred. That is, if a small change in signal quality can be detected, then this effect will indicate the presence of an intruder. Discriminant analyzers incorporate intelligence into the logic circuits of detection systems to better differentiate between active signals and background noise. Thus, these "smart" detection systems are able to discern signals against predetermined criteria to accept or reject the detection signal.
- The function of an alarm in a detection system is to indicate that an anomalous signal has been detected. The signal may have been generated by the presence of an unauthorized person or action, and it indicates that a response is required to investigate the anomalous incident. However, the issue of unwanted alarms, where spurious signals are generated by sources other than actual unwanted intruders or actions, requires the authenticity of the alarm condition. It is necessary to have an understanding of the reliability (false alarms through instability of a device) and validity (unwanted alarms through environmental sources) of the detection system to achieve optimum effectiveness for the protection of assets. The discrimination between an actual attack on the detection system and a spurious

signal from the surroundings will determine the validation level of the system. The incorporation of intelligence into the discrimination function of a detection system will reduce the frequency of unwanted alarms.

Classification of Intrusion Detection Systems

Security intrusion detection systems can be incorporated as electronic barriers in a DiD strategy to detect the presence of unauthorized persons in a secure area. These detection systems can be applied to perimeters on fences and walls, on open ground and sterile zones, buried beneath the ground surface, inside buildings, on doorways, on walls, in rooms, and under floors. Garcia (2008) proposed that the ideal intrusion protection boundary is a *sphere* enclosing the asset to be protected; that is, all directions surrounding the asset are being monitored for detection. There are strengths and weaknesses of performance for all types and forms of detection systems, and so security detection technologies continue to be modified and developed to increase sensitivity and reduce false detection rates. Standard or well-developed detection technologies can be categorized as single or multidimensional in function.

Point Detectors

Point detectors operate at a particular location and can be considered as zero-dimensional detectors in a DiD strategy. They are used in access control to respond to unauthorized entry at doors, windows, pathways, and hatches. Some examples of point detectors are reed switches that are located on doors to detect opening, and pressure pads beneath surfaces to detect the removal of works of art.

Linear Detectors

Linear detection technology includes one-dimensional sensors to monitor fences, walls, doorways, and pathways. These detectors include visible and infrared laser beams such as tripwires, microphonic cables mounted on fences, fiber-optic cables on fences and under surfaces, e-field systems on fences, and leaky cable detectors buried under ground.

Area Detectors

Detection systems that monitor horizontal or vertical areas in two dimensions will detect the presence of unauthorized persons located in the area or who pass through the vertical two-dimensional area. Examples of area detectors include vibration detectors on walls or safes, break-glass detectors on windows and glazing panels, and motion detection systems. A two-dimensional detection field is established by the detectors from signals generated somewhere on a surface. Also wide-area detection systems can employ multiple linear sensors that contribute to the extended region of surveillance. The advantage of this approach is that difficult terrain can be monitored within a larger-than-normal area.

Volumetric Detectors

The presence of persons can be monitored in an exterior environment or within the confines of a building or facility by the application of volumetric intrusion detection systems. The detection of movement by three-dimensional monitors can locate the persons within a predetermined region in both exterior settings and interior volumetric space. Movement of people can be detected by systems through the Doppler effect, attenuation of a beam, or receiving a signal (e.g., near-infrared radiation) from the presence of an intruder. Examples of volumetric detection systems include microwave, ultrasonic, active infrared detection, and passive infrared detection. The extent of volumetric detection depends on the strength of the signal generated and the sensitivity of the receiving detector element in a system. However, these limits of detection of volumetric systems continue to be extended through the development of new sensing surfaces in solid-state devices. Interior limits are determined by the radiating field generated by the source and the physical surfaces in facilities such as walls, panels, and doors (Jones and Smith, 2005).

Interestingly, Garcia's (2008) approach to the classification of external intrusion sensors employs a five-method taxonomy of the security systems:

• Passive or active.
• Covert or visible.
• Line-of-sight or terrain-following.
• Volumetric or line detection.
• Application.

This classification of intrusion detection sensors can be compared to the hierarchy of intrusion detection systems that has been discussed. However, for a detailed account of security technology and the application of intrusion detection and access control systems, consult Garcia (2006, 2008).

The conversion to digital signaling from traditional analog technologies has greatly enhanced the capability of intrusion detection systems for the protection of assets. The adoption of sensors with digital output signaling has allowed comprehensive signal processing with a quantum step in intelligence level that can be integrated in the system.

BARRIER AND OPEN GROUND DETECTION

Fences and walls have the capacity to carry intrusion detection systems to enhance the capability of the DiD strategy for the protection of assets. Similarly, open ground both within a defense area and external to a perimeter fence often requires area detectors to ensure that all attack paths into a facility have been covered. These intrusion detection systems generally have sensors that respond to movement, vibration, breaking of beams, or intrusion into magnetic and electric fields (Smith, 2006). Some of the more interesting sensor systems can include:

• *Microphonic sensor cable:* This type of cable can be mounted on fences and walls and will sense the movement of a fence or cable when it is disturbed by an intruder climbing the barrier.
• *Fiber-optic cable:* The technology of this cable class detects movement of a fence through attenuation of the light beam intensity through flexing of the cable. That is, slight bending of the cable changes the amount of light transmitted along the fiber-optic cable through light leakage at the bending points. Also, fiber-optic cable can be buried underground (or

under car parks) to detect the presence of an intruder through the weight of the person on the cable, which changes its shape or configuration.

- *Leaky cable:* Coaxial cable with some of its shielding removed can produce an electric field that extends above the surface of the ground. The presence of an intruder into this field will distort the field and register an alarm condition.
- *Seismic detection:* Geophones consist of conducting coils and permanent magnets can be mounted in strings on surfaces or buried underground. This form of technology is very sensitive to movement or vibration, and is able to detect the presence of intruders through minute disturbances and vibrations.

Movement and vibration sensor detection systems sense intrusion by converting mechanical vibrations on surfaces caused by intruder activities to electrical signals. These signals are processed by the system's discrimination circuits, and are classified as hostile by producing an alarm, or as benign from a nonthreatening source. The performance of the sensor depend on its placement on the barrier or structure so that a strong mechanical link or coupling is made between the sensor and the barrier.

Trends in movement and vibration detection systems are toward universality of mechanical coupling between the sensors and the fabric of surfaces, so that the detection system will bond to all forms of materials. That is, the surfaces of the fabrics become the sensors for intrusion detection through contact or proximity. The reliability and validity of intrusion detectors are being enhanced by the application of further intelligence into the analysis component of the system to discriminate unwanted signals from producing false alarms.

Laser Intrusion Detection

High physical security breaches have the possibility of occurring on critical infrastructure as conventional intrusion detection either fails or is compromised due to security management inadequacies. Conventional detection systems in a DiD strategy comprised of CCTV, night vision systems, radar, and security patrols have been shown to be inadequate in preventing attacks, partly due to the late detection of a system breach or failure. Thus, breaches can be better prevented or minimized if the detection of unauthorized persons or vehicles occurs at a long standoff range, providing time for appropriate detainment by a tactical response group.

Current laser intrusion detection systems typically have a laser scanner using servo motors and rotating mirrors to deflect a laser beam toward the region of interest. Although this principle addresses the issue of sensor deterioration and finally breakdown over time, it does suffer from wear and tear, and will eventually fail and require maintenance.

However, a laser intrusion detection system has been devised with no physical moving parts, so as to remove the mechanical fail factor in its operation. The optical laser scanning system for intrusion detection uses an *optical cavity*, which has been developed to produce multiple exiting beams from only one entering beam, thus providing an array of laser beams over an area under surveillance (Sahba et al., 2006a). This static approach to beam propagation over an area of surveillance depends on the optical cavity, with multiple total internal reflections of the laser beam within the cavity, and partial transmissions at the optical cavity surfaces.

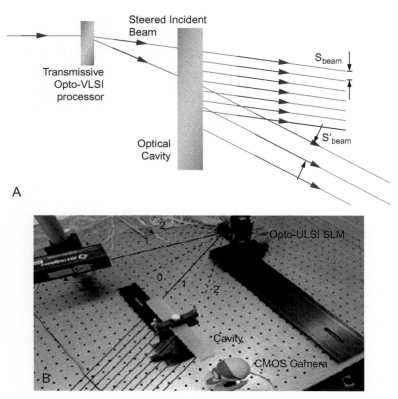

FIGURE 6.5 (a) The schematic ray diagram of the laser beam and optical cavity. (b) The optical bench configuration of the laser beam and optical cavity.

The schematic ray diagram of the laser beam and optical cavity are shown in Figure 6.5(a), where the direction of a single laser beam is controlled and relocated by an opto-very large scale integration (VLSI) processor onto the optical cavity, where through multiple internal reflections a many-beam output is produced. The optical system has been designed to achieve maximum production of exiting laser spots over a wide field of view of surveillance (Figure 6.5b).

The application of the optical laser scanning system for intrusion detection using an optical cavity to produce a multibeam output is shown in Figure 6.6. The beams produced by the optical cavity impinge on the intruder, and reflect back to a camera that detects the presence of the person. The captured reflected beams will produce an alarm to alert a tactical response group to intercept the intruder (Sahba et al., 2006a). The system also has the capability to locate the position of the unauthorized intruder by a ranging technique. Also, by repeated measures of the location of the intruder, the system can determine the speed and direction of travel of the intrusion. Spectral analysis of the captured beams reflected from the surfaces of the intruder can produce important information (Figure 6.6) about the intruder and include:

- Materials of the clothing worn by the intruder.
- Skin tone of the intruder.

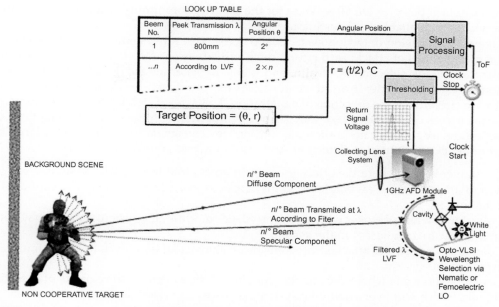

FIGURE 6.6   Schematic diagram of the laser intrusion detection system with range and spectral analysis capacity.

- Whether the intruder is wearing metal or carrying metal objects.
- Materials of the footwear of the intruder.

The prospects for remote spectroscopy from spectral analysis may also indicate if hazardous or dangerous materials such as explosives are present (Sahba et al., 2006b).

TESTING SYSTEMS

The purpose of testing and evaluating security systems and the components of the systems is to assess whether security technology that has been specified in a DiD strategy has the capability to perform according to specifications. The testing and evaluation of sophisticated security systems has generally remained in the domain of governments in national facilities and the commercial security industry through manufacturers and security engineering consultants. The production of testing protocols and industry standards has been developed by national organizations and professional security and engineering bodies in the appropriate security fields. The purpose of testing is to investigate and evaluate the design and function of security technology (Smith, 2005). Generally the intentions of these testing facilities are to:

- Provide a rigorous test and development facility.
- Assess, analyze, and report on security technology.
- Initiate development in establishing protocols and standards for security technology.
- Provide research and education in security technology.
- Provide a commercially available research and test facility.

Not all test facilities provide all services for the security community, but across the industry all services are available from testing facilities.

Generally, intrusion detection systems and access control systems are vulnerable to two different categories of attack: zero-effort attack and adversary attack. For a zero-effort attack an intruder avoids detection by stealth, and is able to penetrate the defense ring with no detection alarm. The intruder in an adversary attack has produced, developed, or manufactured devices to circumvent the detection of penetration. This type of attack may take the form of an imitation access card for entry, or may require tampering with the power or data links on a detection device, or may neutralize the sensing device signals to prevent detection. Other types of attacks on intrusion detection systems and access control systems are:

- Circumvention is where the attacker can gain access into the security system.
- Repudiation is where an employee gains access to the security system and confidential data.
- Collusion is where the user with access privileges modifies the system parameters to allow an attacker to gain access to the system.
- Coercion is where the attacker threatens or blackmails an employee to grant him or her access to the system.
- Denial of service is where the attacker may flood the system with requests of detection signals, which will overwhelm the system resources and deny the legitimate users access, or deny detection of an intruder.

An evaluation methodology has been developed and comprises a number of discrete stages in the process of testing security equipment:

- The development of a defeat evaluation methodology, which will require client approval before the methodology can progress beyond this stage.
- Commercial evaluation of the security device or system, so that a detailed account of the capability of the equipment is determined.
- Performance testing of the security device or system is conducted to assess the level of operation and performance of the equipment.
- Defeat testing of the equipment to assess its capability to prevent an attack on the integrity of the device. The physical integrity of the device is assessed by defeat testing, by both nondestructive and destructive methods. The technical integrity is assessed by interrogating the source of supplies, by environmental attacks and by verification attacks.
- Detailed reporting of the testing and assessment process is required to establish the reliability and validity of the security equipment.

When intrusion detection sensors are relied upon for perimeter and open-ground protection, three factors need to be considered for the design and management of the system. These decisions include which sensors to use, where to deploy the sensors, and how to interpret each sensor's alarm condition in real time (Peck and Bates, 2006). Each of these factors relating to sensors needs to be assessed according to an evaluation plan under similar conditions to which they are expected to function. Thus, site-specific decisions are required to achieve an effective DiD intrusion detection design for the protection of assets. The testing function of security sensors is a crucial process in the development of an intrusion detection system that exhibits reliability and validity in its purpose of application.

A Model for Testing

The testing of security equipment is a major component in the validation of the data acquired from intrusion detection devices and access control systems. With security policies and procedures in mind, the overall aim of security equipment testing and evaluation is to recommend a *best-fit* security equipment solution to a security problem. That is, not all intrusion detection security products are deemed suitable for all intrusion surveillance needs. A compromise is needed to best fit security detection systems to the asset protection task required by the security management plan. A best-fit solution goes beyond the functionality and capabilities of security equipment and extends to the degree to which the security equipment adequately addresses security risks, how well it integrates with operations and organizational policies, and how scalable the equipment is to cover an organization's dynamic security risk levels. Then the function of testing is to assess the capability of the equipment to determine its suitability for application in a specific context in the security management plan.

Security equipment testing and evaluation is not an independent process that can be engaged in without consideration of the threat and risk associated with an asset. Therefore, equipment testing and evaluation need to be considered within a formal risk management framework, such as the standard ISO 31000. Without a formal framework, such as that provided by AS/NZS 4360:2004, security equipment testing and evaluation can recommend inappropriate security equipment that inadequately protects against risks, poorly integrates with organizational operations, is not accepted by its users, and potentially impacts overall organizational performance. Security equipment testing and evaluation is an imperative component in the management of security risks for the protection of an organization's assets.

A model has been developed for testing security equipment and its evaluation in the context of its application in a security plan (Figure 6.7). The model proposes a five-stage plan with two levels of testing:

1. Intelligence acquisition and analysis.
2. Development of plan.
3. Client liaison.
4. Execution of plan.
5. Reporting.

The two levels of testing according to the five stages of the testing process are:

Level 1: The laboratory environment, which determines if the security equipment is technically and physically capable of meeting the needs of the security plan.
Level 2: Operational or simulated operational environment, which assesses the suitability of the equipment to perform within its intended environment in its intended role. That is, the assessment of equipment in actual or simulated conditions in which it is expected to function.

Level 1 testing is performed in a controlled laboratory environment, where factors that usually vary in the operational environment of the device are largely controlled. These factors include environmental conditions, operational activities, equipment operation, platform of operation, length of operational time, subject diversity, and other factors according to the

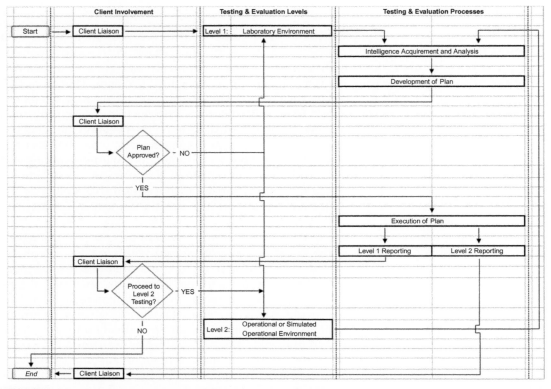

FIGURE 6.7   Model for the testing and evaluation of security equipment. *(Reprinted from Jones and Smith, 2005.)*

mode of operation of the device. Laboratory testing is ideal in the preliminary testing and evaluation stages, as it allows the security equipment to be isolated from a network, and repeatedly tested, thus allowing the reliability and validity of the sensor's performance to be evaluated (Jones and Smith, 2005).

Assessing the reliability and validity of security equipment is a major objective of level 1 testing under this model. The reliability of the equipment is its ability to repeatedly produce the same results under the same circumstances, while its validity is its ability to produce the results the manufacturer claims it can produce. Level 1 testing will provide the client with an indication of how reliable the detection device is, and whether it may be applied in the relevant security strategy according to the security management plan. However, level 1 testing will not inform the client if the security equipment is suitable for operation within its proposed environment.

Level 2 evaluation will depend on the outcome of level 1 testing, and will be conducted in an operational or simulated operational environment, where the conditions are similar to those in which the device will be expected to perform—that is, windy, wet, humid, dry, dusty, hot, or cold conditions. The equipment will be fully deployed and operated on a small scale, to evaluate the suitability of the security equipment to operate in its intended environment.

If operational testing is not possible, then a simulated operational environment will be employed. Government test houses employ several remote testing locations for the assessment of equipment in rough-weather environments.

Stage 1: Intelligence Acquirement and Analysis

The acquirement and analysis of intelligence is the most important stage of the security equipment testing process, as it outlines the aims and objectives of testing methodologies to be developed. That is, the more relevant the information that can be acquired and accumulated into the intelligence, the more defined, precise, and accurate the security equipment testing methodologies. The gathering of intelligence to plan the testing and assessment methodologies is an important phase of the process, and will allow the tester to seek information to address the following questions:

- Does the client already have one or more items of security equipment to be tested, or should we source the appropriate security equipment?
- What will be the financial, operational, logistical, political, or other constraints?
- In what operational environment will the security equipment be employed?
- What are the demographics and technology acceptance issues in regards to the users?
- What is the current security equipment solution? What are user attitudes toward this solution and how well does this solution work?
- What are the security equipment priorities: usability, security, functionality, scalability, ease of use, durability? What are these priorities for both the users and the management?
- What specific security classification standards or grading systems must the equipment be tested and evaluated against?
- What decisions will be made by the client as a result of testing an evaluation?

Thus, intelligence acquirement and analysis is a critical stage in the testing process as it establishes the boundaries and the extent of testing for a particular purpose (see Figure 6.7).

Stage 2: Development of Plan

The collection and analysis of the intelligence concerned with the security equipment provides a foundation for the commencement of the development of the plan. At this stage, the aim and objectives of testing and evaluating the security equipment should be clear, and there should also be unambiguous recognition of which elements and characteristics of the security equipment need to be tested and evaluated (see Figure 6.7). Thus, some recognition of the constraints of the device should be considered as the plan is developed to meet the needs of the client.

Stage 3: Client Liaison

The proposed testing and evaluation plan is presented to the client for approval. The proposed plan meets the needs of the client and the completion of testing will provide data upon which decisions can be made. If the client disapproves of the plan, then further investigation is needed through the intelligence acquirement and analysis stage, and so recommences the testing cycle (see Figure 6.7).

Stage 4: Execution of Plan

Upon approval of the testing and evaluation plan by the client, the plan is executed, and test data are generated for analysis and reporting to the client (see Figure 6.7).

Stage 5: Reporting

The client should receive a detailed testing and evaluation report providing results and an interpretation of the data. This report will provide the client with both a qualitative and quantitative assessment of results, with comments on the quality and functionality of the detection device. At level 1 testing, a recommendation should be presented as to whether to proceed to level 2 testing, where environmental conditions will be imposed on the equipment similar to the actual conditions for the application of the device (see Figure 6.7). Level 2 testing will inform the client if the equipment is appropriate for the proposed security protection of the client's assets.

It is necessary for the testing regime to also consider the *reliability* and *validity* of the data and outcomes from the results. It is important for the respective concepts of reliability and validity to be given considerable status in the testing and evaluation process, as without these functions being addressed, the outcomes of the testing will be uncertain.

RELIABILITY

The concept of reliability is the degree of confidence in which a testing regime can repeatedly yield the same results. The objective of reliability, in security equipment testing, is to measure whether a set of results is sufficiently reliable to be accepted as accurate, consistent, and dependable. This outcome of testing requires the ability to be able to reproduce the same results time again, ensuring that they are not an improbable occurrence.

VALIDITY

Validity is the degree of confidence in which outcomes from an application of the device can assess what they purport to assess (Haslam and McGarty, 1998). That is, we need to be assured that the results from testing are in fact the expectation of results according to the manufacturer or other acknowledged group.

Before results can be considered valid, they must first be shown to be reliable. Results can be reliable and valid, reliable and invalid, unreliable and invalid, but never unreliable and valid. That is, while high reliability does not warrant validity, results cannot achieve validity without reliability. So the aim of security equipment testing and evaluation is to produce results that are both reliable and valid. If this outcome cannot be achieved, then the testing results will need to be discarded.

Reliability and validity are crucial to the credibility and effectiveness of test results. This view has been supported by Wegner and Spyridakis (1989), who consider the issues of evaluation methodologies that have been developed by equipment usability assessors that have not addressed the reliability and validity of data produced by the testing methodologies. Concerns have been raised over the credibility and effectiveness of the results produced from the testing process. Wegner and Spyridakis propose that the concern for reliability and validity will enhance the credibility and effectiveness of usability testers. Thus, the testing and evaluation model presented for the assessment of security equipment must be considered within a framework of reliability and validity.

CONCLUSION

The application of security technology to the protection of assets depends on the requirements and conditions of the security management plan. That is, the function of security technology within a security protection strategy is to support the security management plan. Also, the application of security technology must be congruent with appropriate theories and principles for the protection of assets, and is required to be integrated with design and planning. The security principles of DiD and CPTED both support the application of security technology within the contexts of the principles of the protection of assets. An understanding of critical path analysis and EASI will allow security management to assess the quality of the security strategy in the protection of assets for their organization. The principles of universal element conceptual mapping are an advanced approach to understanding the reliability and validity of a security strategy, and provide security managers with the ability to extend their knowledge of a security system.

The necessity to detect the presence or activity of unauthorized persons in an area of interest requires appropriate sensors according to risk and the environment. Applications of sensors on barriers and in open ground are familiar technologies for the detection of unauthorized persons. However, the application of multibeamed laser intruder detections systems provides a technology to detect the presence of a person and analyze the reflected beams of the intruder to determine location, movement, and information about the intruder.

The testing of security technology is an important facet of a security plan and design in asset protection. Testing is necessary to determine the appropriateness of an item of equipment for a particular task in a security function. A testing model has been presented in this chapter to evaluate both the reliability and validity of security technology in the context of its application in a security strategy.

Further Reading

Gill, M. (Ed.), 2006. The Handbook of Security. Palgrave Macmillan, Houndmills, Hampshire.

References

Alach, Z., Smith, C.L., 2006. Theoretical considerations for modelling physical security risk. Journal of Information Warfare 6, Edith Cowan University, Perth, Western Australia.

Armstrong, D., 2005. A model for the evaluation of barriers and containers and their resistance to physical attack. In: Proceedings of the IEEE 39th Annual 2005 International Carnahan Conference on Security Technology. Las Palmas, Spain, pp. 263–266.

Armstrong, D., Peile, C., 2005. Perimeter intrusion detection systems performance standard. In: Proceedings of the IEEE 39th Annual 2005 International Carnahan Conference on Security Technology. Las Palmas, Spain, pp. 33–36.

Campbell, K., 2003. Security concepts for gated communities and residential towers. In: INTERSEC 2003 Conference. World Trade Centre, Dubai, January 2003.

Garcia, M.L., 2006. Vulnerability Assessment of Physical Protection Systems. Butterworth-Heinemann, Boston.

Garcia, M.L., 2008. The Design and Evaluation of Physical Protection Systems, second ed. Butterworth-Heinemann, Boston.

Haslam, S.A., McGarty, C., 1998. Doing Psychology. Sage Publications Ltd, Wiltshire.

Jones, D.E.L., Smith, C.L., 2005. The development of a model for testing and evaluation of security equipment within the Australian Standard /New Zealand Standard AS/NZS 4360:2004—Risk Management. Paper presented at the SET Conference on Counterterrorism. Canberra, Australia.

Lockyer, K.G., 1996. Project Management and Project Network Techniques. Pitman, London.

Peck, L., Trachier, G., 2004. Security technology decision tree tool. In: Proceedings of the IEEE 38th Annual 2004 International Carnahan Conference on Security Technology. Albuquerque, New Mexico, pp. 91–98.

Peck, L., Bates, R., 2006. Force protection sensor selection. In: Proceedings of the IEEE 40th Annual 2006 International Carnahan Conference on Security Technology. Lexington, KY, pp. 34–46.

Purpura, P., 2002. Security and Loss Prevention, fourth ed. Butterworth-Heinemann, Boston.

Sahba, K., Alameh, K.E., Smith, C.L., 2006a. A proposed motionless laser scanning architecture for perimeter security. In: Proceedings of the IEEE 40th Annual 2006 International Carnahan Conference on Security Technology, Lexington KY, pp. 9–16.

Sahba, K., Alameh, K.E., Smith, C.L., Paap, A., 2006b. Cylindrical quasi-cavity waveguide for static wide angle pattern projection. Optics Express 15 (6), 3023–3030.

Smith, C.L., 2003. Understanding concepts in the defense in depth strategy. Paper presented at Security Technology, 2003. In: Proceedings, IEEE 37th Annual 2003 International Carnahan Conference on Security Technology, Taipei, Taiwan, Republic of China. pp. 8–16.

Smith, C.L., 2005. The security systems research and testing laboratory at Edith Cowan University. In: Proceedings of the IEEE 39th Annual 2005 International Carnahan Conference on Security Technology. Las Palmas, Spain, pp. 308–311.

Smith, C.L., 2006. Trends in the development of security technology. In: Gill, M. (Ed.), The Handbook of Security. Palgrave Macmillan, Houndmills, Hampshire.

Wegner, M.J., Spyridakis, J.H., 1989. The relevance of reliability and validity to usability testing. IEEE Transactions on Professional Communication 32 (4), 265–272.

Integrated Identification Technology

OBJECTIVES

- Distinguish between the concepts and principles of detection, recognition, and identification in the domain of security surveillance technology.

- Characterize the access control principle of something you are, know, or have for applied security.

- Explain the functions of the major components of an access control system for the protection of assets.

- Identify the ancillaries that are required to support the primary components and functions of an access control system.

- Explain how access control systems can be integrated with building control systems in large facilities.

- Explain the functions of smart cards in the domain of building management systems.

- Compare and contrast the effectiveness of the range of access cards for the security of assets.

- Be aware of the modes of attack on biometric identification systems.

- Describe the management and social factors that should be considered in the selection of a biometric system for asset protection.

- Explain the principle of multimodal biometric systems as a strategy to reduce the effect of attacks on this access control technology.

- Identify the functions and operations of intelligent CCTV in detection technology.

- Develop a strategy for the application of intelligent CCTV in the protection of a national infrastructure.

INTRODUCTION

The continued development of security technology and its applications for the protection of assets will depend on understanding the principles of its operation and functions in safeguarding the people, information, and assets of an organization. National security, economy, and growth require quality security technology and security management to protect the critical infrastructure of an organization. Therefore, an understanding of the quality of security technology, their applications, and management will determine the relevance and level of security available. An emphasis on the context of the security is necessary for technology to be applied within a *security management strategy*. Thus, the management of the technology will ensure the suitability of this approach for an effective security application in the protection of assets.

Because security technology has the capability to enhance a protection of assets strategy, it is necessary to determine the role of the technology in providing security. This chapter is concerned with the *detection*, *recognition*, and *identification* of persons who are either authorized or unauthorized to be present at a particular location in a facility. Following the detection of a person, it is necessary for recognition and then identification of the individual to determine the authorization status. The principles of access control are presented and discussed, with the importance of the credentials of codes and cards, and the merit of *biometric identification* is considered. Methods of attacks on biometric systems are described, with multimodal biometric security systems presented as a means of countering attacks. Intelligent CCTV is developing a strong contribution to the strategy of assets protection for an organization. Types of intelligent CCTV are presented as positive approaches to automated surveillance for a security strategy. Thus, the management of these security technologies will better protect the assets of an organization and its people.

BACKGROUND

The successful application of automated surveillance in security for monitoring and apprehension of intruders requires a model that is capable of detection at one end of a spectrum, and identification at the other end. Such an approach bridges the detection and locating of an individual through intrusion detection methods, to the identification of an individual using biometric methodology at a distance. Two similar models that can be applied to automated surveillance are:

1. Automatic target detection and recognition approach (Schroeder, 2002), where a model is proposed that includes detect, discriminate, classify, recognize, and identify. This model has direct application to target detection in a military domain.
2. A methodology for tracking systems (Musa and Watada, 2008), which proposes detection, tracking, object representation, and recognition. This approach to intrusion detection through surveillance can be normally applied to individuals who may or may not have authorization to be present at a location.

These two approaches to surveillance can be integrated into a model that has the components of detection, recognition, and identification (DRI) as the major factors in the application of imaging to asset protection. These factors represent the important stages of the process of detection in intrusion detection, and the recognition or identification in access control.

Detection

The process of detection means the localization of the object (or person) when it first enters the imaging device's field of view. That is, when a person is initially in the field of view of the camera or sensor, the analytical component of the surveillance system is able to indicate that a new object is present in the environment of the previous image frame. Thus, a comparison between successive image frames has identified the presence of the new object, and therefore has detected the person. Then, the detection process needs to detect the object in every successive frame of the surveillance system to track and invigilate the person. The method used by the military for target detection is to reliably differentiate targets from clutter. Thus, features of target signatures are analyzed to separate them from background. The probability of detection (PD) needs to be high so that targets are not missed. As well, detection systems for people also require imaging signatures of individuals so that appropriate objects are initiated for tracking. These approaches include:

- Background subtraction method has been employed by most tracking surveillance systems (Yilmaz et al., 2006).
- Disparity templates of images were used by Beymer and Konolige (1999) for the detection process of humans in the field of view.
- Object classification and motion matching was used for the detection of a pedestrian and bicycle on a road by Qui et al. (2003).
- Edge information and skin tones were used by Siddiqui and Medioni (2006) as visual features of video imaging to detect the limbs of humans.

Present-day solutions for object detection use hybrid methods that use a variety of methodologies to best detect the initial presence of individuals in the field of view of detection technology. As well as the detection of the physical presence of people, the detection of object behavior or object activity should also be included in the process of localization. Thus, the process of detection is an important factor in automatic surveillance for intrusion detection, access control, biometric identification, and CCTV analytics.

Recognition

The concept of recognition in a surveillance model or paradigm requires the system to determine the category or class of an object according to a set of parameters. Object recognition can be discussed in a number of contexts in visual perception models so that the class or category can be determined before object identification can proceed. There are several models that can be considered when understanding the process of recognition in the context of surveillance:

- *Template theories* claim that patterns or templates of objects are stored in long-term memory so that matching can recognize the object being observed. This is a limited approach to recognition as ill-defined categories will not be met.
- *Feature theories* propose that patterns consist of a set of specific features or attributes. The process of pattern recognition starts with the extraction of the features or attributes from the visual stimulus presented by an object and then the set of attributes is compared to the information stored in memory for recognition to be gained (Eysenck and Keane, 2002, p. 84).
- A *computational theory* for object recognition was proposed by Marr (1982) where a series of representations or descriptions are provided with increasing detail about the object to be recognized. Marr (1982) identified three major kinds of identification:
  - Primal sketch as the two-dimensional description of the main light-intensity changes from the object including information about edges and contours.

- A two-and-a-half-dimensional sketch includes a description of the depth, making use of shadows, texture, motion, and binocular disparity. This description is observer-centerd or viewpoint-dependent.
- A three-dimensional representation describes the shape of the object in three dimensions with relative positions being independent of the viewpoint of the observer. Marr (1982) proposed that object recognition was achieved by matching the three-dimensional model representation constructed by visual information against a catalog of three-dimensional model representations stored in long-term memory.
- Biederman (1990) extended Marr's theory of object recognition by proposing a recognition-by-components approach, where object components of basic shapes are used. Biederman proposed that there are 36 basic shapes or geons, which may be blocks, cylinders, spheres, arcs, and wedges. Thus, all shapes can be constructed from geons, and so recognition of objects is achieved through the geons that can construct the object.

Thus, classes of objects are visually recognized according to their characteristics, attributes, or features that allow them to be associated with a class or category. These attributes or components have properties of association, so that common features or attributes determine the particular class that an object will belong to. It should be noted that a particular object may belong to two or more categories, as it may have overlapping attributes; for example, an object can be a chair and a stool at the same time.

The principle of recognition in biometrics is a little different, as it is a pattern-recognition system according to physiological features or behavioral characteristics that a person possesses. A biometric system typically operates in one of two modes: recognition or verification, and identification.

- Recognition or verification of a person is achieved when the biometric signature of a person matches the person's biometric signature stored in the system or on a smart card. That is, a one-to-one match of the person's features or characteristics is achieved with the stored biometric signature of that person. The person has been recognized to be who he or she claims to be.
- In identification mode the system performs a one-to-many comparison against a biometric database in an attempt to establish the identity of an unknown individual. That is, the biometric signature of a person is compared to the database's templates of signatures to identify the person.

Identification

The principle of identification is the process by which an individual person is uniquely known for who they are through positive features and attributes of their physiology and behavioral traits. The requirement to identify people is a cornerstone of modern society for citizenship, ownership, family inheritance, and identity. The crime of identity theft is a major concern for law enforcement.

Identification methods derived from biometric characteristics require automated pattern matching, and so are always probabilistic, meaning that decisions are made with some level of uncertainty. Thus, biometric identification has the capacity to connect a person through the measured characteristics to the identity previously recorded in a database. Thus, the identification of the person occurs through measurement by the technology, and as a result the person cannot be identified by this procedure outside of the system. This technique is offered as an alternative to more commonly used and privacy-invasive techniques, such as recitation of mother's maiden name, date or location of birth, or production of a passport or driver's license. It should be noted that not all biometric identification methods are appropriate for every individual, because there are across-individual and within-individual variations in the measure. Also, biometric probabilistic identification cannot align individuals as members of groups, nor identify groups or subpopulations. Also, the establishment of identity does not include medical conditions, age, race, or gender of individuals.

ACCESS CONTROL SYSTEMS

Technological advances have contributed to the popularity of automated electronic access control systems through decreasing hardware costs, increased emphasis on the need for security, and increased opportunity for integration with building systems. Within the security of a facility, an *access control system* (ACS) is a measure or group of measures designed to allow authorized personnel, vehicles, and equipment to pass through protective barriers, while preventing unauthorized movements. The issue of authorization for people in a security facility is important, as it determines who has the right to be present at a particular location in a particular situation. The status of authorization is granted to individuals according to the security management plan, and is not granted according to rank or designation in an organization. That is, the security management plan may decree that a more junior person in the organization has authorization to access a particular area than a senior member of the staff; this is determined by respective duty statements.

Purpose of Access Control Systems

Defense-in-depth (DiD) strategies often employ physical barriers to protect the assets of an organization. However, for authorized persons to gain access to protected areas, they will need to cross the physical barriers through openings such as doors and gates. Since these openings can represent security weak points in a barrier system, it is necessary to manage the transiting of authorized persons through these openings to prevent unauthorized access. The function of automated ACSs employing electronic technology is to manage the movement of authorized persons through DiD barriers and control the access of unauthorized persons (Norman, 2012).

The access control of a facility can be achieved by the application of several approaches for the protection of assets of the organization:

- Psychological or symbolic barriers through design or signage.
- Security staff physically located at entry and exit points.
- Security staff located at central points that monitor and control entry and exit points using intercommunication, videophones, and CCTV cameras.
- Mechanical locking devices operated by keys or codes.
- Automated electronic access control systems.

Each approach has advantages and disadvantages, and the precise method used will depend on the particular application in which access control is required.

Role of Access Control Systems

The role of an ACS in terms of its DiD functions is to deter, detect, and delay intrusions, and facilitate a response through its detection capability. Although some ACSs may incorporate automated response features (e.g., closing or locking doors upon an alarm), these systems primarily introduce more delay into the penetration of the DiD strategy rather than establish an action to indefinitely neutralize an attack. As such, these systems do not negate the need for a human response force.

Access control systems usually feature a locking device on a portal that allows entry through a barrier by an authorized person. Credentials and readers are used to identify and distinguish authorized users from unauthorized users and intruders. A credential is a physical item (e.g., a card), item of information (e.g., a code), or a personal characteristic (e.g., a fingerprint) used by an authorized user, while a reader is an electronic device that examines a user's credential at a portal for authorized entry.

Also, there are ancillaries at the access points that are required to support the primary components and functions of an ACS, including:

- Sensing devices.
- Egress devices.
- Barrier automation devices.
- Cable transfer devices.
- Audible annunciation devices.
- Visual indication devices.
- Signage.

Each portal will usually be connected to a local control unit to perform processing activities affecting that particular portal. In small systems this control unit may be integrated with the reader, while in more complex systems, the control unit will usually be separate and process several portals. Larger systems are generally designed so that control units for portals throughout a facility are linked to each other and to a central control unit (usually a dedicated personal computer) via a network (Norman, 2012).

It is interesting to note that to achieve seamless operations within a facility, ACSs are integrated with building systems, such as:

- Other security systems.
- Building management or intelligent systems.
- Fire and life safety systems.
- Energy management systems.
- Elevator systems.
- Emergency systems.
- Software-based management and database systems.

Facility Access Control Systems

When an authorized user seeks to access a particular door in a facility, the credential is presented to the reader at that door, and the credential is converted into a unique data signal.

Analysis of the signal determines whether or not the user is authorized to gain access at that particular time. An authorized credential is allowed to proceed, and the locking device on the door is released. The door can then be opened and closed by an automatic mechanism. Simultaneously, all the information associated with the access attempt is recorded by the central control unit. When an unauthorized user attempts to open a particular door, the analysis of the data signal will indicate an unauthorized status, and will not unlock the door. Feedback is provided to the central control unit to indicate that the access attempt was unsuccessful, and the attempt to gain access will be recorded by the central control unit (Norman, 2012).

If an intruder attempts to gain access by forcing a door open, then a door contact switch or other detection device will send the signal that the door has been opened to the local controller. An alarm will be generated and a response will be required from the security department. An administrator can access the central control unit and examine aspects of the system, such as the status of portals in the facility, the log of access attempts, and alarms events. The administrator can also change the system settings, enroll new users, temporarily disable an existing user's access, and perform a wide range of security management tasks.

Credentials

Access control system *credentials*, wherever these are tokens, cards, or biometrics, comply with the principle of *something you have* (e.g., a card or token), *something you know* (e.g., a password), and *something you are* (e.g., a biometric signature). The application of this principle (Figure 7.1) from tokens to biometric signatures produces a perception that the security system becomes more secure. Within a security context, biometric may be considered the highest level of identification as "biometric characteristics is the true identifier of a person" (Smith, 2006, p. 624); however, taking such a theoretical approach with a biometric system can lead to systems that are prone to technical attack or simple defeat through system vulnerabilities (Brooks, 2010).

The traditional approaches to the identification of persons for authorized entry include the following functional methodologies of codes and cards for access identification:

* *Codes*, include personal identification numbers (PINs), passwords (as alpha or alphanumeric), and encryption keys. The theoretical level of security is determined by the number of possible code combinations, with more characters being equated to increased security. In practice, however, code security is largely determined by the ability of the users

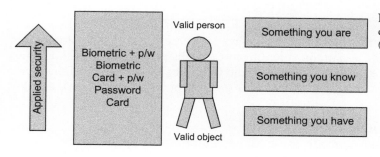

FIGURE 7.1 Access control: perceived level of applied security. *(Reprinted from Brooks, 2010.)*

to keep it secure. Therefore, code- and password-based systems are more likely to be defeated with prior knowledge of the code rather than by trial-and-error attacks.
- *Cards*, come in the form of ID badges, keys, airline tickets, driver licenses, magnetic stripe cards, proximity cards, Wiegand cards, and the various types of smart cards.

However, these two forms of authorization for access do not positively identify an authorized person at the access control point. Thus, personal identification systems based on knowledge and possession offer limited security since these methods can be compromised—knowledge and possession identification systems only respond to input or tokens and not the actual authorized person. There are limitations on the use of PINs and passwords, as experience has shown that the sheer volume of these codes are too great to be retained by an individual's memory, and these codes should not be recorded! Psychologists claim that the average person can retain in memory only four randomly generated eight-character alpha-numeric passwords. This limitation of the human memory restricts the application of passwords as an identifier (Smith, 2006).

Biometric Signatures

The characteristics of an individual can provide identification of the person through personal features or attributes and is based on physical and behavioral characteristics of the person. Thus, *biometrics* refers to the measurement of biological traits of individuals, and the application of these measurements to the identification of people. The two main operational modes of a biometric system are *identification* and *recognition*, and *verification*, where the following principles are required:

- *Identification mode:* There is no claim of identity for the user, and the system must search the entire database to find the highest probability of a match. This comparison is a one-to-many search of a biometric database for comparison.
- *Recognition or verification mode:* The user has a known identity, and the system searches the database to find the corresponding match for verification. This comparison is a one-to-one match to verify the identity of the person.

In summary, the combination of these identification methods provides higher levels of security for access control and identification of personnel. Thus, multi-identifying modes provide additional levels of protection for access to restricted areas.

CARDS

Cards can be classified according to a variety of physical and electronic technologies that have the capacity to store a code as a unique identification for the person. These technologies can include physical, optical, magnetic, and electronic technologies as the principles upon which unique information or coding is stored. Some examples of types of cards that employ these technologies are:

- *Physical technologies:* Hollerith cards.
- *Optical technologies:* embossed, barcode, infrared, holographic, and optical cards.

- *Magnetic technologies:* magnetic slug, magnetic sandwich, magnetic stripe, and Wiegand cards.
- *Electronic technologies:* proximity and smart cards.

From this range of cards, some have found acceptance in security access control, and as such, provide the necessary capabilities to withstand attack, and some even to withstand sustained attack against unauthorized entry. A selection of these cards is discussed here according to their features, modes of operations, and levels of security that they provide for asset protection.

Infrared Cards

Infrared cards feature a barcode that is imprinted inside the card and is not visible to the human eye. When placed in a reading device, infrared radiation is illuminated on the card, causing the barcode to cast a shadow that is scanned by the reader. These cards are much more difficult to reproduce, and therefore offer much higher security than standard barcode technology.

Holographic Cards

Holographic cards feature a holographic pattern that is embossed and read by an infrared laser. The holograms are difficult to copy, and so they provide higher security for authorization. These cards are used for ACS applications, and more recently for telephone cards.

Optical Cards

Optical cards function in a way similar to compact disc technology, where a code is burnt in digital format into the card substrate and read by a laser. These optical cards have become widely used in ACS, and, although expensive, are appropriate for high-security applications.

Magnetic Stripe Cards

Magnetic stripe cards use the same conventional magnetic recording technology used for audiotapes, and are currently used with credit and debit cards. They consist of a standard coercivity plastic card to which a strip of magnetic tape is applied. This standard tape strip contains three magnetic tracks that are used to store the card's code data. The card is usually presented to the reader by swiping or inserting it into the reader, which obtains the card's code using a magnetic head that detects the magnetic field generated by its strip.

The advantage of magnetic stripe cards is that their codes can be changed after manufacture by reprogramming, and as credit and debit cards, they can also feature text and images and be used as identification badges. Disadvantages arise because these cards require swiping or insertion into a reader resulting in wear over time. In general, magnetic stripe cards offer a relatively low level of security.

Wiegand Effect

The Wiegand effect produces an electromagnetic output when electric pulses are induced in twisted wires as they pass through a magnetic field. Wiegand tokens consist of many small pieces of twisted magnetic alloy embedded into a plastic token in codified positions usually arranged in two rows or columns. A Wiegand reader generates an alternating magnetic field that induces the Wiegand effect when a token is presented. The reader then detects the resulting electric pulses, which represent the code formed by the positioning of the wires within the token.

Wiegand cards and tokens have advantages over magnetic stripe technology, as they cannot be corrupted by magnetic fields, and Wiegand pulses can be detected over a longer range than the field created by a magnetic stripe card. Since Wiegand tokens require minimum contact with the reader, and the wires are embedded, there is reduced wear to critical components. A disadvantage of Wiegand cards and tokens is that they are not reprogrammable, since the code is determined when the wires are embedded during manufacture.

Proximity Cards

Proximity cards function on *radio-frequency identification* (RFID) principles, in which identification codes are transmitted and received using RF signals. Proximity cards feature an RF transmitter circuit consisting of a tuned antenna and a microchip that is programmed with the credential's code. Thus, the credential can be presented at a distance from the reader, without actually requiring contact.

Proximity cards can be classified as being either active or passive. Active cards and tokens contain a battery to power the transmitter, and usually transmit their signal constantly, which is detected by a nearby reader in the same way as a normal radio receiver. However, passive credentials do not contain their own power source, and therefore do not transmit any signals until close to a reader. The reader transmits an RF signal, which is received by a passive credential that uses the energy in the received RF signal to power its own transmitter.

A benefit of proximity technology is user convenience where a faster portal throughput rate is achieved through ease of credential presentation. A disadvantage is caused from proximity technology's reliance on RF communication, where its operation can be affected by electromagnetic interference.

Smart Cards

Smart cards are plastic tokens containing integrated circuit chips that can provide an array of functions for security and building management functions. Smart cards can be classified according to the type of chips they contain:

- *Memory only:* These cards contain only a memory chip, and simply store data without providing any processing capabilities.
- *Memory with hardwired logic:* These contain a memory chip and also a logic chip, which can provide encryption and authenticate access to the memory chip.
- *Microprocessor:* These contain a microprocessor chip and read/write memory supported by an operating system, which allows sophisticated processing capabilities.

Currently, most smart cards contain a microchip as well as an RF transmitter circuit, a battery if needed for memory, and processing or active communications. However, usually the required power is supplied by the reader. When smart cards are used for ACS applications, the code is stored in the card's memory, and the reader obtains its code by accessing this memory. This process is done in the same way as memory access in a computer. A smart card may interface with a reader in one of two ways:

- Contact smart cards feature an exposed chip to allow direct physical contact with the reader. If the reader is of the insertion type, then it will provide power and communications with the card over electrical connections with the chip.
- Contactless smart cards feature a chip that is completely embedded in the card. This reader functions on the same principles as proximity technology, with power and communications being provided via RF signals.

Smart card access control systems provide several advantages for the protection of assets, as the central control computer stores the data for the system, and individual credential verification is not required. The information on the access card has greater security because of its design and function, and the access card allows a broad variety of additional applications for enhanced performance and outcomes. Because of their sophistication, smart cards offer many features and advantages because they are fully programmable, and through their higher data storage capacity, they can have biometric data of a person on their credential.

BIOMETRICS

The traditional forms of knowledge and possession to achieve authorization for access to a facility do not positively identify the authorized person at the access control point. Thus, personal identification systems based on knowledge and possession offer limited security since these methods can be compromised as they only respond to input such as codes or cards, and not the actual authorized person. However, personal characteristics of an individual can provide the factual identification of the person through personal features or attributes, referred to as *biometrics*, based on physical and behavioral characteristics of the person. The availability of biometric identification systems and technology continues to increase, and with the improvement in reliability of the systems to provide repeated measures, and validity to detect a registered person, there is now a positive societal acceptance.

Biometrics refers to the measurement of biological traits of individuals, and the application of these measurements to identify people. Biometric systems use methods of verifying or recognizing the identity of a living person from physiological or behavioral characteristics. As Smith notes, "All persons on this planet are most similar in many ways, but are different from each other in all ways. This consequent allows people to be identified by biometric procedures" (2003, p. 34).

Thus, biometric systems are automated procedures for verifying or recognizing a person's identity from either a physical or behavioral characteristic. Sherman (1992, p. 128) defines biometrics in the following manner:

> The term biometrics strictly relates to the statistical analysis of biological phenomena and measures, but has become widely accepted within the security profession to describe technologies used for personal identity verification.

The concept of identification operationalizes the principle of authorization; that is, for a person to be authorized to enter a facility, perform an activity, receive a service, or attend a function they need to be identified for access. Although this process of identification for authorizing persons has traditionally been linked to knowledge or tokens, the positive identification of a person is best achieved from personal characteristics by recognition of features or behavioral attributes where these characteristics are detectable and quantifiable.

Types of Biometric ID

Biometric characteristics of a person can be either physical or behavioral—physical by their personal being, and behavioral according to how they act. For about a century, the principally measurable characteristic associated with people that was universally accepted as a positive identifier was the fingerprint. Trained experts matched contact data collected using special inks, dusting powders, and tapes. These data consisted of whorls, ridge endings, and bifurcations, and the identification was achieved by the comparison of these features against templates. However, a sensor capable of reading a fingerprint made by pressing the finger against a glass plate has been developed, with the digitized image stored as a computer file. Thus, a set of possible finger biometric identity prints will include a thumb print, full finger print, finger pattern with creases on the underside of the finger, palm print, hand topography, and hand geometry for positive ID. Other physical characteristics that have been investigated as potential biometric identifiers include:

- Finger length (insufficient variation).
- Wrist veins (underside).
- Hand veins (back of the hand) (Cross and Smith, 1995).
- Knuckle creases (when gripping a bar).
- Fingertip structure (blood vessel pattern).
- Hand topography (Vuori and Smith, 1997).
- Ear shape.
- Lip shape.

Other biometric technologies for behavioral characteristics that have been developed and gained some market acceptability included voice patterns, retina scans, signature dynamics, iris recognition, keystroke dynamics, and signature recognition.

Figure 7.2 shows the pattern of blood vessels in the back of a hand illuminated in infrared radiation, with the segmentation of the pattern reduced to a metric that represents the positive identification of the person (Smith, 2003; Cross and Smith, 1995). Again, Vuori and Smith (1997) showed the three dimensionality of the human hand by applying structured light to the object to enhance the shape for positive identification. These examples are illustrative of biometric techniques that can be applied to positively identify individuals.

However, many other biometric identifiers have been considered as biometric IDs, including facial features, the personal characteristics of body odor, retina (Figure 7.3) and iris features (Figure 7.4), and movement gait. In fact, there is a multitude of potential biometric characteristics of people that have been examined for possible unique identification of authorized users; though a smaller range of commercially available automatic biometric identification systems are currently available.

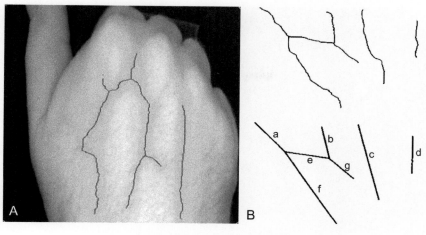

	Length	Angle
a	91.0	123.3
b	80.2	100.0
c	199.3	101.9
d	96.0	90.6
e	76.1	170.2
f	208.0	115.9
g	67.6	128.4

C

FIGURE 7.2 (a) Hand vein pattern in infrared radiation; (b) segmentation of a hand vein pattern; and (c) metric derived from the segmentation of the hand vein pattern. *(Reprinted from Smith, 2003.)*

FIGURE 7.3 Retinal vein patterns.

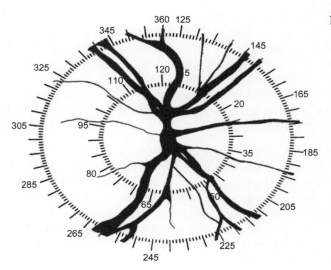

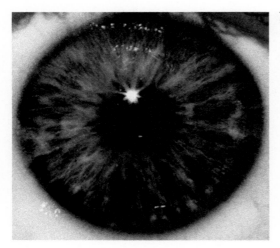

FIGURE 7.4   Iris pattern biometric.

Figure 7.3 shows the retinal vein patterns in the back of the eye, and since these patterns are considered to be unique to individuals, they may be applied as a biometric identifier for positive ID. The retinal vein pattern can be superimposed on a double annular scale where the intersection points on the scale by the veins produce the data that becomes the identifier for the person.

Figure 7.4 shows an image of the iris of a human eye surrounding the pupil of the eye. The structure in the iris can be likened to a bar code and therefore used for identification (Daugman, 2004).

As in all pattern recognition objectives, the issue is the relation between interclass and intraclass variability. That is, the objects can be reliably classified only if the variability among different instances of a given class is less than the variability between different classes. Thus, the variability between repeated imaging of the same iris should be less than the variability between images from a range of irises. The stability of the iris structure is high, and so it is suitable for automatic personal identification as a biometric ID. There is a belief that the iris changes systematically with the health of a person, or the personality of a person. This belief has been discredited (Berggren, 1985; Simon et al., 1979) as being medically untrue, and that in fact the iris maintains relative stability over time.

Individuals can also be identified by their behavioral characteristics—that is, the way they conduct themselves or act. As examples, systems have been designed to use well-understood behavioral characteristics of persons, including:

- *Speech analysis* where the voice print shows the variation in frequency against time when the person said a given word. This biometric ID is difficult to duplicate because of the many human factors involved in the production of sounds. Although we can hear the carrier frequencies as we speak, we are unaware of the higher frequency overtones in our speech, and these frequencies assist in the application of the voice print identification.
- *Signature dynamics:* The distribution of pressure over time when a person completes his or her signature is a unique biometric identifier. That is, the signature is not the identifier, but rather is the pressure applied through the pen to the paper and the pressure pad beneath the paper.

- *Keyboard typing rhythms:* Competent keyboard operators each develop a typing style particular to them. As a result of this unique typing style that each keyboard operator has developed, they can be identified by the typing rhythm that they use while working. The advantage of this biometric identifier is that it continues to be refreshed and updated while the keyboard operator works.

Biometric System

The purpose of the biometric system is to produce an image or a signal that characterizes the biometric feature of an individual as an access control measure. There are three major components in an automatic biometric system to produce the biometric signature for the identification of the person for authorization:

- A device to capture an image or signal of the particular characteristic of the person.
- The compression, processing, and comparison of the image for ID of an authorized person.
- Interface of biometric identification with the access control system.

Each authorized user of the biometric system is required to enroll by presenting the characterizing trait for inclusion in a digital library for future retrieval. This biometric image may be stored as a *template* or *signature*, which will then be a representation of the original biometric image. Some examples of templates or signatures are:

- The lengths and widths of fingers in a hand geometry biometric system.
- The number of swirls in a fingerprint image.
- The structure of the pattern of hand veins under infrared radiation.
- The frequency distribution of a series of spoken words.

These data of the template may be stored in a database for reference and comparison, or encoded on a card for a direct comparison.

The schematic structure of a generic biometric system consists of a sensor, a feature extractor, stored templates, a matching function, and an output application when access is granted. These components of the biometric system represent the minimum configuration for biometric access control.

Sensor: The sensor can have many forms according to the biometric feature being assessed, and can include a camera for facial or iris recognition, a capacitance or ultrasonic pad for fingerprints, a microphone for voice recognition, and an infrared detector sensor for veins in hands.

Feature extractor: The biometric features of interest are extracted from the sensor data to provide a signature template for the biometric of a person. This signature template should have sufficient resolution to provide a unique signature for the person.

Stored templates: Before a person can be authorized for access by a biometric system, the individual must be registered on the system. This process usually involves the biometric feature being recorded three times, with the outputs combined to form a library template for comparison for acceptance or rejection.

Matcher: The function of the matcher is to perform the comparison process between the library template and the biometric signature for the current attempt to gain access through a matching algorithm in the system.

Application device: The application device is able to operate when the system indicates that a positive match has occurred. These devices may provide cash at a dispenser, open a door, provide access to a computer, validate a passport, start a motor vehicle, and operate a credit card.

The selection of an appropriate biometric identifier for authorized individuals to gain access to an asset should have the following properties:

- *Universal:* All persons should have the characteristic.
- *Permanent:* The characteristics should not vary over time.
- *Distinctive:* The same characteristic from different persons should be as different as possible—that is, the interclass variability should be as large as possible.
- *Robust:* Repeated measures of a characteristic of a person should be as close as possible—that is, the intraclass variability should be as small as possible.
- *Accessible:* The characteristic should be easy to present to the sensor.
- *Acceptable:* It should be perceived as nonintrusive by the user.
- *Hard to circumvent:* It should be difficult for an impostor to deceive the system.

These properties of a biometric identifier serve to define the characteristics of individuals so that they may be best identified by their physical characteristics and behaviors. There are several advantages to be gained by the application of biometric technology since it can provide both accurate and secure access to information. This advantage is in contrast to the application of password verification with its many problems that people experience when applying them. Biometric ID can be applied uniformly across a subpopulation, producing constant results with consistency of outcomes.

The acceptability of biometric systems by authorized users has become an important factor in biometric identification operations, where management have imposed biometric ID on a workforce without due consultation. Initially, the few high-end biometric security systems for government and military had limited users, so the willingness of users was not an issue.

However, for mass population usage of a biometric system, the following factors need to be considered:

- The assets of an organization warrant protection. The value or significance of the assets warrants the expense and involvement of staff.
- The biometric system effectively protects the assets. If the justification of the installation of a biometric system is to protect the assets, then the system must be directly associated with the assets.
- The system is not hazardous to the health of the users. It is imperative that the biometric ID system does not impair the health of the staff, and that the staff is assured that there is no health issue with the system.
- The system does not impede movement of authorized users and cause production delays. That is, a biometric access control system is not installed on an access way that is repeatedly used by staff while performing their normal duties.
- Management of the organization are not able to collect personal information about staff from their biometric signatures. That is, personal information on the staff from their biometric data should not be available to anyone, including insurance companies.
- Management of the organization need to decide whether the benefits of the biometric system outweigh the liabilities.

The identification of persons by biometric systems has become a common application of technology in access control systems. To restrict access of persons to facilities, computer systems, financial transactions, information, and high-security areas, it is necessary to identify authorized persons. The reliance upon technologies makes identification of individuals both a demanding and exacting task. Biometric systems are being developed that are more reliable, less expensive, and better designed for personal identification. However, the application and administration of biometric systems are also important and demanding, and require considerable planning within the context of the organization before committing to this form of access control.

Attacking Biometric Systems

Although biometric systems have many advantages in the security of access control, they are also vulnerable to attacks that decrease the effectiveness of their security. Figure 7.5 shows the schematic biometric system for the ID of individuals, with the attack points in the system being indicated relative to the key components of the system. The locations of these attack points in the biometric system are susceptible to compromise through a variety of techniques and procedures that challenge the integrity of the system and validity of the identification decision.

Attack 1: A fake biometric is presented to the sensor. This fake can be in the form of an inanimate object, such as a latex finger, a photocopy of an ear, or a piece of textured card.
Attack 2: Illegally intercepted data are resubmitted by a replay of the information. The resubmission of a previously intercepted biometric signature will gain access.
Attack 3: Feature detector program is replaced by a Trojan horse program, where the feature extractor module is compromised to produce feature values selected by the attacker.
Attack 4: Legitimate features are replaced with synthetic features. Genuine feature values are replaced with the features selected by the attacker.
Attack 5: Override the matcher by replacing it with a Trojan horse program. The matcher can be overridden and modified to output an artificially high matching score.

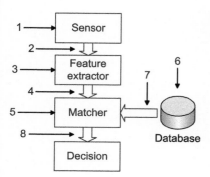

FIGURE 7.5   The schematics of a biometric system with the attack points presented.

Attack 6: Templates in the database library are modified. The attack on the template database can be achieved by adding a new template, modifying an existing template, and removing templates.

Attack 7: Intercept the channel from the templates library. An attack on the transmission medium between the template database and the matcher can replace the signature template data.

Attack 8: Override the final decision. The decision of the matcher output can be changed from reject to accept to gain access to the accesses.

A range of interactive attacks on biometric systems can be performed to disrupt or corrupt the functioning of the system. In *denial of service* an attack corrupts the authentication system by being bombarded with many bogus access requests, until the process can no longer cope with the excess input information. In *circumvention*, the attacker gains unauthorized access to data such as medical records (privacy), or a *subversive attack* where data are changed. In *repudiation*, the attacker denies accessing the system, often by claiming that his or her biometric signature was stolen. In *contamination*, an attacker can surreptitiously obtain biometric data of legitimate users by lifting a latent fingerprint, producing a Gelatine overlay and using it to access the system (Figure 7.6). In *collusion*, a legitimate user with access to the system (perhaps the system administrator) is the attacker who illegally modifies the system. In *coercion*, the attacker forces the legitimate user to access the system.

It is common for biometric systems to have live detection in an attempt to reduce vulnerabilities in certain types of biometric sensors. For example, camera (optical) sensors are more user friendly as they can provide greater feedback instructions; however, these are considered the least secure with relatively simple collusion attacks being successful (Brooks, 2010). Live detection attempts to overcome this limitation by validating the presented biometric. As a finger is presented, the sensor pads detect an inductive or capacitive charge across the pads, caused by finger moisture. Therefore, defeating this type of live detection is simply a matter of licking or wetting the inanimate object before presentation.

The degrees of vulnerability in biometric readers are related to the sensor technology, housing device, and security management system. Defeat methods include the ability to spoof types of sensor readers, enroll and use inanimate objects with collusion attacks, and

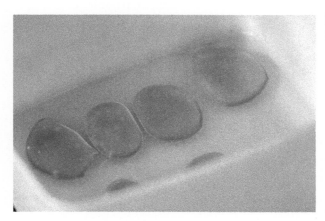

FIGURE 7.6   Replicated three-dimensinal fingerprint overlays.

bypass the biometric reader altogether (Brooks, 2010). For example, some biometric readers do not contain built-in anti-tamper switches, allowing access to the reader output relay and overriding the system decision.

Multimodal Systems

Because of the susceptibility of biometric systems to attack, to either compromise the system or gain access to the asset, it is necessary to devise alternative strategies to prevent the possible threat. An approach that has been taken is to apply multimodal biometric systems that employ multiple biometric applications to simultaneously capture different types of biometric signatures for identification. These applications are a variety of combinations of biometric signatures that can be applied for positive ID for access to assets. The designs of these combinations integrate two or more biometric systems to achieve a positive result for access. The strategies that may apply can include:

- *Multiple sensors:* Several sensors each taking the signature from the same biometric feature, such as the index finger.
- *Multiple biometrics:* Several sensors each taking a signature from different biometric features, such as the face, index finger, and voice pattern.
- *Multiple units of the same biometric:* Several biometric units each taking the same biometric feature and each making a decision of accept or reject.
- *Multiple snapshots of same biometric:* The same biometric unit takes multiple biometric signatures of the same biometric feature of an individual to compare biometric signatures.
- *Multiple representations and matching algorithms of same biometric:* Several biometric units each taking the same biometric feature and fusing the matching result before a decision is made.

The multimodal approach to improving the reliability of biometric systems requires several (two to about five) parallel systems where the same or different biometric features can be *simultaneously* applied and processed to achieve access to the protected assets. Thus, multimodal biometric designs have presented a possible mechanism to greatly improve the reliability of biometric access control through employing a parallel processing approach to the reduction in error in wrongful access and to reduce the threats according to known attack points in a biometric system (Ferrer et al., 2006). However, this approach does require correct application by the design, the administrator of the system, and the user. It may only be suitable for high-security applications since considerable time is needed to access the system (Ferrer et al., 2007).

INTELLIGENT CCTV

The digital enhancement of CCTV systems has provided a more effective and increased capability of surveillance imaging systems for security applications. The development of enhanced CCTV systems through automation and intelligence has converted these systems into powerful and responsive management tools (Garcia, 2008). Thus, the integration of computer processing and CCTV images has produced a powerful device for the detection of intruders. There is a trend for CCTV to be further integrated with other access control and surveillance technologies to develop an effective multifunctional system for the protection of assets (Garcia, 2006). Computer vision technology is transforming the principles, applications, and products in video surveillance and intelligent CCTV. This approach to intelligent vision technology is best applied to large outdoor sites and facilities such as airfields, refineries, electrical generation power plants, and seaports (Haering et al., 2008). These large facilities are ideal for such intelligent CCTV and video surveillance systems, where constant strategic surveillance is needed to maintain the integrity of the sites as national infrastructure locations.

Video content analysis (VCA) or video analytics (VA) is a recent aspect of intelligent CCTV that shows the range of analytical applications (or functionalities) that include the following functions:

- *Dynamic masking:* Used to block a part of a video signal to maintain privacy of an individual.
- *Egomotion estimation:* Used to determine the location of a camera by analyzing its output signal.
- *Motion detection:* Used to determine the motion of objects or people in a video scene.
- *Object detection:* Used to determine the presence of a type of object, which leads to object recognition. These objects or entities include people or vehicles, and may be used for fire and smoke detection.
- *Recognition:* The recognition of objects such as people or vehicles can possibly provide identification of the objects.
- *Style detection:* Applied in the settings where the video signal has been produced, and detects the style of the production process.
- *Tamper detection:* Determines whether the camera or output signal has been tampered with.
- *Video tracking:* Determines the location of persons or objects in the video signal, through analysis of an external reference grid.

This diverse range of applications of VCA can generally be found through the availability of commercial products, with a range of successes; functionalities of motion detection and people counting are popular systems. A number of these video analytics applications are functional in the security domain, together with comparable audio analytics.

Video motion detection (VMD) is a form of intelligent CCTV where a camera system is used as a means of intruder detection. As analysis of computer vision advances with processing power, so does the ability of these systems to digitally assess the presence of intruders within the field of view of an imaging system. The earliest intruder image processing algorithms engaged a frame differencing technique where the previous frame is compared to the current frame to seek a difference. That is, if a difference in the two imaging frames is present, then the object under observation has moved. This technique still forms the foundation for some of the current sophisticated surveillance systems. Stored sample frames from the imaging device are compared to subsequent frames to identify changes in image detail. Some problems that occur with this approach to VMD are:

- No concept of image understanding since all pixels in the image have equivalent importance.
- The intelligence of the domain knowledge is not exploited since there is no ability to take advantage of the image information in the comparison frames.

- No knowledge of the target and its movement since only a difference in image structure is detected.
- Camera movement and weather effects can deteriorate the effect since these anomalies can be interpreted as motion in the scene's field of view.

VMD systems have the capability of presenting several detection zones simultaneously on a screen, with a change in condition on any of the zones activating an alarm and commencing recording. Due to changes in lighting conditions VMD is more suited to interior applications, as the movement of shadows and wind-blown objects tend to cause unwanted alarms. However, exterior applications of VMD have been developed to minimize negative features by filtering out unwanted alarm conditions.

Similarly, multiple video camera systems can be applied to the surveillance of large regions by human observers and more recently by intelligent functions in the imaging analysis capacity of the VMD system. As there is a limit to the capability of a human observer to perceive and maintain contact with multiple objects of interest in the field of view, there are automated systems that detect, locate, and track multiple targets as they move in the field of view. Multiple cameras can be applied in a couple of ways to the surveillance of the region:

- Spatially adjacent cameras extend the coverage of the surveillance.
- Overlapping fields of view of multiple cameras provide redundancy of images, so as to minimize the ambiguities of occlusion, and maximize the accuracy of position determination.

The simultaneous appearance of images of targets to be tracked in two or more cameras can be used to minimize the effects of occlusion, as it is unlikely to occur in both views at the same time. The images on different cameras of the same target are achieved through a mapping function that relates the location of a pixel in one view with the same pixel in the view from other cameras. This pixel mapping function is called *homography*, and can be determined by locating a minimum of four equivalent points in two views (Ellis, 2002). However, the points must lie in the same plane, but this condition is often satisfied for surveillance systems in constructed environments, where tracked targets will share a common ground plane.

The trend of CCTV toward a management information system (MIS) is rapidly progressing, where CCTV is a multipurpose tool in the management of the security of an organization (Brooks and Smith, 2002). Some applications of intelligent CCTV include:

- Real-time surveillance of objects and persons in the field of view.
- Multiple tracking features, including the detection of movement against the normal flow of movement.
- Dormant systems that activate on detection of the presence of a threat.
- Wireless links for detection systems allows remote area monitoring with intelligent CCTV.

The function of intelligence in CCTV is to detect, identify, classify, and track targets and objects in a surveillance field. Interestingly, intelligent CCTV can track the movement of people traveling the wrong way in crowded environments, such as airport security exits where the entry of a person through an exit will breach the security of the facility. Intelligent imaging of a scene allows the doorway to be designated as a tripwire that is only activated in one direction. In this case, the tripwire activates into the room, while it does not activate when a person walks out of the room. This form of intelligence in CCTV is most effective in interior scenes, and has been applied in exterior environments with mixed success.

Intelligent CCTV can detect the removal of objects by comparing images both before and after an event. Usually these systems can be programmed to compare before and after at selected time intervals and the after image can indicate the location of the object that has been removed. In general, there is a trade-off in the choice of approaches for detection, tracking, and identification. Usually if a technique is employed for ease of detection, then it suffers in tracking, and is unable to identify the object or individual.

CONCLUSION

The management of security technology to detect, recognize, and identify persons for authorization is an important function in asset protection. Different areas of surveillance technology, such as intrusion detection, CCTV, biometrics, and surveillance tracking systems, use a range of terms for the functions of identification. This chapter has standardized terminology to that of *detection, recognition,* and *identification,* as the stages of locating unauthorized persons in secure areas. The major systems of surveillance technology are access control including codes and cards, and biometrics presents certain challenges for security managers when applied to major facilities and national infrastructure. The management of CCTV surveillance systems is an important component in a security management plan, and the introduction of intelligent CCTV allows surveillance enhancements to be applied in maintaining a rigorous security regime.

The management of technology that has the capacity to identify individuals in a security context is an important utility in a security plan. The access control systems applying codes and cards have evolved to moderate security levels, but smart cards and biometric identification have the potential to provide high-level security for substantial assets. The integration of surveillance technologies with each other, and with building management systems, provides the direction for current systems design for national assets and information repositories. Also the integration of access control technology with intelligent CCTV has the potential to initial development of the next generation of security surveillance technology for asset protection. The challenge for security managers will be to include these technologies into a seamless system that protects the people, the information, and the properties of organizations and communities in the national interest.

Further Reading

Gill, M. (Ed.), 2006. The Handbook of Security. Palgrave Macmillan, Houndmills, Hampshire.

References

Berggren, L., 1985. Iridology: A critical review. Acta Ophthalmol. (Copenh) 63 (1), 1–8.
Beymer, D., Konolige, K., 1999. Real-time tracking of multiple people using stereo cameras. In: IEEE Frame Rate Workshop. Artificial Intelligence Center, SRI International, Menlo Park, CA.
Biederman, I., 1990. Higher-level vision. In: Osherson, D.N., Kosslyn, S., Hollerbach, J. (Eds.), An Invitation to Cognitive Science: Visual Cognition and Action. MIT Press, Cambridge, MA.

Brooks, D.J., 2010. Assessing vulnerabilities of biometric readers using an applied defeat evaluation methodology. Paper presented at the *Proceedings of the 3rd Australian Security and Intelligence Conference*, Perth, WA.

Brooks, D.J., Smith, C.L., 2002. Public street surveillance: A psychometric study on the perceived social risk. In: Hutchinson, W. (Ed.), Proceedings of the 3rd Australian Information Warfare and Security Conference 2002. Perth, Western Australia, pp. 29–42.

Cross, J.M., Smith, C.L., 1995. Thermographic imaging of the subcutaneous vascular network of the back of the hand for biometric identification. In: Proceedings of the IEEE International Carnahan Conference on Security Technology. London, United Kingdom, pp. 20–35.

Daugman, J., 2004. How iris recognition works. IEEE Transactions on Circuits and Systems for Video Technology 14 (1), 21–30.

Ellis, T., 2002. Multi-camera video surveillance. In: Proceedings of the IEEE 38th Annual 2002 International Carnahan Conference on Security Technology. Atlantic City, NJ, pp. 228–233.

Eysenck, M.W., Keane, M.T., 2002. Cognitive Psychology, fourth ed. Psychology Press, Hove, UK and New York.

Ferrer, M.A., Travieso, C.M., Alonso, J.B., 2006. Multimodal biometric system based on hand geometry and palm print texture. In: Proceedings of the IEEE 40th Annual 2006 International Carnahan Conference on Security Technology. Lexington, KY, pp. 92–97.

Ferrer, M.A., Morales, A., Travieso, C.M., Alonso, J.B., 2007. Low cost multimodal identification system based on hand geometry, palm and finger print texture. In: Proceedings of the IEEE 41st Annual 2007 International Carnahan Conference on Security Technology. Ottawa, Ontario, Canada, pp. 52–58.

Garcia, M.L., 2006. Vulnerability Assessment of Physical Protection Systems. Butterworth-Heinemann, Boston.

Garcia, M.L., 2008. The Design and Evaluation of Physical Protection Systems, second ed. Butterworth-Heinemann, Boston.

Haering, N., Venetianer, P.L., Lipton, A., 2008. The evolution of video surveillance: an overview. Machine Vision and Applications 19 (5, 6), 279–290.

Marr, D., 1982. Vision: A Computational Investigation into the Human Representation and Processing of Visual Information. W. H. Freeman, San Francisco.

Musa, Z., Watada, J., 2008. Video tracking system: A survey. ICIC Express Letters 2 (1), 65–72.

Norman, T.L., 2012. Electronic Access Control. Butterworth-Heinemann, Boston.

Qui, Z., Yao, D., Zhang, Y., Ma, D., Liu, X., 2003. The study of the detection of pedestrian and bicycle using imaging processing. Intelligent Transportation Systems 1, 340–345.

Schroeder, J., 2002. Automatic target detection and recognition using synthetic aperture radar imagery. www.ips.gov.au/IPSHosted/NCRS/wars/wars2002/.../schroeder (accessed 2012).

Sherman, R.L., 1992. Biometric futures. Computers and Security 11, 128–133.

Siddiqui, M., Medioni, G., 2006. Real-time limb tracking with adaptive model selection. Proceedings of the International Conference on Pattern Recognition 4, 770–773.

Simon, A., Worthen, D.M., Mitas, J.A., 1979. An evaluation of iridology. J. Amer. Med. Assoc. 242, 1385–1387.

Smith, C.L., 2003. The science of biometric identification. Australian Science Teachers Journal 49 (3), 34–39.

Smith, C.L., 2006. Trends in the development of security technology. In: Gill, M. (Ed.), The Handbook of Security. Palgrave Macmillan, Houndmills, Hampshire.

Vuori, T.A., Smith, C.L., 1997. Three-dimensional imaging systems with structured lighting and practical constraints. Journal of Electronic Engineering 6 (1), 140–144.

Yilmaz, A., Javed, O., Shah, M., 2006. Object tracking: A survey. ACM Comput. Surv. 38 (13), 1–45.

8

Knowledge Management

OBJECTIVES

- Understand the development of knowledge from information and how knowledge contributes to better security.

- Be aware that knowledge management comprises strategies and practices applied in an organization to consolidate the corporate understanding of information of the entity.

- Know that there are a range of knowledge management strategies to produce effective knowledge for the entity.

- Understand the need for intelligence in the development of the security management plan for the protection of a facility.

- Know the functions of the components of the intelligence cycle, and how these components contribute to the intelligence product.

- Be aware of the issues associated with the development of intelligence product through the intelligence cycle.

- Know that security intelligence is a process that gathers and analyzes information on criminal and adversarial behavior to reduce the effects on an organization.

- Be aware that espionage is the acquisition of information and intellectual property through secretive and illegal methods.

- Understand that the vetting process endeavors to validate a person's identity and ensure his or her integrity.

- Be aware that predictive profiling is applied to threat mitigation from adversaries according to their modes of operation.

INTRODUCTION

The *security management plan* is a major constituent of security strategies for organizations and entities. Security managers are responsible for the initiation and development of a security plan, and need to draw appropriate information from many sources to satisfy the security requirements to protect their organization's assets. A security plan will assess the security risks and security threats to an organization so that suitable strategies are applied to potential adversaries. The acquisition of information for risk and threat assessments is achieved through knowledge management, and the attainment and processing of the information is crucial for an effective security management plan.

The organization and dispersal of knowledge can be achieved through *knowledge management*, which develops knowledge bases, expert systems, knowledge repositories, and group decision support systems. Therefore, knowledge management assists in improved performance, competitive advantage, innovation, and integration of sources of knowledge. As a result, the development of knowledge management systems will be strategic assets that aid the effective distribution of information and knowledge among authorized groups. It is considered that knowledge management systems will enhance the ability of information and knowledge managers to better distribute knowledge to appropriate analysts and experts for production of intelligence.

Intelligence is a fundamental process in the domain of security management, and is a critical element in effective decision making for the protection of assets. Intelligence can support the security risk management and security threat assessment processes. As intelligence is both a product and a process, it determines how data and information are converted into useful knowledge (Clauser, 2008).

A form of data gathering in situations or on people is *predictive profiling* to identify suspicious behavior in specified environments. Predictive profiling attempts to identify suspicious indicators according to characteristics of particular adversarial methods of operation. That is, by observing the behavior of people in a security-sensitive location, an estimate of the threat level can be produced. Thus, predictive profiling can be applied to determine whether a person, object, or situation represents a major threat to an organization.

The management and processing of information are important processes in the protection of assets of an organization. By producing intelligence from data and information, and managing that knowledge, security outcomes will be enhanced. That is, the security of an organization is dependent on the quality of the knowledge derived from the relevant intelligence.

Knowledge and intelligence are distinct concepts, but both support organizational security. For example, knowledge may be considered an underlying concept that can encompass paper information (the traditional view), electronic information (the contemporary view), and individual and corporate information (explicit and tacit). Whereas, intelligence is a process to better use information to gain value and improve knowledge.

KNOWLEDGE

The gathering of information usually means the gathering of data, and data are values of qualitative or quantitative variables usually obtained by measurement. But data in its raw state has limited value, and requires processing to a form that has usefulness or application. However, data can be presented in tables and visualized in graphs. Data as a concept can be considered as the lowest level of abstraction from which information and then knowledge can be derived.

For data to become information, it must be interpreted to have meaning, which may be derived from a range of contexts. That is, information may take meaning from technical, formal, or daily-living contexts. Because people gather data, it is people who impose patterns upon it. As a consequence, these patterns are viewed as information that can then be collated as knowledge. The interpretation of data into information will depend on the understanding of the data by an individual, and the insight of the individual's perceptions of the associations of the data to form information. Therefore, while information necessitates an understanding of the relations among data, it does not provide the underlying meaning or *theory* for the relationship. As a result, information is derived from data and has the capacity to provide some output from its application, but does not generate understanding or knowledge until it can be associated with other information from diverse contexts.

The constructs of patterns from associations of information have the potential to represent knowledge. By understanding the patterns of information within a domain of data, knowledge is realized and understood through these patterns and their implications. A characteristic of patterns representing knowledge tends to be self-contextual—that is, the pattern generates its own context rather than the context of the contributing information. Also, knowledge that is derived from patterns of information provides a high level of reliability or predictability of the application of the knowledge. This argument was also discussed in Chapter 1 where the scientific method was presented as a means of understanding data gathered within a controlled context. Thus, information patterns that represent knowledge have a self-contained consistency, which is not a characteristic of information.

The concept of wisdom is derived from the understanding of the foundation principles responsible for the patterns in the domain representing knowledge. Thus, wisdom can be thought of as a *truth* idea that will remain through time. These foundation principles are universal and are completely context-independent. That is, the wisdom of the domain does not rely on location, time of day, or environmental conditions; the wisdom of the domain is true under all conditions.

The sequence of acquiring understanding from data, to information, to knowledge, and finally to wisdom can be described as an emergent continuum, where the progression does not occur in discrete stages of development. The progress of development of the continuum depends on the rate of understanding of an individual within the domain. Thus, the progress of the development is influenced by the amount of partial understanding of the relations that represent information, the patterns that represent knowledge, and the principles that are the foundation of wisdom.

Learning occurs by connecting new information to patterns that we already understand. There is an idea that the complexity level for understanding within a domain exists between the extreme concept levels of *complication* and *mundane*. These concepts can be explained by information and knowledge that is highly differentiated and integrated and is more complex. High levels of differentiation without integration support the complicated, while information and knowledge that is highly integrated without differentiation yields mundane. Therefore, we tend to avoid the complicated and are not interested in the mundane, so the level of complexity that exits between these two alternatives is the option that is most appealing to us.

Knowledge Management

Knowledge management comprises strategies and practices applied in an organization to consolidate the corporate understanding of the information of the entity. These strategies and practices are applied to identify, represent, distribute, and adapt the knowledge of the organization through insights and experiences for the common good of the entity. The corporate knowledge of the organization resides either with individuals or groups of like individuals as processes or practices.

The objectives of an organization through the management of knowledge can be achieved through improved performance, competitive advantage, innovation, sharing of experiences within the organization, and integration within the organization. Thus, knowledge management can be considered as a strategic asset of the entity through the availability of corporate knowledge to all at the appropriate authority level.

The dimensions of knowledge management are considered to be strategy, process, and measurement, where these dimensions provide an integrated model upon which individuals in an organization can both contribute and avail knowledge for the benefit of the organization. Therefore, some important outcomes have been identified from the integration of the dimensions of the knowledge management model:

- Cultural norms that influence people are critical activators for successful knowledge creation.
- People of an organization are the primary resource for the dissemination and application of knowledge.
- Cognitive, social, and organizational processes are necessary for a knowledge management strategy.
- Measurement, benchmarking, and incentives are essential for the knowledge management process.
- Measurement, benchmarking, and incentives have the capacity to drive cultural change with regard to knowledge in an organization.

Therefore, programs that develop knowledge management strategies in an organization have the capability to benefit both individuals and organizations if the programs are purposeful, concrete, and action-oriented.

A range of approaches to knowledge management have developed through both theory and practice of the domain:

- *Technocentric* knowledge management approach has an emphasis on technology, which enhances knowledge dissemination and creation.
- *Organizational* knowledge management approach is concerned with the design of an organization to best facilitate the knowledge processes.
- *Ecological* knowledge management approach is concerned with the interaction of people, identity, knowledge, and environmental aspects as a complex adaptive system.

Therefore, modern knowledge management can be considered according to a selection of models and paradigms, such as community of practice, social network analysis, intellectual capital, information theory, complexity science, and constructivism. But it should be emphasized that whichever approach is applied, the outcomes need to be practical for an organization to benefit from the implementation.

Knowledge can be categorized according to a dimension that distinguishes between tacit knowledge and explicit knowledge. Internalized knowledge can be represented by tacit knowledge and is knowledge that an individual may not be consciously aware of, such as riding a bicycle. However, the knowledge that a person consciously holds in mental focus is known as explicit knowledge. This form of knowledge can be readily communicated to others as it represents active cognition for the individual.

Hayes and Walsham (2003) applied perspectives of content and relational facets to knowledge and knowledge management. Thus, the content perspective claims that knowledge can be easily stored as it can be codified. But the relational perspective of knowledge makes it difficult to disseminate away from the location where the knowledge is developed. Therefore, internalized tacit knowledge is converted into explicit knowledge to share or disseminate it.

A model was proposed by Nonaka and Takeuchi (1995) where knowledge follows a cycle where implicit knowledge is converted into explicit knowledge. Then within the knowledge cycle, explicit knowledge is reinternalized into implicit knowledge. So with the internalization and externalization of knowledge, Nonaka and Takeuchi (1995) were able to show that the functions of knowledge management of dialog, team building, learning, and linking explicit knowledge can be achieved.

Another framework for the consideration of knowledge distinguishes between *new knowledge* and *established knowledge* within a group, organization, or community. Thus, collaborative environments such as social computing tools can be used for both knowledge creation and knowledge transfer.

Strategies

Organizations have employed a range of *knowledge management strategies* to produce effective knowledge for their entity. As knowledge can be accessed at three stages in the knowledge management process—before, during, and after—a selection of strategies is available to generate the new knowledge for an organization. Strategies have extended from requiring content submission to be mandatory, to incorporating incentives into performance measurement plans. Thus, push and pull strategies can be applied to knowledge management within an organization. Whether rewards as an incentive are successful in knowledge management is still an open question as an appropriate strategy.

An example of a *push* strategy involves actively managing knowledge by individuals explicitly depositing their knowledge into a shared knowledge repository such as a database. This knowledge repository is available to all individuals in the group to retrieve on a needs basis.

Another approach is the *pull* strategy where individuals request knowledge from an expert pool associated with a particular domain. This ad hoc approach allows experts to provide specialized knowledge to individuals or small functional groups as the knowledge is needed and can be an efficient application of resources.

However, many other approaches to the acquisition of knowledge in knowledge management strategies can include:

- Incentives as a reward for sharing knowledge.
- Cross-project learning as a means of sharing knowledge.
- Project reviews across functional groups to inform individuals of the new knowledge that has been generated.
- Mapping of knowledge within a corporate subdomain, and the mapping of knowledge repositories within an organization for access by all groups.

- Access to expertise and communities of good practice within an organization.
- Expert directories for knowledge seekers to approach knowledge resources.
- Systems to allow the transfer of best practice within an organization.
- The systematic evaluation and planning of competences of individuals within an organization.
- The distribution and physical locations of individuals within a knowledge domain can either reinforce or inhibit knowledge sharing.
- The establishment of knowledge repositories through records, databases, and catalogs.
- The measurement and reporting of intellectual capital provides explicit knowledge for a particular organization.

For example, a security director may have many security managers working across a broad region within a large organization. Each security manager captures local threat information, but how is this threat information maintained as an effective commercial network for the organizational threat assessment? Such collection of information could be a simple database, but such a system has to be assessable to other authorized staff within the organization and integrated into the security risk management process.

The selection of approaches for the application of knowledge management in an organization indicates the extent of the need for effective management to ensure that these strategies can be realized. The intellectual capital that resides within an organization is actualized by the knowledge management strategies that are applied according to the organization's requirements.

Motivation to Apply Knowledge Management

Why would an organization consider adapting a knowledge management approach to the sharing and transfer of knowledge between its domain groups? What structural and efficiency advantages are derived from such an approach? Some considerations that are needed within the organization's management approaches would be:

- The availability of increased knowledge content for the development of future products and enhanced services.
- Achieving shorter new product development cycles.
- The facilitation and management of innovation.
- Achieving advantage from expertise within the organization.
- Improving the networking capability through connectivity both within and outside of the organization.
- Encouraging innovative thinking by individuals in the organization.
- Intellectual capital and assets in the organization are able to be utilized to the advantage of the entity and the individual.

The success of these approaches is yet to be fully tested, and the capacity of knowledge management to enhance outcomes will be determined through research.

The physical management of knowledge systems is presently being achieved through search and retrieval semantic technologies that allow ease of interrogation for knowledge disclosure. Generic technologies for the management of knowledge systems include groupware, document management systems, expert systems, semantic networks, relational and object-oriented databases, simulation systems, and artificial intelligence (Gupta and Sharma, 2004). Recent applications of social computing tools such as bookmarks and blogs provide a more unstructured approach to transfer, capture, and creation of knowledge. As these approaches are text-based they represent explicit knowledge transfer, and therefore require condensation to obtain meaningful applicable knowledge.

In a security management application, an applied knowledge management system should be formulated to integrate the many elements of security information. The system may include:

- *Document control system* to formalize the development, publication, and change management of documents such as policies, procedures, and guidelines.
- *Incident reporting system* that allows all staff to report incidents. Such a system could integrate with the health, safety, and environmental systems as an online system.
- *Threat register* to record the many reported and identified threats, with dates of reviews, assessment levels, information of sources, and their reliability and validity.
- *Criticality register* to record the identified critical functions and assets, with dates of reviews, assessment levels, information of sources, and their reliability and validity.
- *Risk management register* to record the many identified risks, with dates of reviews, assessed consequence and likelihood levels, information of sources, and their reliability and validity.

Knowledge Management Systems

The role of the knowledge manager has evolved from the maintenance of knowledge repositories to that of influencing the culture of their organization for improved sharing of knowledge, collaboration, and innovation. As a result of the advancement of the knowledge manager's capacity, the functions of knowledge management within an organization interact with departments such as quality control, sales, human relations, and operations.

The knowledge management system supports the creation, capture, storage, and dissemination of information within an entity. The justification of the development of the knowledge management system is for employees to have ready access to an organization's knowledge base of facts, sources of information, and solutions. For example, having a common repository to a database on lessons learned will allow others to learn from past experiences. Sharing the information can lead to more effective outcomes, and produce new or improved knowledge.

Figure 8.1 shows the structure of a generic knowledge management system with the processes needed for knowledge generation shown as inputs, and functions of the process shown as outputs.

The input function is achieved through knowledge capture and knowledge access via a knowledge database, which has the capability of generating new knowledge for application. The output function of the framework allows knowledge to be shared among groups, and acquired by groups or individuals. The output also facilitates the transfer and networking of knowledge within and among groups, and within and among internal and external entities.

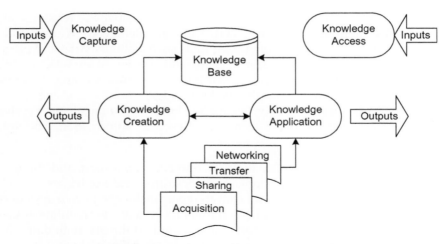

FIGURE 8.1   Knowledge management framework.

The achievement of the generic knowledge management system may be acquired through the development of existing systems that have been adapted for the knowledge management functions. Thus, by adapting an existing system for knowledge management, all the hard-won reliability and validity functions and performances are maintained and sustained. These systems that have been adapted may be:

- *Document based:* Technologies that permit the creation, management, and sharing of formatted documents such as distributed databases.
- *Ontology or taxonomy based:* Technologies that process and manage documents that have the capability to summarize the document, and present usable information in the form of terminologies.
- *AI technologies:* Artificial intelligence technologies that apply a customized representation scheme to represent the problem domain. That is, AI systems are capable of learning processes in knowledge management through appropriate training, and therefore have the capacity to improve the efficiency of an operation.
- *Network maps:* The development and application of network maps are able to display the flow of communication amongn groups and individuals. Thus, the mapping of data, information, and knowledge flow within an organization is essential for effective communications within and among management levels.
- *Social computing tools:* Applications of social computing tools, such as Facebook, instant messaging, chat rooms, and video conferencing, to the development and evolution of knowledge management systems are becoming effective within an entity. These systems support the gathering, representation, processing, application, and dissemination of information that can be distributed across social communities, such as teams, function groups, organizations, and markets.

Thus, knowledge management systems have the functions of knowledge capture, access, creation, and application.

The distinguishing features of a knowledge management system include:

- *Purpose:* A knowledge management system will have an explicit knowledge management objective such as collaboration, sharing good practices, a strategic advantage, or a competitive advantage.
- *Context:* A knowledge management system should process knowledge from information that is meaningfully organized, accumulated, and presented in a context of creation and application.
- *Processes:* Knowledge management systems have been developed to support and enhance knowledge demanding processes in projects. These processes can include creation, construction, identification, capture, acquisition, linkage, structure, visualization, transfer, maintenance, and retrieval. Also, when the process is associated with the knowledge life cycle where knowledge becomes of no use and needs to be removed from the system.
- *Participants:* Individuals can be actively involved in the knowledge networks supported by knowledge management systems. However, this involvement is not a necessary requirement as knowledge management systems are designed for knowledge to be developed collectively. Thus, the distribution of knowledge leads to continuous change, reconstruction, and application in different contexts, by different participants with differing backgrounds and experiences.
- *Instruments:* Knowledge management systems support instruments that allow the processes of knowledge management to proceed. That is, instruments applied in knowledge management processes of capture, creation, sharing, expertise locators, corporate knowledge directories, and skills management systems are collectively components of knowledge management systems.

Thus, knowledge management systems can be applied in a wide range of cooperative, collaborative, and hierarchical communities; virtual organizations and networks; and entities where participants and individuals are active in extracting and generating new knowledge for the benefit of an organizations.

Knowledge management enhances the value of a corporation by identifying their assets and expertise. As a consequence, the identification of assets and expertise allows for the efficient management of the organization's resources. The role of security management in this context is critical in the protection of the intellectual assets. Thus, to achieve secure knowledge management, the security management team must have secure strategies, processes, and metrics. That is, the security strategies and security processes need to be both reliable and valid, and the metrics must include support for security-related information (Birtino et al., 2006).

Knowledge Management Issues

The management of knowledge in an organization is crucial for the effectiveness and well-being of the organization. Corporate memory in an organization is important for the functioning of the entity, and could include knowledge relating to their products, processes, management, and technologies. The principle of a common corporate memory ensures that knowledge generated in one department is available in other departments for the advancement of the organization. The function of knowledge management includes knowledge capture, storage, and dissemination, and involves new applications for the knowledge according to existing information infrastructure in the organization. These applications could include:

- Knowledge repositories where databases allow the storage and retrieval of explicit research, technical, and management knowledge in text format for general understanding and comprehension—for example, a security management incident reporting system.
- Best-practice systems where knowledge repositories used for the exposition, storage, and retrieval of business best practices are accessible on a need-to-know basis. These systems make available the lessons learned in projects to be available to others. For example, document control where specifications, scope of works, procedures, and the like are controlled for management issues, with hierarchical copies of past versions.
- Expert networks within an organization can be established by individuals with specific expertise in a professional area for electronic accessibility by others in the organization. The function of an expert network is to provide appropriate responses to enquiries relating to the domain of the expertise for professional colleagues within the entity—for example, the threat assessment from expert groups, including their assessments, source data, and likely outcomes.
- Communities of practice are organizational networks for groups within the organization, the members of which share common professional interests and wish to communicate on issues relevant to the common goals of the organization. These self-organizing groups may work in dispersed geographical locations, and can take advantage of knowledge management applications. These systems are appropriate for industrial associations such as ASIS International, but are also suitable for local organized special-interest groups.

The applications of knowledge management principles to the *specific issues* of an organization will determine the effectiveness of the process within the entity, and therefore the appropriateness of the knowledge management style.

The management of these issues is an important process conducted by practitioners, researchers, and business managers. Issue management is the process of identifying, organizing, and monitoring a collection of issues so that their evolution and resolution are acknowledged and integrated into an organization's management structure. The process of issue management involves grouping issues into closely related sets, and then assigning appropriate individuals or groups within the organization the tasks of resolving the issues for the benefit of the management team. Common and important issues of knowledge management that should be considered include:

1. How to use knowledge management to provide strategic and tactical advantage.
2. How to maintain the currency of organizational knowledge.
3. How to motivate individuals to contribute their knowledge to a knowledge management system.
4. How to identify the organizational knowledge that should be captured in a knowledge management system.
5. How to assess the financial costs and explicit and implicit benefits of knowledge management.

6. How to verify the efficacy, legitimacy, and relevance of knowledge contributed to a knowledge management system.
7. How best to design and develop a knowledge management system.
8. How to sustain the progress of a knowledge management system in an organization.
9. How to ensure knowledge security.

These knowledge management issues are indicative of many issues raised by several thousand knowledge management respondents in a study by King et al. (2002). The study sought to identify the major groupings of sets of knowledge management issues raised by the respondents to develop appropriate processes for management of their organization. A factor analysis based on the similarity of the knowledge management issues produced four main categories to be resolved for effective management: executive/strategic management; operational management; costs, benefits, and risks; and standards. The groupings provided suitable domains of knowledge management issues to effectively improve the management process.

The *executive/strategic management* set of knowledge management issues addressed elements that were important to individuals through a strategic view and included potential benefits and potential pitfalls. These issues indicated an interest in knowledge management's potential for enabling their organization to compete at a new level of sophistication, influencing creativity and innovation within the communications network of the organization.

Operational management issues address the processes of how to identify the knowledge available in an organization. These issues also include the processes by which to capture knowledge in a knowledge management strategy, and how individuals will relate to the capture of knowledge. Also, the issue of the ability to design a knowledge management system with its tools and applications to successfully address the needs of an organization should be considered.

Costs, benefits, and risks issues address how much funds, time, and human resources an organization should be able to invest in developing a knowledge management system, and how much it can expect in return in financial and nonfinancial benefits.

Standards issues in an organization are concerned with the knowledge management technology and communications network both in terms of definition and technical validity, such as the integration of technology from several vendors and proprietary applications with nonproprietary systems.

These groupings of issues associated with the construction, development, and management of knowledge management systems indicate that they may be successfully accomplished by individuals or small groups responsible for the maintenance and advancement of the components of a system. Each individual or group could be responsible for the implementation or incorporation of experience relevant to each issue in an organization's management beliefs and values. Also, the system will benefit from focused research on aspects and components of the design of the knowledge management system.

INTELLIGENCE

Intelligence in its traditional form is the product of collection, evaluation, analysis, and synthesis of information. Thus, intelligence is produced to assist policy makers and planners to make effective decisions. Commercial corporate intelligence is applied at the company or organizational level for the planning of the protection of assets through security. Therefore, the purpose of intelligence is to enhance the security of an organization, and so the efficiency and perhaps the prosperity are increased according to the goals and objectives of the entity. When intelligence is stated in terms of security its intention is to provide a relative security advantage by better protecting the assets of the organization. That is, intelligence provides the knowledge about adversaries and their attack methods that will allow planning to neutralize the effect of their imposition on the organization. Ideally, intelligence will enhance the abilities of the security managers to better design policy and develop security planning for the organization. However, the output from intelligence needs to be considered as probabilistic with limits on the ultimate effectiveness of the output. As Foster (1994, p. 1) states:

> Elite decision makers in organisations and groups must often make difficult decisions in conditions of extreme environmental and cognitive uncertainty. In order to assess the risks derived from seemingly random events or from people or organisations that may have the intent and capability to cause adverse consequences, intelligence collection and analysis systems are often utilised.

The role of intelligence in security management has become a most important function in the protection of assets of an organization. Present thinking is that as crime becomes more sophisticated, the professionalization of security requires the need for serious analysis of crime relevant to the organization being protected. Such analysis provides the foundation for a thorough assessment of the threat and permits the security manager to develop a security strategy to counter the risks exposed by the intelligence. Therefore, the development of an intelligence assessment culture in an organization will benefit from the quality of the security management plan through appropriate countermeasures to the expected crimes anticipated from the intelligence process. It is recognized that intelligence plays a major role in compliance within government and national security. However, intelligence also has a significant function in law enforcement and corporate security.

Intelligence Cycle

Traditionally, intelligence has been produced by a series of stages in a process termed the *intelligence cycle*, where data and information are subjected to analysis to produce knowledge that is useful in the protection of an organization and its assets. The threats to these assets may be external to the organization, or internal within the management of the entity. Therefore, the application of the intelligence cycle as a component in the planning phase of the security of the organization is crucial in the effective development of the security management plan.

The intelligence cycle is a model that describes the process by which data and information can be meaningfully converted or developed into intelligence that will benefit the organization or the nation. In terms of security, the intelligence cycle is the process by which information about threats to an organization is gathered and assessed to determine the likelihood that it will eventuate (Gill and Phythian, 2006). The intelligence cycle is an iterative process by which information is gathered, analyzed, and activated to remove or reduce the threat level according to the following phases of the process:

- Direction and planning of the activity.
- Collection or gathering of data and information.

- Processing of data and information.
- Analysis to produce meaningful intelligence.
- Dissemination of the intelligence to the clients.
- Feedback to intelligence producers on quality of the intelligence.

These components of the intelligence cycle (Figure 8.2) provide information for the security management plan, and the feedback component of the cycle permits the cyclic model to recommence the process again. However, the cyclic nature of the process ensures that it is as effective as its weakest link in the methodology, or the degree to which each node in the cycle is accomplished to completion. Thus, the intelligence cycle is repeated until the intelligence requirements have been satisfied. Nevertheless, in reality the cycle is not wholly sequential; rather, all components are carried out simultaneously.

Direction or *requirements* of the intelligence process will be determined by a decision maker in an organization. Identifying the requirements for the organization will mean identifying the policy and security issues in which intelligence will contribute to the improved performance of the entity. The requirements will usually result from a priority approach to the many issues of the organization. As a result, as intelligence capabilities are usually limited, priorities need to be set. The question of who sets these priorities for the production of intelligence will probably be determined by senior management and the security manager, as the production of intelligence may be an expensive process.

Collection of the data and information necessary for the security management plan can be retrieved from a wide variety of sources. In response to the chosen requirements for the organization, intelligence personnel develop an intelligence collection plan. This plan will include the relevance of available sources and methods, as well as relevant intelligence from other agencies such as police, fire departments, government administration areas, industry groups, and crime research organizations. Some requirements will be better met by specific types of collection, while other requirements may need several types of information gathering. Again, these decisions on collection capabilities are a key issue since the decision of how much can or should be gathered to meet each requirement must be made.

Interestingly, organizations will be able to access human intelligence (HUMINT) through employee records, clients, and the like. Imagery intelligence (IMINT) can be gathered from Google Earth and other such data. Open-source or publicly available intelligence (OSINT) can include newspapers, periodicals, crime reports, specialist databases, and foreign broadcasts. Today, web-based open sources are readily available using such sites as Facebook, LinkedIn, blogs, and many other programs.

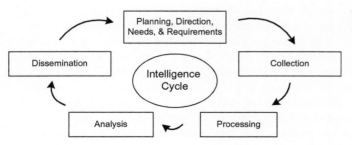

FIGURE 8.2   The intelligence cycle for application to a security plan.

Processing and *exploitation* of the information that has been gathered potentially produces intelligence. That is, the collected information in the previous stage is not intelligence. It is only after effective analysis that the product of intelligence is made available. Transformation of large volumes of data to a form appropriate for the production of intelligence that can be used effectively in an organization includes:

- Translations.
- Decryption.
- Interpretation of information stored on film and magnetic materials.
- Application of highly technical photographic and electronic processing.
- Data reduction through statistical procedures.

An evaluation of the relevance and reliability of the collected data and information needs to be conducted to determine the value of pursuing that line of exploration.

Analysis and *production* of the output from processing will include the integration, evaluation, and analysis of all available data and information. The preparation of a range of intelligence products will include timely, single-source, and issue-oriented reports for immediate action, and longer-term, all-source products that will be used for the future development of an organization. Analysis establishes the significance and implications of the processed information, and integrates it with other incongruent items of information to identify patterns. These patterns can be interpreted in terms of the significance of newly generated knowledge within the active operational domain. Analysts will draw on three major sources of knowledge: logic, specific knowledge of the content, and lessons learned from previous analyses (Grabo, 2002). The work of analysts, who are subject-matter experts, consider the reliability, validity, and relevance of the information and integrate it into a coherent whole. These experts organize the evaluated information into context and produce intelligence for the protection of the organization.

Dissemination is the process by which the finished intelligence product is passed to the consumers or clients for application. The finished intelligence products can take many forms depending on the requirements of the clients and its potential applications. The level of necessity will have a bearing on the form of the intelligence product and this is usually determined by the organization. At this phase of the intelligence cycle, producers or users can reinitiate the first phase again, so that the cycle commences again.

Feedback can be a further phase in the intelligence cycle where either the client or the decision maker from the initial stage provides feedback to the team, where revised requirements of the process are needed and a further cycle in the intelligence process is instigated.

It is interesting to note that the traditional intelligence cycle is widely accepted as it follows a conventional paradigm for problem solving. The standard approach seems to be that by following a sequential, orderly, and linear process, an appropriate outcome will be achieved. That is, by progressing from the question to the solution, an outcome is achieved that satisfies the intention of the process. By applying analysis to data that are systematically gathered, the process is analogous to classic problem solving. However, it is claimed by Clarke (2010) that intelligence practitioners do not apply logic sequential processes to the production of intelligence, but rather apply cognitive processes that see previous stages revisited to consolidate a "hunch." That is, the individual might perform some analysis on some data, and then revisit the data collection phase to reinforce an idea that has credibility. As a consequence, the linearity of the process appears not to be in logical progression, but rather on a needs basis to fulfill the requirements of the phases of the intelligence cycle.

In conducting analysis, intelligence analysts are essentially information translators, whose function is to collate and review information, and to provide reliable intelligence in an operational format for a security management plan (Joseph and Corkill, 2011).

Professional intelligence analysts are required to make complex judgments at the micro-, macro-, and meta-levels that optimize decision making for the client for particular circumstances and within a specific context (Corkill, 2008). Intelligence analysts process complex matters including moral and ethical issues, which may question values, beliefs, and assumptions. The outcomes from these analyses may impact individuals through to national security levels.

Finally, issues associated with the team approach to the production of intelligence have imposed pressures on the intelligence analysts:

- The glut of information from the data collectors imposes an overload of data for analysis—for example, today with the excessive and ease to information via the Internet. Techniques need to be developed to filter the data so that it can be effectively treated for analysis. Therefore, the quality of the filtering process will determine the ultimate quality of the final product.
- The client demand for more detail about intelligence targets is imposing greater stresses on the team.
- The overanalysis of information can distort the intelligence to such an extent that decisions are made on incorrect information.
- The dissemination of intelligence from the analysts encounters barriers in the communication stream, so that the decision maker does not receive all or some of the intelligence product. These barriers may be psychological or physical obstacles to communications within an organization.

These issues associated with the production of intelligence have the effect of hampering a security manager in making decisions on the security of his or her organization. The skilled security manager will devise strategies to eliminate or reduce the effects of these issues.

INTELLIGENCE IN SECURITY MANAGEMENT

The application of intelligence to support and plan the processes for security and security risk management has enhanced the quality of the security management plan for the protection of assets. Thus, security intelligence, or SYINT, is a process that gathers and analyzes information on threat behavior to reduce or minimize the effects on an organization. For a security manager to successfully design security strategies against threats to an organization, the nature of these threats must be known. The application of intelligence allows a security manager to develop appropriate security strategies through the development of risk and threat assessments. Intelligence may be applied for planning, business case development, risk management, and investigation management where a security manager needs value-added information to make decisions in the interest of his or her organization. Thus, the security manager must have a constant flow of value-added information on intelligence and other relevant sources, which are based on sound research and analysis as evidence to support the security management plan.

Security Intelligence

The supporting function of a SYINT capability to the security plan is to provide timely, accurate, and relevant intelligence to decision makers. That is, a security manager does not encounter major complications with information overload, underload, or message distortion. Therefore, the security manager has an increased opportunity to make decisions with reduced cognitive or environmental uncertainty. This approach to planning is a rational decision-making model, where decisions are optimized, through application of information relevant to the decision at the time.

Security intelligence provides a security manager with knowledge upon which business plans, budgets, and strategic and tactical security plans can be developed, justifying directed resources to protect the assets. The application of SYINT has the capacity to allow security decisions to be more effective as it is a capability multiplier, permitting the security function to be proactive and decreasing the required time to respond to a risk or threat. The analysis and assessment of threat constitute a primary function of intelligence. Thus, security intelligence analysis has the major purpose of the identification and assessment of a threat, with the favored model of threat being based on *intentions* and *capabilities* of a threatening entity. That is, the product of intent and capability produces the threat to be considered in the management plan. Therefore, if either intent or capability is assessed to be zero, then the threat level does not exist.

A SYINT capability will increase the knowledge of all aspects of a threat description—that is, where, why, and how the threat will manifest itself relative to the security of the organization. The SYINT capability will reduce the environmental and cognitive uncertainty in which the security manager and the organization will make decisions and assessments. It will also lower the level of uncertainty of the potential threat capability and intent. Thus, the assessments made by the security manager will be more objective and less subjective.

Internal and External Threats

An organization's major threat to its assets is from within the entity, and as such is always a concern for the management and security manager. However, initiating SYINT for an internal threat within an organization is much easier, since collecting information is accomplished from existing corporate databases. Usually, a greater reduction of an internal threat can be achieved than that for external threats.

Gathering SYINT on external threats is more difficult, and requires greater expenditure of resources. However, the allocation of resources to SYINT will allow a security manager to combat theft, industrial espionage, and sabotage. Therefore, the application of knowledge systems will allow comprehensive reporting of threats and enhance the security manager's ability to respond to external threats.

The amount of time and effort invested in the SYINT program will really determine the degree of support that SYINT provides for a security manager. Obviously, careful planning and development should be applied early in the program, with regular assessment to ensure that it is *fit for purpose*. Quality sources of information and the capability to analyze and interpret the output from the intelligence process are necessary components of a successful strategy. Thus, a key to success is the appropriate and effective training of personnel engaged in the SYINT program. Inadequate skills and knowledge of the task through a lack of training will cause a degeneration of the program.

Espionage

A working definition of *espionage* is intelligence activity directed toward the acquisition of information through clandestine means and prohibited laws of the country in which the act is committed. Thus, espionage is the acquisition of information and intellectual property through secretive and illegal methods. However, this context means that the act of espionage will differ between jurisdictions according to the appropriate laws of the state.

Open-source information gathering is legal for an organization, even though it might be conducting competitive intelligence activities against its commercial adversaries. Open-source data and information may be procured from the public domain:

- Governmental departmental reports.
- Industrial and corporate reports.
- Privately sponsored database.
- Press and Internet sources.
- Specialist newspapers.
- Satellite imagery.
- Trade shows and professional meetings.

However, the clandestine collection of information is the commencement of the industrial espionage process. The intention of espionage is to collect information without being able to be identified, and not to be able to identify the process. Many of the techniques of operation are illegal and could include wiretaps, breaking and entering, and blackmail threats. Legal strategies may include pretext interviews, false job interviews, and following people, but may lead to offenses. These methods are certainly unethical.

The threat of espionage or intelligence requires strategies for negating attacks on the information of organizations. Some protective measures that can be applied to the information of an organization are:

- Vetting of personnel and staff background checks ensure that staff employed are who they claim to be, and that they are not a threat to the organization.
- Classification systems in the organization, where important information is segregated and protected.
- Communications security.
- Physical protection of information.
- Regular briefing of engaged staff on the need and merit of protecting the information of the organization.

The process of industrial espionage is practiced by governments and corporations alike, and as a consequence the information of organizations requires protection. Because the striving for competitive advantage in both the private and government is active, the need for information vigilance is paramount.

VETTING

Vetting of personnel and staff background checks ensure that staff employed are who they claim to be, and that they are not a threat to their organization. *Personnel security* (PERSEC) is a process of ensuring that an individual is not a security risk; this process is developed according to the prevailing security policy of the organization. Vetting is a common type of PERSEC and is based on the evaluation of an individual's character, attributes, background, and actions (Defence Vetting Report, 2007).

Insider Threat

Both internal and external threats to an organization are real, and need to be strongly considered in the protection of assets of the entity. Internal threats to an organization are more difficult to counter, and so strategic planning is essential to minimize the effect of this threat (Shaw et al., 2009). Factors associated with an insider threat are:

- *Stressors:* Personal and situational stressors may lead to insider risk, such as embarrassment, betrayal, workplace conflict, family issues, and financial stress. These stressors may lead to impaired judgment, reckless behavior, and vindictive behavior, such as espionage, theft, fraud, and sabotage. A life event such as substance abuse, suicide, or divorce may trigger the action of an individual's decision to commit espionage.
- *Motivation:* Specific factors that can motivate a person to harm their organization are if a person is unhappy, the crime is easy to commit, there is an opportunity for the intervention, and there is a reward for the action. Also, increased motivation to commit a crime may result if there is an intellectual challenge, to satisfy curiosity, or to gain personal advantage. Individuals commit espionage to fulfill complex emotional needs, or a combination of emotion and financial needs (Brooks et al., 2011).
- *Personality factors:* These factors are important in terms of prevention, where general weaknesses of greed, impulsiveness, vindictiveness, paranoia, and sensation seeking are relevant to the insider threat. Those engaging in espionage often suffer from the personality disorders of *antisocial personality disorder* and *narcissistic personality*. Therefore, a person with antisocial personality disorder rejects rules, lacks feelings of guilt, is manipulative, and seeks immediate gratification. Their ability to develop loyalty is compromised, as they have little ability to develop a commitment to persons or entities. Meanwhile, a person with narcissistic personality has unjustified feelings of importance or self-esteem, a sense of entitlement, and a lack of empathy for others. These people are overachievers with a high self-image and a drive to be successful.

The insider threat in an organization needs to be considered, particularly in the protection of information assets. Therfore, the importance of vetting as a tool for the assessment of identity, integrity, and character should be considered for individuals in key positions in the organization (Muldoon, 2008).

Security Clearance

The vetting process has two primary aims: to validate a person's identity and to ensure their integrity. The crime of identity theft is prevalent, and likewise individuals also assume others' identities. Integrity confirms the honesty of a person and determines their security vulnerabilities. These integrity assessments are achieved through police checks, referee checks, and security assessment interviews. The purpose of the interview seeks to confirm the suitability of the person for a security clearance if engaging with government departments and entities. There are five levels of security clearance: restricted, confidential, secret, top secret (negative vetting), and top secret (positive vetting) (Defence Vetting Report, 2007). The positive vetting process involves an intensive enquiry into an individual's life until compliance for clearance has been established beyond reasonable doubt. Therfore, a top secret classification requires an intrusive process of evaluation of a person needing access to information of the highest national security significance (Hennessy and Brownfeld, 1982). Meanwhile, negative vetting is less intrusive and only aims to identify a person's background and lifestyle.

The *Protective Security Manual* (Attorney-General's Department, 2010) outlines the evaluation of suitability for clearance is founded on the suitability indicators of maturity, responsibility, tolerance, honesty, and loyalty.

- Maturity is appraised by analyzing an individual's capacity for honest self-appraisal, personal life choices, hobbies, capacity to cope with stress, and their engagement with drugs and alcohol.
- Responsibility is evaluated by assessing a person's history of financial responsibility and general personal history such as that regarding work, educational background, and security records.
- Tolerance is assessed by examining a person's appreciation of a broad perspective, such as an ability to accept other people's life choices and to respect other cultures.
- Honesty is determined by examining whether a person has a history of unlawful behavior.
- Loyalty is evaluated by considering a person's commitment to the democratic process with their loyalty to their nation.

People may be subject to challenging circumstances that can cause negative psychological, social, and physical consequences. As a result, people who are unable to cope with these challenging circumstances may indulge in a range of negative behaviors, for example, substance abuse and violence. These risk factors have a destructive influence on the indicators for a security clearance, and as such will cause difficulties within an organization. The requirement for an internal security clearance within an organization will depend on the corporate policies of the entity.

PREDICTIVE PROFILING

Predictive profiling is an observational technique applied to the operational profiles of criminals or terrorists for the identification of *suspicious indicators* (Figure 8.3) in a protected environment. This type of profiling can be applied to threat mitigation from the adversaries according to their modes of operation. That is, by understanding the methodologies of aggressors in a security context through accumulation of intelligence, their behaviors and actions can indicate threats to an asset. Thus, when predictive profiling is applied to a situation, a person, or an object, its purpose is to identify suspicious indicators that associate with an adversary's known method of operation. Predictive profiling has the potential to be effective in most security environments and the ability to enhance the protective security according to most security prerequisites.

A suspicious indicator is a signal that has the potential to predict a method of operation, or a deviation from normal behavior, from the observed behavior of the situation, person, or object. Therefore, the observed deviations in behavior can be interpreted as a threat to be assessed, and have the potential to cause harm to the assets (people and information) in a secure environment.

Behavioral psychology generally determines the factors in the domain of suspicious indicators, and although these factors are not well defined, they are derived from the attributes of attire, accent, life story, documents, mannerisms, and appearance, among many possible specific indicators. Because the context of the security environment can vary greatly, there is no predetermined suspicious indicators listing; rather, the trained observational skills of the assessor must determine appropriate suspicious indicators for the security environment undergoing surveillance. Thus, proactive security engaging predictive profiling has the following stages of engagement:

- *Detect suspicion:* Surveillance techniques by technology or humans provide information for assessment on deviant behavior.
- *Determine method of operation:* Analysis of the behavior can indicate the criminal or terrorist methodology in the security context.
- *Deploy against threat:* Identification of the adversary through predictive profiling allows activation of the security management plan according to the known capabilities of a threat.

FIGURE 8.3   Suspicious indicators in a predictive profiling methodology.

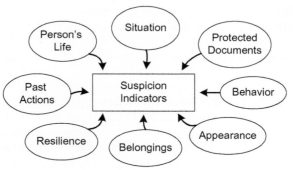

The objective of predictive profiling is to determine whether a situation, person, or object is a threat to the assets of an organization. It may not be possible to assess the level of threat from the suspicious indicators, but the level of threat can be ascertained from follow-up interviews with the individuals involved in the behavior.

Successful predictive profiling employs processes to fragment criminal and terrorist methodologies into planning and executive phases to better intercept the action before it is instigated. The term *aggressor's methods of operations* (AMO) is used to describe the procedures developed by adversaries to breach the security of a facility or public structure. A security department can develop its own suspicious indicators database by *red teaming* the facility to seek the behavioral characteristics for predictive profiling. Therefore, relevant suspicious indicators are available for administration and staff to maintain vigilance for criminal and terrorist presence.

Predictive profiling emphasizes the application of questioning techniques to detect and determine adversarial motivations and intentions beyond observed suspicious indicators. The purpose of probing questioning of individuals, who have been identified by suspicious indicators, is to refute the suspicion that has been observed. This style of questioning is contrary to that experienced in law enforcement where aggressive inquisition to prove guilt is conducted. The questioning following identification by suspicious indicators is in a customer service style to invoke cooperation. Therefore, appropriate training is required for officers to engage in friendly inquisitive conversation with a suspicious person to gain information that can refute the apparent suspicion. Interestingly, this style of questioning reinforces a positive image of the security industry in dealing with others.

CONCLUSION

The evaluation of information through the intelligence process is a critical component in accessing knowledge for security management. The intelligence analyst functions within a process known as the intelligence cycle; data are collected, processed, and disseminated as intelligence products to the clients. The application of the intelligence products by the corporate security manager to the protection of assets of an organization will ensure the relevance of security strategies to the known threats to the organization. The recent development of sophisticated knowledge management systems allows security managers to access and distribute information and intelligence to appropriate expert groups within their organization to contribute to the security management plan.

The need for vetting of personnel within an organization has been discussed in terms of an evaluation of an individual's character, integrity, attributes, background, and actions. Integrity confirms the honesty of a person and determines his or her security vulnerabilities. These integrity assessments are achieved through police checks, reference checks, and security assessment interviews. Similarly, those in a different context, protective profiling examines the characteristics of an individual with regard to known behaviors according to suspicious indicators of criminals and terrorists.

Further Reading

Gill, M. (Ed.), 2006. The Handbook of Security. Palgrave Macmillan, Basingstoke, Hampshire.

Logan, K.G., 2010. Homeland Security and Intelligence. ABC-CLIO, Santa Barbara, CA.

Prunckun, H., 2010. A Handbook of Scientific Methods of Inquiry for Intelligence Analysis. Scarecrow Press, Lanham, MD.

Walsh, P.F., 2011. Intelligence and Intelligence Analysis. Routledge, New York.

References

Attorney-General's Department, 2010. Protective Security Manual (PSM). Attorney-General's Department, Canberra, Australia, 2010.

Birtino, E., Khan, L.R., Sandhu, R., Thuraisingham, B., 2006. Secure knowledge management: Confidentiality, trust, and privacy. IEEE Trans. Syst. Man Cybern. 36 (3), 429–438.

Brooks, D., Corkill, J., Pooley, J., Cohen, L., Ferguson, C., Harms, C., 2011. National security: A propositional study to develop resilience indicators as an aid to personnel vetting. In: Proceedings of the 3rd Australian Security and Intelligence Conference. Edith Cowan University, Perth, WA, pp. 35–43.

Clarke, R.M., 2010. Intelligence Analysis: A Target-centric Approach. CQ Press, Washington, DC.

Clauser, J., 2008. An introduction to intelligence research and analysis. Revised and edited by Goldman, J. Scarecrow Press, Lanham, MD.

Corkill, J., 2008. Professional intelligence judgment artistry. In: Proceedings of the 1st Australian Security and Intelligence Conference. Edith Cowan University, Perth, WA, pp. 17–25.

Defence Vetting Report, 2007. Defence Vetting Report, Oct. 22, 2007. Defence Teaming Centre Inc, Canberra, Australia.

Foster, K.J., 1994. Crucial success factors in achieving cost effective security solutions. Security management: Towards 2000. In: Proceedings of the 1994 National Conference, Sydney, 15–16 March, 1994 and Melbourne, 17–18 March, 1994. pp. 21–32.

Gill, P., Phythian, M., 2006. Intelligence in an Insecure World. Polity Press, Malden, MA.

Grabo, C.M., 2002. Anticipating Surprise: Analysis for Strategic Warning. Joint Military Intelligence College: Center for Strategic Intelligence Research, Washington, DC.

Gupta, J.N.D., Sharma, S.K., 2004. Creating Knowledge-based Organizations. Idea Group Publishing, Boston.

Hayes, N., Walsham, G., 2003. Knowledge sharing and ICTs: A relational perspective. In: Easterby-Smith, M., Lyles, M.A. (Eds.), The Blackwell Handbook of Organizational Learning and Knowledge Management. Blackwell Publishing, Malden, MA, pp. 54–77.

Hennessy, P., Brownfeld, G., 1982. Britain's cold war security purge: The origins of positive vetting. The Historical Journal 25 (4), 965–973.

Joseph, J., Corkill, J., 2011. Information evaluation: How one group of intelligence analysts go about the task. In: Proceedings of the 4th Australian Security and Intelligence Conference. Edith Cowan University, Perth, WA, pp. 97–103.

King, W.R., Marks, P.V., McCoy, S., 2002. The most important issues in knowledge management. Commun. ACM 45 (9), 93–97.

Muldoon, S., 2008. Employment Risks in a Security-sensitive Environment. Australian Institute of Criminology, Canberra.

Nonaka, I., Takeuchi, H., 1995. The Knowledge Creating Company: How Japanese Companies Create the Dynamics of Innovation. Oxford University Press, New York.

Shaw, E.D., Fischer, L.F., Rose, A.E., 2009. Insider Risk Evaluation and Audit. Technical Report 09-02, U.S. Department of Defense.

Business Continuity Management

OBJECTIVES

- Describe the process of business continuity management.
- Distinguish the benefits of business continuity management to an organization.
- Characterize the term *crisis*.
- Compare and contrast the four phases of a crisis: prodrome, acute, chronic, and recovery.
- Categorize the four generic business continuity management stages: emergency response, continuity response, recovery plans, and restoration plans.
- Explain each response plan within an overarching business continuity management process.

- Within a business context, recognize the various organizational drivers for business continuity management.
- Be able to implement a business continuity management plan.
- Be able to correlate the crisis phases, business continuity management stages, and response plans within a timeline of activities.
- Model a forecast of a crisis using a business impact assessment.
- Critically discuss each essential element of a business continuity management plan.
- Explain the relationship between security and business continuity management.

INTRODUCTION

The occurrence of a disaster usually overwhelms those affected by it, particularly when there has been no planning or preparation. Even in situations that are repetitions of previous calamitous events, people often seem to be unprepared. The annual flooding of certain rivers or other extreme weather events offers a prime example. People and organizations will be repeatedly devastated, but each time they are no better equipped than the time before (Walsh and Healy, 2004, pp. 10–11). Nevertheless, with some preplanning and a little thought such disruptive risks can be better managed. Events such as terrorism incidents, natural disasters, and pandemics can all be better managed using business continuity management (BCM).

BCM is a practicing domain in its own right, neither subservient to risk management nor solely providing crisis management or first-response plans. BCM is informed by risk management and provides a means to manage disruption-related risks. Such disruptive risks within an organization are those that:

- Have a significant impact on critical business process, capability, or output.
- Exceed, for a period of time, the routine capacity of management.
- Cannot be cost-effectively mitigated.

BCM allows an organization to understand and, importantly, articulate critical organizational objectives that must be achieved and maintained. Once these objectives are better understood, processes, resources, and their availability can be considered to safeguard these objectives in times of crisis. A BCM framework should pose the questions of what can happen; what does it mean to us; what is critical to the organization, project, or team; and what do we have to do before, during, and after an adverse event or crisis?

Effective BCM should lead an organization to:

- Stabilize any disruption as soon as possible.
- Continue or resume operations that are critical to organizational objectives.
- Expedite the return to normal operations as soon as possible.
- Capitalize on any resulting environmental opportunities caused by the event.
- Increase additional risk with confidence (Standards Australia, 2010).
- Provide a cost-effective risk mitigation strategy.
- Improve organizational resilience.

CRISIS

BCM respond to disruptive risks, which manifest as a crisis, disaster, adverse incident, or natural event. A crisis can be defined as a "crucial stage or turning point, especially in a sequence of events," extended to "an unstable period, especially one of extreme trouble or danger" (Angus and Roberston, 1992, p. 231). This definition provides a negative cognition, similar to those that define *risk*. Nevertheless, when handled appropriately a crisis can become an opportunity. The BCM function must be prepared to capitalize on any opportunity that may present.

The aim of managing a crisis is to return an organization to its normal activities as soon as possible, learning from the experience and, therefore, becoming more resilient. Consequently, crisis management and BCM are closely interrelated. Thus, emergency planning and response, particularly from respective emergency management agencies, should be considered within the BCM context. Furthermore, some organizations often think that BCM relates solely to information technology; however, this is not the case, as BCM should encompass all organizational activities. Finally, many consider BCM as just a set of response plans, whereas

TABLE 9.1   Typical Disruptive Risks Events Suffered by a Sample of U.K. Businesses

Event	Disruptive Risks					
	2006 %	2007 %	2008 %	2009 %	2010 %	2011 %
Extreme weather	9	28	29	25	58	64
Loss of IT	38	39	43	40	35	34
Loss of people	29	32	35	24	28	34
Loss of site access	13	13	16	13	22	26
Loss to telecoms	24	25	30	23	20	20
Supply chain disruption	10	13	12	9	13	19
Loss of key staff	19	20	21	14	15	18
Loss of utilities	—	—	—	—	15	16
Occupational Health and Safety incident	13	17	17	16	14	15
Negative publicity	16	19	18	14	9	11
Damage to profile/image/brand	8	11	10	11	7	10
Environmental incident	5	6	7	7	5	7
Pressure group protest	7	7	6	7	6	6
Industrial action	6	7	7	7	4	6
Fire	5	6	5	5	4	4

BCM can allow an organization to learn from past crises and respond sooner to a developing crisis.

There are many likely disruptive risks, for example, from malicious cyber attacks to damage of a corporate brand. A sampling of U.K. business managers were asked to list their disruptive events over 12-month periods (Woodman and Hutchings, 2011, p. 10), with events such as extreme weather, loss of IT, and loss of people leading the list of most disruptive organizational risks (Table 9.1). Without appropriate BCM, an organization is more likely to suffer from a disruptive risk.

FOUR PHASES OF A CRISIS

A crisis may commence long before an organization is aware that they are entering a crisis event. Nevertheless, there may be clear signals that an organization—that is aware of what to look for and what action to take—can take steps that will allow them to divert a potential crisis. A crisis can have as many as four distinct phases (Figure 9.1), namely prodrome, acute, chronic crisis, and recovery phases.

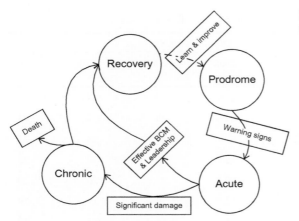

FIGURE 9.1   Four phases of a crisis, from warning to death or recovery.

Prodrome Phase

The prodrome phase is the precrisis or warning stage. For example, many may consider an earthquake as an "act of God" that has no warning, although there is usually some degree of seismic data that may not have been interpreted and communicated effectively. A crisis is best managed during the prodromal phase, as it is easier to manage a crisis before it becomes acute. If the symptoms of a pending crisis can be identified, an organization can react with greater efficiency and implement corrective measures immediately.

Acute Phase

The acute phase has the crisis occurring and damage has resulted, and the organization commences damage control. It is this stage of a crisis that most people refer to when speaking of a crisis. How much damage control is applied will depend on the organization, the incident, and the organization's ability to respond. The organization will try to limit its exposure to damage and risk. If the crisis cannot be controlled, perhaps the outcome or location of the crisis may be influenced to reduce the impact on the organization.

The acute phase is often characterized by the speed at which events move and may appear to be the longest phase; however, the following chronic phase is generally the longest. While the prodromal phase tells you that trouble is building, the acute phase lets you know that it has erupted. For example, during the acute phase the earthquake causes the ground to shake, buildings to collapse, and injury, deaths, and loss results.

Chronic Crisis Phase

The chronic crisis phase may be considered the postmortem or clean-up phase. After an extended period of time, the crisis will either destroy the organization or the organization will manage to begin to return to its precrisis level of capability. If the crisis has been well managed, it will be a time for the organization to gain value from the crisis and its associated stress. If the crisis has been poorly managed, it may be a time of upheaval, bankruptcy, and takeover bids. The chronic crisis phase can be significantly shortened with effective BCM and leadership.

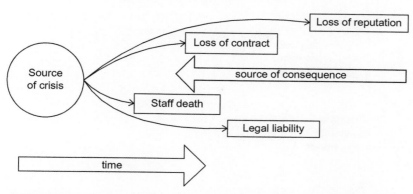

FIGURE 9.2   Source of a crisis, with many resulting and varied consequences.

Recovery Phase

The recovery or resolution phase is when the organization has returned to normal operations, equal or superior to the period prior to the crisis. The aim of BCM is to arrive at this phase in the shortest time possible. An appropriate BCM function should move the organization in crisis directly from the prodromal phase to recovery.

The duration and intensity of each phase will depend on the organization's health, readiness to react, the ability of the BCM function, and resilience. In one case, the prodromal phase may last several weeks, while in other situations the whole crisis cycle may take less than 24 hours. Each crisis needs to be managed on its merits and based on the individual situation.

Not all crises will have all four phases. In some cases the prodromal symptoms will be recognized and the organization will move directly to crisis resolution. Such an approach may result in the BCM process not even being activated. The key concept is recognizing the symptoms, in much the same way as one recognizes they are developing a cold.

Crises have a tendency to be cyclical in nature, come in multiples, and, much like the "source of risk," one crisis source will result in many consequences (Figure 9.2). When an organization or its managers are unprepared, managers will focus on what they feel most comfortable managing. This approach may result in the managers not addressing the root cause or source of the crisis.

Those managing the crisis must be able to determine what requires priority action and what can wait. Among the many symptoms, managers must be able to ascertain the root cause and address that problem. Such an approach is supported by a structured and preplanned process, considered business continuity management.

BUSINESS CONTINUITY MANAGEMENT

There are many reasons for developing, implementing, and maintaining a BCM function (Figure 9.3). A BCM plan may be developed as a risk mitigation strategy to manage a highly unlikely, but significant disruptive risk. There may be a corporate governance need within an organization, a significant catalyst of BCM. Customers, regulators, and insurers may require

FIGURE 9.3 The drivers for business continuity management.

an organization to adopt BCM, although the requirement from insurers for an organization to implement BCM has reduced over recent years (Woodman and Hutchings, 2011, pp. 16–17). Finally, the security manager may instigate BCM as part of their security management emergency response group.

BCM may be defined as the "availability of process and resources in order to ensure the continued achievement of critical objectives"(Standards Australia, 2004, p. 2). Furthermore, according to the British Standard BS25999-1, BCM is

> "A holistic management process that identifies potential threats to an organisation and the impacts to business operations that those threats, if realised, might cause, and which provides a framework for building organisational resilience with capability for an effective response that safeguards the interests of its key stakeholders, reputation, brand and value-creating activities" (citied in Woodman, 2007, p. 2).

BCM is the integration of what have traditionally been discrete functions, such as emergency evacuation plans, first-responder plans, crisis plans, and IT recovery plans. Today, BCM is a formal process to manage disruptive risk, ensure business sustainability, maintain business success, and improve resilience across the whole organization. To achieve these outcomes, the BCM function must (Standards Australia, 2004, p. 2):

- Understand the organization's critical objectives.
- Identify the barriers or interruptions that may be faced achieving these critical objectives.
- Determine how the organization will continue to achieve its objectives, should interruptions be realized.
- Test and measure controls for responding to mitigating these interruptions.

The application of BCM is defined by the type, size, and industry of an organization. For example, BCM is more common in the public sector (66%) and listed companies (60%), as opposed to private companies (44%) and voluntary companies (41%). The size of the organization also directs the likelihood of applied BCM. For example, 62% of larger organizations and

42% of medium organization have BCM, with only 34% of smaller organization having BCM. Finally, finance and insurance (80%) and the utilities sector (76%) have a high application of BCM, with education (36%) and construction (29%) at the other end of the spectrum (Woodman, 2007, pp. 15–16).

Risk Management and BCM

BCM is not subservient to risk management, but rather is a function that can support risk management with a mitigation strategy. BCM can be carried out as a standalone process, with its own embedded risk assessment process. Nevertheless, a more effective approach is to use risk management as the "informing" process, much like a threat assessment informs the "likelihood" component of security risk management. For example, a low-likelihood and high-consequence (disruptive) risk may be treated wholly by BCM. The loss of a facility for an extended period from either fire or flood may be difficult to physically protect beyond general fire and life safety systems; rather, BCM can be used to identify and address the feasibility of hot sites, supply contracts, costs, and lead-time to mobilize, and, importantly, the critical need for that facility.

Corporate Governance and BCM

BCM, risk management, and security management are integral and dynamic components of effective corporate governance. These various functions support the board and senior managers to manage uncertainties as effectively as possible, ensuring the sustainability of an organization.

ESSENTIAL ELEMENTS OF BUSINESS CONTINUITY MANAGEMENT

The degree of effect, who responds, and the resulting action will be dependent on the disruptive risk. For example, some crises will involve external first-responding agencies such as the fire department or police, who will take command of the situation until resolved within their realm of responsibility. From that point, the organization will resume responsibility in such areas as facility clean-up, media liaison, business resumption, recovery, and, finally, restoration. In addition, the timeline from prodrome to restoration will vary depending on the organization's resilience to the type and severity of the crisis, from minutes to years. Some crises could result in an organization not returning to their precrisis condition for years after a crisis incident, whilet others may be resolved in days.

In BCM, there are four generic response plans and activities (Figure 9.4). In the first instance, emergency response will activate the BCM process, triggered by the event or its prewarning. This initial stage is defined within the prodromal phase and results in a high level of management activity to stabilize the crisis, through detection and response. Emergency response is closely followed by continuity response, defined within the acute phase and where response continues in an effort to contain loss. A high level of management activity continues in stabilizing the crisis, but also is extended to maintain critical business functions.

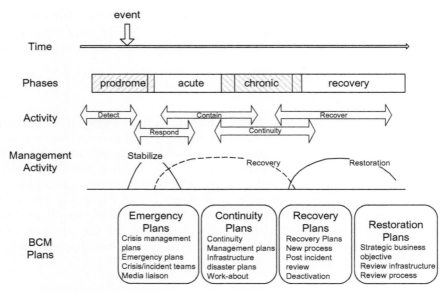

FIGURE 9.4   Business continuity management overview and timeline.

Later, recovery is activated and defined within the chronic phase, to either recover or fail. Management activities focus on recovery from the crisis to get the organization back to a position of precrisis. The concluding part of recovery is the deactivation of most of the response plans, with lesson learned and improvements applied. Finally, and much later, restoration completes the BCM process, where the organization has recovered but seeks a better way to do business.

BCM Plans

The emergency response stage is the initial response, which normally encompasses the first 24–48 hours, focusing on the protection of people and assets from immediate harm. This stage will include response plans such as the crisis management plan, emergency management plan, incident response team, and media management plan. Typical security plans that support this initial emergency response would be procedures such as fire evacuation plans and improvised explosive device (IED) threat plans.

The continuity response stage considers the elements to keep the critical business functions operating during the crisis, which can encompass periods from four hours to many weeks or even months. This second stage makes available prepared processes, resources, and controls to allow an organization to maintain its critical business output at an acceptable level.

The recovery stage considers the core operational activities necessary to reestablish the business, which can encompass periods from weeks to months. Such tasks include organizational improvements, new processes, postincident review such as lessons learned, and BCM deactivation. The principal purpose of this stage is to gain a progressive reestablishment of operations back to a precrisis period. In addition, if achieved to a reasonable level, it would be expected that operations will exceed precrisis levels with "improved capability and performance" (Standards Australia, 2004, p. 20).

The restoration stage considers strategic activities for any major infrastructure or organizational changes, which can encompass periods from many months to years. There may be a refocus of strategic and business objectives (Standards Australia, 2004, p. 3). For example, in a kidnapping case an organization may review their need to operate in certain geographical markets. The principal purpose of this stage is to implement strategic changes to the organizations from lessons learned in the period following the crisis.

BCM FRAMEWORK

BCM, like the security management plan, should take a formal and structured approach aligned to an organization. The purpose of BCM is to plan, organize, staff, lead, and control people, assets, and resources to proactively counter a disruptive risk.

The complexity of BCM plans will depend on organizational expectation and requirements. Each BCM plan or part thereof is to some degree modular, where the BCM framework should be built to best suit the organization, its risk appetite, culture, and operating and strategic environment. Nevertheless, unlike the security management plan that does not provide a "how-to" approach, the BCM plans should provide a clear articulated guide to deal with each disruptive risk.

The BCM framework (Figure 9.5) should take logical steps for the assessment, development, and propagation of suitable response plans.

Define the Context

Defining the context starts BCM—establishing the process, resources, and capability. Tasks include gaining senior management support and written endorsement, articulating the need for BCM, and setting up a project team or BCM manager. BCM requires resources, for example, hiring a BCM manager to facilitate the process or setting up a project team with relevant and skilled staff can be a significant cost.

The project team or BCM manager will need to consider such aspects as how the process is to be carried out and in what time scale, what assessment methods are to be used, will a "standalone" risk management task be used or will risk management be integrated into the BCM framework, and who the stakeholders are and who will undertake the BCM task.

Critical Business Objectives

Critical business objectives articulate what is vital for an organization to maintain its core business outputs. Consider the organization as a system, with inputs (resources, people, assets, information), transformations (manufacture, produce, service), and outputs (goods, services). What elements within the systems are vital to maintain the critical business goods and services outputs?

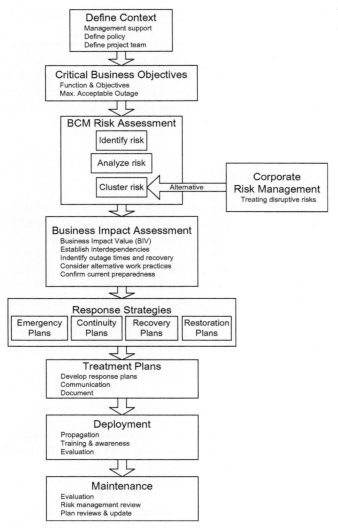

FIGURE 9.5 Business continuity management framework.

To develop an understanding of these critical business objectives you must ask the "what if" questions, such as "What are the key critical business objectives?" and "What are the critical activities that are essential for the business to operate?" If these business objectives and activities were lost, how long would it take for them to be restored? Unfortunately, the possibilities of "what if" questions are endless and some parameter must be set. The role of the BCM project team or manager is to set these parameters during the process.

Through a process of meetings, workshops, brain-storming sessions, corporate plans, annual reports, and executive statements, these elements need to be listed, and aligned with capacity and capability. The outcome of this stage is to gain a common understanding of critical functions and processes that support core business objectives (Standards Australia, 2004, p. 17).

Thus, for each identified disruption, determine the maximum acceptable outage time (MAO) for each critical function. The MAO represents the maximum time that the organization can continue to tolerate this loss of capability (Standards Australia, 2006, p. 10).

Risk Assessment

Risk assessment may use either an embedded risk assessment process or the output from the corporate risk management process. What method is used will depend on the organization, task, project team, and complexity of the environment. Risks that are treated with BCM are, in general, ones that could cause a significant disruption.

Disruptive risks need to be clustered into source or common failure modes. For example, risks such as fire, flood, and IED are treated quite separately, but from a BCM perspective they all result in a loss of facility access. If the facility is critical, for example, as a primary distribution center, then these three risks are equally disruptive; however, if the loss of facility access only becomes critical after 24 hours, then you would expect the IED (unless exploded) to be resolved. So the fire and flood risk are parceled together as loss of facility access for greater than 24 hours. The clustered or common mode failure risks are then used to assess the business impact of these potential risks.

Business Impact Assessment

The business impact assessment or crisis forecasting provides an analysis of how significant disruption may affect an organization's outputs and what capabilities may be required to address such disruptions. There are a number of distinct requirements in determining both current resources and the essential minimum level of resources to continue to operate, along with the impact of risk disruptions in both financial and nonfinancial terms. The likelihood of an event and the business impact or consequence of the threat, if realized, are two components in measuring the business impact.

In addition to identifying the impact of disruptions and the maximum acceptable outage time, articulating interdependencies assist in understanding business impacts. For example, what are the effects to the supply chain, who and how do internal and external stakeholders relate, are there alternative work practices, and what are the current processes in place that may treat such disruptive risks?

Response Strategies

The BCM process is now at a stage where information has identified what is critical to the business, what disruptions may occur, the impact if these disruptions are realized, and the current state of affairs. BCM response plans can now be developed to address disruptions at each crisis phase. These response plans include the initial emergency response, closely followed by continuity response, and later recovery response, with the final restoration response concluding the BCM process.

During this stage there are a number of aspects that should be considered to direct response plans, such as:

- Legislative, regulative, and other legal requirements that must be addressed.
- Suitability of alternative plans.
- Cost of plans.
- Creeping risk (residual risks that raise the consequence, for example, fitting vehicle immobilizers increased the interaction between car theft and victims, increasing breaking and entry, bag snatching, and assault).
- Capability of the organization to implement plans (Standards Australia, 2006, p. 11).
- Benefits and limitations of the plans.

Treatment Plans

Treatment plans can now be developed and documented to address a disruptive risk, divided into relevant response plans. Consider that BCM plans need to be read by staff who may not have been involved in their development, so plans need to be written in simplistic language. Plans must be comprehensive and have clarity, but not be overly long. Do not make assumptions that the reader knows core needs, and ensure that each plan has some degree of flexibility, as a plan may just get you to the starting point.

Plans need to meet the organizational needs and the proposed treatment strategy, so although plans are not generic in format, they do contain a number of predefined sections (Table 9.2).

Communication should be built in to the various response plans. The degree of complexity of communication will depend on the type and scope of the planned disruption, so in some plans the communication strategy may be relatively minor, whereas in others it could be significant. The principal purpose of the communication strategy is to communicate with internal and external stakeholders in a transparent and concise manner, have an orderly flow of information management, and build a robust dialog with those who need or seek information.

TABLE 9.2   BCM Treatment Plan

Section	Content
Cover page	What type of BCM plan, title, date, owner, control document record
Contents	Table of contents
BCM plan	Details of the plan: emergency, continuity, recovery, or restoration Trigger event(s) Staff responsibilities
Response plan	Procedures: what steps to take
Contact	List of relevant contacts Callout list
Technical plan	Specialized departmental plans, such as IT, finance, security
Resources	Internal and external list and resource contacts

Deployment

Once the BCM plans have been developed, they need to be propagated and relevant staff made aware. Propagation needs to achieve a number of objectives, such as communicate to staff that the organization has incident plans, train staff on the plans and raise their awareness, and undertake evaluation of the plans to ensure that they are achievable.

All staff can be made aware of BCM plans in procedures such as employment inductions or, more specifically, as part of their job description. Staff who have a direct responsibility or role in plans need to undertake training. Training will not only make those responsible staff more aware of the plans, but also give them confidence in the plans, allow plans to be improved, and, ultimately, ensure staff better manage an incident.

The evaluation of plans can take a number of approaches and these all need to be used. An evaluation could include a desktop review, desktop scenarios, notification exercises, call-out exercises, or live scenario exercises. The approach to evaluation will depend on the organization and its degree of significance to disruptive risks. Nevertheless, all forms of exercises allow some degree of evaluation, improvement, and confidence in the plans.

Maintenance

An active and regular maintenance program is required to ensure that plans are fit for purpose (Standards Australia, 2006, p. 13) and have not decayed. Personnel need to understand the requirements for BCM plans and that resources and processes to perform the plans are appropriate. Evaluation of plans achieves this task to some degree, but additional maintenance is required. Regular audits, review of the threat environment, and update of the criticality register and risk register need to be carried out. This information has to feed back to the various BCM plans to allow these plans to realign to the organization's critical and at-risk objectives.

BUSINESS IMPACT FORECASTING

When assessing disruptive risks, an assessment of the likelihood, business impact value (BIV), and period of failure can be made. The BIV may be assigned a numerical scale between 1 and 5, which estimates the ramifications and impact of the crisis (Table 9.3).

As with risk assessment, the BIV forecasting reflects the participant's bias and perception. Individuals and departmental managers' crisis may not be a crisis to others. If the crisis affects your department, look at it from your perspective; however, if conducting BCM for the whole organization, an organizational perspective will be required. Such an approach will mean interviewing management and key personnel, as well an assessment workshop. Some questions that you may wish to ask include:

- What are your key business objectives?
- Are there any critical nodes of activity?
- What is the acceptable level of outage (–i.e., MAO) for a critical section, for example, four hours, one working day, three working days?

TABLE 9.3 Business Impact Value

Scale	Rank	Financial Impact	Implicit (Qualitative) Impact
Catastrophic	5	Financial loss > 10% of operating budget	Total loss of operations Impact across all critical business functions Immediate board intervention required
Major	4	Financial loss > 5% of operating budget	Significant degradation of operations Impact on multiple critical business functions Immediate senior executive intervention required
High	3	Financial loss > 3% of operating budget	Substantial degradation of operations Impact on multiple business functions Substantial executive intervention required
Moderate	2	Financial loss > 1% of operating budget	Moderate degradation of some parts of operations Impact on single business function Local management intervention required
Low	1	Financial loss < 1% of operating budget	No measurable operational impact
Unknown	U	Impact and resulting consequence being realized is unknown	Consequence of harm being realized is unknown

- What is the disruptive risk of the crisis escalating in intensity? How intense will the crisis become, and how quickly may the crisis escalate?
- What are the regulatory or legislative requirements? Will the crisis be monitored by a regulatory body (e.g., emergency response agencies)?
- To what extent would the crisis impact on normal operations?
- Is the organization a victim or a culprit? As discussed in risk management, this issue can impact on the media's attention and resulting public's perception of the organization.
- If the threat of a crisis is realized, what will be the impact on the organization's financial outcomes?

Establishing the BIV is important, but so is establishing the likelihood of the crisis occurring. Likelihood can be expressed as a percentage, such as 70% (0.7) chance of occurrence, or as a qualitative descriptor (Table 9.4). The greater the chance of the disruptive risk being realized, the more attention it should receive; although, if the disruptive risk occurs on a regular basis it is likely that there are already procedures to deal with such a "regular" event. It is sometimes more prudent to plan for nonprobabilistic events, such as low likelihood and high consequence. Such disruptive risks are better suited to treatment by BCM.

The third criterion is the period of failure. Most organizations can stand some loss of critical objectives for a period of time; however, once a certain period is reached the loss of that service or product becomes significant. Typical assessment periods to consider may be four hours, one working day, three working days, or one week.

As with risk assessment, the BIV takes precedence or has a greater weighted value than the likelihood of the impact. That is not to say that a BIV of 4 with a probability of 2% should not

TABLE 9.4   Likelihood Scale

Scale	Rank	Description	Percentage
Certain	5	The impact will be realized	Over 99%
Very high	4	The impact is highly probable	>50%
High	3	The impact is moderately probable	>10%
Medium	2	The impact is probable	>1%
Low	1	The impact is improbable	<1%
Unknown	U	Likelihood of impact is unknown	Unknown

TABLE 9.5   Business Impact Matrix to Rank Disruptive Risks

Likelihood	Business Impact Value				
	Low	Moderate	High	Major	Catastrophic
Certain	High	High	Very high	Extreme	Extreme
Very high	Moderate	High	High	Very high	Extreme
High	Moderate	Moderate	High	Very high	Very high
Medium	Low	Moderate	Moderate	High	Very high
Low	Low	Low	Moderate	High	High

receive less attention than a BIV of 2 with a 90% probability. One of the methods of preventing too many errors in assessing the priority of a crisis is the business impact matrix (Table 9.5), which takes the same form as the risk assessment matrix (see Table 3.5). The BIV and likelihood of impact measures can be summed using the business impact matrix to produce a ranked crisis from low to extreme.

The assessed crisis needs to be documented and, if appropriate, BCM response plans developed. This process should be documented, controlled, and monitored using a BCM crisis register (Figure 9.6).

LEARNING FROM A CRISIS

Even though many organizations may be owned and managed by individuals who apply their "own" unique processes, many disruptive risks are not unique to that organization. For example, the loss of utility power for longer than 48 hours will have a similar effect on many different organizations. Depending on the organization and at certain periods, disruptive risks and their impacts can be highly specific. But in general, risks are similar across

Disruptive risk source	Impact	Owner	BIV	Likelihood	Risk score	Ranking	Existing controls	Treatment Plans
Provide a descriptor of the risk source	*What impact will this risk have?*	*Who "owns" the risk (i.e.) manager*	*Table 9.3 (a)*	*Table 9.4 (b)*	*a*b*	*Table 9.5*	*List current control measures*	*List proposed plans, who, when & where*

FIGURE 9.6   BCM crisis register.

different organizations regardless of their industry, operations, size, or location. It is therefore likely that:

> Any risk event, disruption or failure that occurs in one organisation will have a propensity to occur in a similar organisation for a similar reason.
>
> Although organisations may appear to be individually unique, if they possess similar underlying systems, structures, process, etc., they will all be open to common modes of failure. *(Standards Australia, 2004, p. 12)*

We can therefore learn from past events, from internal groups within our own organization, associated professional bodies, and neighbors. Isomorphic learning principles are a useful tool that allows us to learn. Isomorphism means *similar* and four areas of isomorphism that may be used include:

- *Event isomorphism:* Two separate events take place and manifest themselves in two completely different ways, but lead to the creation of identical hazardous situations.
- *Cross-organizational isomorphism:* Two organizations with different owners, managed and staffed by different people, but in the same industry and using similar systems, are prone to similar problems.
- *Common mode isomorphism:* Two organizations in different industries, but using similar products, techniques, tools, or procedures, are prone to similar hazards.
- *Self-isomorphism:* In an organization so large as to have many subsections providing the same basic service, the difficulties and crisis suffered by one subunit will most likely be reflected in other subunits.

COMMON ELEMENTS OF BCM

When developing BCM plans for a disruptive risk, they must be written to provide clarity and authority. Written plans require a system of clear and concise procedures that provide detailed instructions as to what will be done, by whom, and under whose direction. During a crisis, confusion and chaos can be expected, so there is little room for individuals to make free-ranging decisions. Thus, the organization needs to respond because each person must know not only their own responsibilities, but what they can expect from others.

Any response needs to take considered decisions to direct limited resources, rather than misdirecting these resources. These aspects must be defined in advance of the crisis, rather than while it is occurring. Having a detailed plan will ensure the appropriate people, equipment, and facilities will be available in time of a crisis.

Some of the more common elements of BCM include strategies for maintaining or recovering core services and products, IT back-up arrangements, remote working, site emergency plans, contact escalation, moving staff to alternative sites, media response, and securing alternative utility services (Woodman and Hutchings, 2011, p. 18). Nevertheless, there are many other elements that need to be considered, such as the appointment of a BCM manager and project team, designating an appropriate authority, a clear chain of command, allocating facilities, resources and financial support, team training, communication and liaison, succession, welfare, self-sufficiency, testing the plans, restoration, and updating to reduce decay.

Even the best BCM plan cannot guarantee that a disruptive risk will not be realized, but it will limit the damage and return the company to usual activity as soon as possible. A faster return to normal operations will, in itself, produce significant savings for the organization.

Applied BCM Planning

Managing a crisis is the same as any other management function, although exceeding the normal capacity of management. The BCM response team must be able to implement the crisis plan and guide the organization through the crisis. For this reason, the response team members must be capable of making decisions, both personally and in their organizational role.

There is no point in having a plan if people are not going to make a decision and act upon the plan. Caution must be taken during the decision-making process to avoid "analysis paralysis." Paralysis occurs when a decision maker makes decisions, but does not implement them, or makes the easy decision that does not address the core or source issue. This factor is dangerous, as people assume decisions are being made and the crisis is under control, when in fact the latter has not occurred.

Appointment of BCM Coordinator

An appropriate person at the executive or senior management level needs to drive the BCM process, supporting the BCM coordinator. The BCM coordinator assumes responsibility for the BCM process, strategy, and plans, and acts as the facilitator. It may be appropriate that this person be the security manager.

Formation of BCM Committee

The formation of a BCM committee allows all departments to become involved and participate in the BCM process. The committee should be composed of representatives from all key departments or divisions in the organization and they should be senior personnel within their representative areas.

Designate Authority

Each BCM plan should clearly establish who is in control of managing each type of crisis, whether this type of crisis is within an emergency, continuity, recovery, or restoration response. Due to the dynamic nature of some disruptive risk and need for rapid mobilization to ensure continuity of operations, designated authority for these two initial plans are important. If there are a variety of crises that face an organization, there may be different people in charge for different emergencies. Nevertheless, for simplicity and so everyone knows who is in charge, a single person who manages all crises is desirable. The members of the BCM response team can vary for different crises.

To maximize the outcomes from BCM and produce significant benefits, senior management need to take an active role. For example, senior managers will already be effective leaders, have a better understanding of corporate objectives, staff will better respond when asked, and when senior executives speak to the media it carries greater weight. The use of senior executives is the norm in most organizations with 46% of senior managers taking responsibility for BCM, as opposed to 26% from the board, 14% from BCM teams, 4.5% from operational staff, and 3.5% from the risk department (Woodman, 2007, p. 10).

Establish a BCM Chain of Command

In supporting the designated authority, there must be a chain of command during a crisis. This chain must be clearly published, so everyone is aware who is responsible to whom and for what. In addition, if people are removed from their normal place of work for the duration of the crisis, they must have someone to replace them in their normal duties. If this is not done, they will continue to be involved in routine activities and this involvement will decrease the ability of the response members. Personnel involved in the crisis need to be able to focus on the crisis, which will not occur if they are involved in daily management issues. Chain of command should be designated by appointment, rather than name. That way if someone is on leave or ill, their second in charge can take over.

Designate Equipment and Facilities

Both facilities and equipment must be available for use during a crisis. A center from which the crisis is controlled should be designated and resourced to enable any incident to be managed effectively. For example, resources should include communications, computers, IT connectivity, display boards, break-out rooms, restrooms, and kitchen facilities.

An alternative location should be selected and resourced in case the primary location cannot be used, either as a "cold-site" or, if required, a "hot-site." A cold-site is a facility or center that can be mobilized with resources after a period of approximately 24 hours, whereas a hot-site can be activated within 1 hour.

Resource and Finance

How will the crisis operations be resourced and financed? This issue will become important if the organization's finances are affected by the crisis or the crisis involves the unusual expenditure of funds, such as paying a ransom or renting facilities and equipment. These aspects are some of the management issues of a crisis that need to be considered in the BCM planning stage.

Establish and Train BCM Response Teams

Establish and train BCM response teams for the various plans. Training will assist staff to better understand these various plans, be more effective in their activation and application, and lead to a more resilient organization. Sixty percent of organizations with BCM plans provide staff training (Woodman and Hutchings, 2011, p. 20), although this level should be higher and include general and nonspecialized staff.

While not inclusive, examples of BCM response teams and their roles may include:

- *Crisis management team:* Responsible for the management (and leadership) of the crisis when a BCM plan is activated. Staffed by trained and skilled staff from relevant departments.
- *Crisis management support team:* Responsible for providing logistics, setting up the command center, and maintaining logs of activities and key decisions.
- *People management team:* Responsible for welfare issues including critical incident stress management.
- *Media liaison team:* Responsible for information dissemination and media advice to the crisis manager, led by a senior corporate executive as the media spokesperson.
- *Specialist teams:* Depending on circumstances and individual organizational needs, specialist teams such as IT, finance, technical, rescue, legal, and salvage should be established.
- *External agency liaison team:* Responsible for liaising, as necessary, with emergency response agencies.

Response teams may need to work 24 hours a day to manage the crisis and must be available throughout the crisis. This extensive demand may require specialist training to ensure team members can function in an area outside their normal job.

Emergency Communications

Communications are vital for an organization to function effectively—in particular in today's IT-driven world of emails, digital media, Google maps, social media, and the like. Thus, the ability to communicate within the organization and the outside world becomes paramount. The response team must ensure emergency communications facilities are available and resilient, in particular, IT connectivity.

Communication procedures with outside agencies need to be addressed. Who will be the point of contact between the organization and outside agencies? One person should be designated, as multiple points of contact may result in confusion and an agency getting several differing stories from the organization. The various plans must clearly state which position in the organization will communicate with the outside agency, including their contact details.

Liaison with External Agencies

Assistance with the development of an organization's BCM plans can be gained from most external emergency agencies. Therefore, early liaison with these agencies will enable some of the plans that are under formulation to be integrated with external emergency services. Agencies that could be consulted include, but are not limited to:

- Local and federal police departments.
- Fire and emergency services department.
- Ambulance services.
- Emergency services.
- Local hospital.
- Other nearby organizations (mutual aid scheme).
- Local government.

Public Relations and Media Liaison

BCM plans should incorporate clearly defined plans for responding to the media at times of disruption. The media can be a great assistance or a hindrance to an organization, depending on how they are handled. For this reason, the response team must consider how relations with the media will be managed. Any staff member who may need to liaise with the media needs to be trained and be in an appropriate senior level position with the organization. Information to the media should be approved for release by the response team, in conjunction with the media liaison team. Nevertheless, media communication is often neglected, as according to Woodman and Hutchings (2011, p. 4) only 50% of those with BCM included plans to deal with the media, even when 61% stated that reputational risk is a bigger disruptive risk than financial loss.

A senior corporate executive should be designated as the media liaison spokesperson. Thus, appropriate measures need to ensure that the prompt release of accurate information concerning the incident is made available to the media (in some events, after prior consultation with the police). Refusal to release such information or the slow dissemination of details to the public could result in adverse reporting and confusion, which could lead to subsequent difficulty for the organization.

There should be awareness by the response team and, in particular, the media liaison team, that certain crises will attract far greater media and public attention. The type of crisis that will raise social concerns involve questions such as who is to blame, whether the perpetrators tried to cover up the event, or who was really at fault. Furthermore, human interests that effect children, those who cannot protect themselves, or the underprivileged, and links to high-profile issues, personalities, and sex, will raise the profile of the crisis event. Finally, pictures or video coverage of a crisis event increases the signal value, making the media more interested.

The crisis consequence and likely level of media interest should be considered during the BCM assessment stage and addressed in the treatment plans. Such awareness allows the BCM plans and particularly the communications plans to be far better prepared. Developing appropriate media response to various disruptive risks could be ideally suited to specialist media experts.

Management Succession

Since a crisis can strike at any time, a member of the BCM response team may not always be available. For this reason, arrangements should be made to have personnel delegated to these duties and available at all times. Such access will necessitate the establishment of a "duty roster" or similar callout program. Consequently, complete details such as home address and contact telephone numbers will need to be maintained at some central point, for example, the security control room.

An essential element in management succession is that not only must the delegated official have responsibility for the implementation of the response plan during their "tour of duty," but they must also be given the appropriate authority. Such authority allows that person to take whatever action they deem necessary to promptly activate the plan without losing time seeking approvals.

Medical and Welfare Provisions

The medical welfare of staff and those most affected needs to be given some consideration, dependent on the assessed crisis. Such welfare includes both physical injuries and psychological effects during and after the crisis. Consider aspects such as the capacity of on-site medical and first-aid care, level of first-aid training, alternative routes for emergency services to reach and depart the site, and who can be contacted regarding psychological support and other welfare matters.

Emergency Warning System

Emergency situations need to be communicated to staff within the facility. Such emergency communication should use the existing facility or site emergency warning and intercommunication system (EWIS), which will have fire and life-safety embedded warnings. However, the BCM response team needs to have access as well, or know how to use this system on an ad hoc basis, depending on their communication requirements. The EWIS consists of an electronic system throughout each building that consists of a public address system, sirens, and lights. In addition, all staff must know what action to take in the event of the EWIS being activated.

Self-sufficient Emergency Capability

It must not be assumed that local police, fire department, and ambulance service will be able to help with every emergency. Other emergency commitments may delay their arrival, and if an organization is located in an isolated or remote area, the response time may be lengthy. Consequently, the organization may need to consider being self-sufficient in the areas of firefighting, first-aid, and security, at least until the arrival of emergency services. The establishment of a site fire team, first-aid trained personnel, auxiliary security personnel, and even rescue teams may need to be considered, particularly at industrial and manufacturing facilities.

Emergency Shutdown

In the event of an emergency and a resulting ordered evacuation, it is important that a planned program for the emergency shutdown of equipment is implemented. Otherwise, the continued operation of certain equipment may lead to further complications if left unattended, for example, furnaces, boilers, conveyor belts, and crushing machinery. Furthermore, there should also be consideration for the securing of sensitive or classified material. The responsibility for a systematic shutdown should be assigned in the relevant response plan.

Mutual Aid Scheme

An organization may not have the resources to cope with some disruptive risks without assistance from outside sources, whether these are the emergency services or others within a mutual aid scheme. The cooperative assistance of other organizations is an important element in contributing to the quick recovery of an organization suffering from a crisis in a related industry or locality. Thus, a scheme can be a significant benefit for those operating in partnerships in small or highly specialized industries and in remote or overseas locations. Mutual aid is a formal agreement to provide each other with personnel, equipment, and other resources to assist in the effective handling of certain crises.

Evaluation of BCM Response Plans

Once deployed, response plans should not have their first test in an actual incident. Plans must be evaluated before an actual crisis occurs to identify deficiencies. No matter how well planning is carried out there will be points for improvement, which will only be highlighted during a test. Not only will the evaluation reveal deficiencies and enable them to be rectified before a real event, it will also provide personnel with valuable training and familiarization that they would not otherwise receive. Woodman notes, "Eighty percent of those who had rehearsed their BCM response plans said that the rehearsals had revealed shortcomings" (2007, p. 9).

The evaluation of plans can take a number of approaches and these all need to be used at some time or other. Evaluations could include a desktop review, desktop scenario, notification exercise, callout exercise, or a live scenario exercise (Standards Australia, 2004, p. 26).

- *Desktop review:* Conducted as the initial evaluation of the developed plan and just after deployment. The review involves an evaluation of the plan to ensure that it meets business objectives, treats the disruptive risk, is current from a risk assessment perspective, and provides logical procedures. The benefit of this review is that it is relatively cheap and rapid.
- *Desktop scenario:* Involves a walkthrough of the plan, carried out within a predefined scenario. The review involves a series of questions relating to the deployment of the plan within the scenario. The benefit of this review is that it is cheap to carry out, but provides a greater challenge to the plan and its participants, resulting in greater improvements.
- *Notification exercise:* Involves a predefined and warned verification of the notification parts of the plan, assessing the accuracy, currency, and utility. The benefit of this review is that it is relatively quick and cheap to carry out.

- *Callout exercise:* Involves a verification of the notification parts of the plan, without any warning. The review again assesses the accuracy, currency, and utility of the plan. The benefit of this review is that it challenges relevant personnel and provides a real-time validation of their ability to respond when a plan is activated.
- *Live scenario exercise:* Involves conducting a real-time scenario evaluation of the plan, from activation (callout), personnel response (desktop), to the plan deactivation. The benefit of this review is that it challenges both the plan and relevant personnel within a real-time scenario; however, this evaluation is the most expensive and takes considerable effort.

The approach to evaluation will depend on the organization, and its degree of exposure and appetite to disruptive risks. Nevertheless, all forms of testing allow some degree of evaluation, improvement, and confidence in the plans.

Updating the BCM Plans

In a changing environment, risk management reviews need to be integrated into BCM to ensure that response plans still meet their assessed risk treatment strategy. Furthermore, regular BCM evaluations will not only identify deficiencies and provide training opportunities, but will also indicate where plans are failing to meet expectations. If the plans are not meeting expectations, they will need updating. Examples of such situations are changes in personnel, additions (or deletions) to facility structure, variations in hazards being experienced at a site, and changes in the internal or external threats. Updating the plans is essential if they are to remain as an effective management tool in case of a disruptive risk being realized.

Postincident Review

Regular evaluations and updates will improve the BCM plans, but a true test of any plan is in a realized disruptive risk. After such an event there should be a postincident review that evaluates the response and management of the crisis, considering what worked well and what was not as effective. For example, a successful managed event can lead to improved identification of strengths and weakness in an organization, provide indices that could signal future crises, facilitate learning, improve organizational moral and teamwork, allow objective and specific reviews of the event, support proposals for additional resources, and demonstrate that the response plan was effective in maintaining the critical business objectives of the organization. Furthermore, improved organizational and consumer confidence can be gained, raising the resilience of the organization, whereas an unsuccessful crisis may lead to loss of staff, loss of information, reduced business, and, eventually, bankruptcy.

SECURITY AND BCM

Security has traditionally taken an emergency and crisis approach with security management, for example, managing IED or fire evacuation plans. These response plans still need to remain important; however, security has to take a greater corporate leadership role. A security manager can either be the owner of the BCM function or a stakeholder. As a stakeholder, the security manager will be involved in the BCM committee, take part in assessment workshops, and write his or her own security-related response plans. However, as the facilitator, the security department should be the corporate leader for BCM, value adding to the security function.

Security currently has an involvement in BCM, but this could be greater. For example, within U.K. corporations the IT function (65%) is the most significant stakeholder in BCM, followed by facility management (57%), human resources (56%), risk management (53%), finance (52%), and then security (45%) (Woodman, 2007, p. 7). Such level of involvement should be increased, as security is ideally suited to provide such a function.

Security's role will depend on the crisis, but responsibilities may include:

- Activate steps to ensure the safety and security of life, information, property, and other assets.
- Activate and operate the Emergency Control Centre.
- Maintain the emergency information log.
- Deploy security personnel to predesignated locations, such as control of access points.
- Source and deploy resources to respond to the crisis.
- Maintain contact information for employees, expert consultants, vendors, and suppliers.
- Brief internal and supporting staff on the crisis.
- Communication with and support external agencies.

Nevertheless, security should take a far more strategic role in the management, application, and ownership of corporate-wide BCM.

CONCLUSION

Business continuity management provides an organization with a function and processes to maintain its critical business objectives during and after a disruptive risk. A disruptive risk may be a crisis, disaster, or natural event that affects either the organization or their external operating environment. Such events may have a significant impact on many parts of the critical business process, capability, or output for an extended period of time, beyond the normal capacity of management. Nevertheless, a crisis may be defined as a critical stage or turning point in a sequence of events, which can lead to significant loss or, alternatively, an opportunity.

Most crises will comprise of four phases, namely the prodrome or warning phase, the acute or damaging phase, the chronic phase that leads to death or recovery, and, finally, the recovery phase. These phases integrate into the disruptive risk timeline, highlighting the degree of management activities and the various BCM response plans that are activated along the disruptive timeline. BCM is made up of four distinct response plans that, at a broader level, comprise of emergency, continuity, recovery, and restoration plans.

The BCM framework provides a structured approach to assess the need for each response plan. Thus, assessment uses inputs from the risk management process, supported by BCM-specific tools such as a critical business assessment and business impact assessment. The business impact assessment, like risk assessment, formulates a ranked scale using either financial or implicit impact, the likelihood of the event, and a defined period of failure.

When BCM is applied, there are many common elements. These elements include the appointment of a BCM manager or project team; designating appropriate authority; a concise chain of command for each response; addressing the need for facilities, resources, and financial support; training the response teams; and communication and liaison. Furthermore, aspects such as management succession, ability to be self-sufficient, evaluating the response plans, and updating BCM to reduce response delay needs consideration. It is important that without risk assessment reviews, evaluations, and maintenance, plans are likely to decay.

BCM is generally applied in an organization due to a number of corporate drivers such as governance and compliance; the need to mitigate a disruptive risk; and customer, regulator, or insurer requirements. Nevertheless, BCM does provide an organization with a number of benefits in stabilizing disruptive incidents, ensuring continuity of operations, improving sustainability and business performance, providing the ability to capitalize on events, better prediction of future crises, and increased resilience. Security should be the organizational facilitator or, at least, a significant stakeholder in the BCM process.

Further Reading

International Organization for Standardization, 2007. ISO/PAS 22399:2007 Societal Security—Guideline for Incident Preparedness and Operational Continuity Management. International Organization for Standardization, Geneva.

Websites

Business Continuity Institute, http://www.thebci.org/.
Charted Management Institute's Annual Business Continuity Management Surveys, http://www.managers.org.uk/.
U.K. Cabinet Office, National Security Community Resilience Resources and Tools, http://www.cabinetoffice.gov.uk/content/community-resilience.

References

Angus and Roberston, 1992. Dictionary and Thesaurus. HarperCollins, Sydney.
Standards Australia, 2004. HB 221: Business Continuity Planning. Standards Australia International Ltd, Sydney.
Standards Australia, 2006. HB 293:2006: Executive Guide to Business Continuity Management. Standards Australia International Ltd, Sydney.
Standards Australia, 2010. AS/NZS 5050: 2010 Business Continuity: Managing Disruption-related Risk. Standards Australia International Ltd, Sydney.
Walsh, T.J., Healy, R.J., 2004. Protection of Assets: Introduction to Assets Protection. ASIS International, Alexandria, VA.
Woodman, P., 2007. Business Continuity Management: The 2007 Business Continuity Management Survey. Chartered Management Institute, London.
Woodman, P., Hutchings, P., 2011. Managing Threats in a Dangerours World: The 2011 Business Continuity Management Survey. Chartered Management Institute, London.

CHAPTER

10

The Future of Security

OBJECTIVES

- Understand how the processes of security can be applied as a predictive strategy for security planning.

- Understand that futures studies seek to determine the likelihood of future events and trends for the protection of assets.

- Be aware that a range of alternative futures are achievable according to the current trajectory of the concepts, principles, and theories as portrayed by trends and predictions.

- Realize that wild-card predictions for the future are a low probability and potentially high-impact risk that have the capacity to change the direction of a well-established and stable trend.

- Be aware that future technology will see the greater use of mobile devices and telecommunications for ease of connectivity.

- Be aware that future technology will witness artifical intelligence, and smart and multifunctional sensors in smart facility automation.

- Realize that alternative futures of intelligence can be considered to challenge current assumptions and strategies in the protection of assets.

- Understand that alternative futures of intelligence in security will indicate the need for change to address the expected new types and levels of threats to organizations.

- Realize that higher educational standards will be required for security to be considered as a profession in the future.

- Understand that managerial strategies applied to security in the future will emphasize the need for professional education of participants.

INTRODUCTION

Security science is presently being considered as an emerging discipline that can be founded on logic and applied as a rigorous set of ideas that have been tested and modified to strengthen the outcomes of the protection of assets. An understanding of the concepts and principles of security science will permit the development of theories of security being

Security Science – The Theory and Practice of Security
http://dx.doi.org/10.1016/B978-0-12-394436-8.00010-2

analogous to the theories of the formal sciences. By understanding the processes and outcomes of security through theories that have been applied and tested, it will be possible to use the theories of security as predictive tools for applications of the protection of assets. The development and application of the scientific method that was discussed in Chapter 1 provides an indication of the power of the predictive capacity of logical thought to further enhance the development of the discipline of security science. In this manner, the logical structure of the discipline of security is assured and security science will be properly considered as a suitable body of knowledge to be applied to the protection of people, information, and material assets.

Acknowledging that security is currently on an upsurge in terms of effectiveness and development, consideration will be given to short-, medium-, and long-term directions for security in the protection of assets. By considering the future objectives of security science, better decisions for forward planning of major security projects and functions will be possible for national infrastructure ventures. What are the future directions of security science or organizational security? What are the new emerging ideas and practices for security? What are the important factors that may affect future national security? Medium- to long-term planning of the security function in the national context will enhance the effectiveness and efficiency of the management of security for national infrastructure, the commercial and financial industry, and the communities in which we reside.

This chapter will postulate on the future of security science in such areas as a developing discipline, increasing legislation and state control, greater professionalism, amalgamation of domains of security (IT and physical security), security management, security intelligence, and security technology. The future development of security theories and security education will enhance the professional capacity of the industry and determine a more secure environment for governments, organizations, and communities.

The security industry has had significant growth in all areas of applications and practice, and this trend is expected to continue. National security and homeland security will continue to have greater significance and their reliance on organizational security will grow, ensuring better integration of these two security practice areas. However, unless the business of security with its many industry associations can improve practice and develop professionalism, growth will be restricted through state control. Other practicing areas such as aviation and maritime security will continue to expand, requiring further specialization to some degree by organizational security practitioners. In addition, some consideration to the ongoing debate of public and private security will be presented.

Security technology will continue to drive security, with areas such as intelligent surveillance gaining greater importance in the industry. Greater use of computing power, wireless connectivity, software design and simulation, software-driven systems, system integration, and nanotechnology will be considered.

BACKGROUND

Trends and predictions in the future progress of security science will necessarily be considered in terms of its past, with forward projections on what might be *possible*, *probable*, and *preferable*, and *wild-card* futures. These types of trends and predictions are considered by *futures studies*, which seek to understand what is likely to continue, what is likely to change, and what is novel. As a result, futures studies seek a systematic and pattern-based understanding of past and present, and seek to determine the likelihood of future events and trends. Futures studies generally are not concerned with short timelines of several years, but rather decades of time to anticipate trends far beyond the business cycle. It is interesting to note that plans and strategies with longer time horizons to be robust to possible future events have been described as *strategic foresight*.

Also, futures studies attempts to gain a world view of the domain with contributions from a range of related disciplines. That is, it seeks to gain a holistic or systemic view of the issues from a broad contribution of associated content spheres. Again, futures studies challenge and dissemble the assumptions that underlie dominant views of the future. As a consequence, the future has underlying assumptions associated with it even though the future has not yet been realized. For example, many predictions of the future of international warfare over the Earth's freshwater supplies are made with analyses of such scenarios, without due consideration of the deep-seated assumptions of such views. That is, with global warming there may be future enhanced rainfall in what are currently drought-affected areas.

Predictability of some domains of knowledge is extremely accurate, with aspects of science such as planetary motion being exceptionally predictable, with future astronomical events most accurately prophesied far into the future. However, it should be considered that much of scientific prediction is neither accurate nor rigorous due to the statistical nature of the behavior of the objects being observed. Thus, science theories such as chaos theory, quantum theory, nonlinear science, and entropy studies all have a random component that necessitates a statistical description of the behavior. As a consequence within the futures studies domain of understanding, there is conflict between predictability and unpredictability of future events. On one hand, it is argued that the future is unpredictable, and can only be predicted by *creating* it. The alternate argument is that probability and modeling of known parameters will allow us to better understand probable futures. However, the complexity of natural systems usually ensures that the modeling of these extensive systems becomes too difficult for meaningful outcomes, and rather only smaller components of large systems can be considered.

The domain of futures studies is drawn from the traditional disciplines, such as economics, sociology, history, mathematics, psychology, and astronomy, and models and methodologies from these knowledge bases are applied in trend and predictive projections. The concept of alternative futures is an attribute of futures studies where prediction can produce a number of possible trends and scenarios that are both stable and rigorous in the outcomes. This approach involves the collection of quantitative and qualitative data about the possibility, the probability, and the desirability of change. Thus, a range of alternative futures are achievable according to the current trajectory of the concepts, principles, and theories as portrayed by the data gathered for trends and predictions. Futures predictions have been derived from extrapolating current technological, economic, or social trends, and recent approaches have included social systems with built-in uncertainties to generate futures scenarios. It is interesting to note that the scientific method is only used sparingly, as repeated and controlled measures are difficult to manage in the quest for better trends and predictions.

The prediction of the future is a worthwhile practice for well-recognized organizations to plan projected scenarios beyond the business cycle. Such areas for medium- and long-term planning could, for example, include population growth, resources depletion, business projection growth, international strategic stability, and city planning. Techniques for predicting the future have been adopted from traditional research methodologies, and could include:

- Causal layered analysis (CLA).
- Delphi method.
- Technology road mapping.
- Simulation and modeling.
- Trend analysis.
- Morphological analysis.

The development of alternative futures scenarios is an important technique to be applied in the quest for trends. People who work within a particular domain of knowledge will have the capacity to consider probable or desirable futures either using qualitative or quantitative methodologies. By examining the range of alternative outcomes for futures, it may be possible to shape the future rather than to just predict it. That is, by scenario testing it may be possible to reduce the range of scenarios and therefore determine a small subset of scenarios that have reasonable reliability and validity associated with them. Thus, potential outcomes may be predicted through an organized and rational approach that allows long-term decisions to be made to shape the future. The practices of *horizon scanning* and *emerging issues analysis* have contributed to better predictability in organizations, and are able to contribute to the risk management strategy of an organization. Almost all businesses (successful and unsuccessful) engage in some form of future prediction, through research and development programs, innovation and marketing research, product development, and competitor progress in the business field.

The occurrence of a *wild-card prediction* for futures is a low probability and potentially high-impact risk that has the capacity to change the direction of a well-established and stable trend in the development of a future. These sudden and unique incidents can cause turning points in the development or evolution of a particular trend. The concept of wild-card events in a development trend has the capability to change or redirect the future as previously described by the predictive trend. Thus, trends have the ability to become mainstream when a sufficient population integrates the ideas of an innovation, project, belief, or action into their daily lives.

Where Is Security Heading?

The protection of assets through the application of organizational security will continue to be an important component of the national, corporate, and community structures and applications for the people of an entity. For the midterm forecasting of the safety and protection of the people, information, and materials of these structures, the need for organizational security will be required.

However, with these requirements in mind, what is the future of organizational security? Perhaps it is thought that security will become better understood, with articulation between the many facets of our current understanding of security. As a consequence, such changes will better equip security professionals in their operational environment, through education and understanding, superior technology to enhance protection, improved management and procedures, better knowledge and intelligence of crime, and executive placement within an organization's management structures. The ability to support mitigation strategies and certain decisions are made through a foundation of science. These many faceted components of change will each take their own discrete development path and so transformations in these aspects may, through appropriate stewardship, enhance the profession, or through poor leadership and management, may condemn security to remain a low-level activity with reduced status and inadequate commitment.

For positive change to take place the future development of security science may need to address a range of components within the domain of the knowledge structures that describe the discipline. However, on a universal view of the future, it is interesting to note that Richard Watson (2008) proposes five major trends for the next 50 years:

1. Ageing and the associated issues.
2. Global connectivity and its impact on communities.
3. The GRIN technologies of genetics, robotics, Internet, and nanotechnology.
4. The environment and its impact on the quality of living.
5. The power shift eastward toward China and India.

While these major trends will be umbrella paradigms for the development of security in the protection of assets, more directed trends can be anticipated for the future of security science:

1. Greater responsibilities for private organizations in areas of ethical dealings.
2. Ever-increasing application of technology to mitigate risks and threats.
3. Increasing technology convergence with areas such as communications, security technology, and information technology and building control systems.
4. Greater corporate understanding of their responsibilities, as has been demonstrated in other discipline areas such as environmental responsibilities and workplace safety.
5. Greater focus on compliance, driven by increasing legislation, social expectations, and self-regulation by the industry.
6. Increase in educational levels across the sector to enhance professionalism of the industry.

The future of security will be dependent on the ability of the industry to address current deficiencies in knowledge, structure, organization, management, and therefore status, and be able to set the trends in directions to enhance the relevant levels of knowledge and understanding for the protection of assets in the future world. As always, the concept of risk plays an important role in setting the future directions for the facets of security, so that a better understanding of risk will enable the trends to be better controlled.

SECURITY IN THE FUTURE

The difficulty in predicting the future is that the outcomes are unreliable, due to the occurrence of *wild-card* events that distort the relatively well-understand trends for the near to mid-future. The greater the predictive leap into the future, the less reliable the outcomes of the trends. However, notwithstanding this severe limitation, an attempt will be made to initiate some discussion on the possible futures of some components of the security domain, to promote knowledge and understanding of security, and leadership in the next generation of security professionals to better serve the needs of nations and communities.

A number of issues for the future of security will be presented to stimulate discussion and assist in the identification of trends for the future. Of the various components of the discipline of security, security technology is both the easiest to predict, and the most difficult to predict: the easiest to predict because of the well-understood evolution of the science and engineering that underlies the applications of devices in security; the most difficult to predict because of the regular occurrences of wild-card discoveries in science and applications of the science in the form of technologies. Also, the futures of a selection of other important components for the security function will be presented, including social, human, management, and intelligence elements.

Futures of Security Technologies

The futures of security technology will be considered with the intent to provide an assessment level of developing and changing technologies likely to be applied in asset protection in the next several decades. The discussion should provide some understanding of potential and developing threats and vulnerabilities of security technologies, through the greater understanding of risk and the application of current and progressing technologies that have yet to be adopted by the security industry. Futures will consider the greater use of mobile devices and telecommunications for ease of connectivity, plug-and-play to facilitate connectivity, single design approach, artifical intelligence, smart and multifunctional sensors, maintenance of such complex systems, and increasing smart facility automation.

The evolution of technology from restricted miltiary development through commercialization, and eventually to commoditization, provides a constant source of fresh technology to community applications. For example, global positioning systems (GPSs), which were once the domain of restricted military applications, now have application in common devices such as mobile phones and cameras. The develpoment of command and control and *forward-looking infrared* technologies in cameras support the idea that defense technologies will continue to enhance the future of security technologies for the community.

Defense Technologies as a Future Indicator

As a consequence, military technology has provided a two-decade indicator of emerging security technology. For example, during the last decade the military focus on battlefield command and control for the individual soldier provided an overview of the current and changing environment. Such command-and-control technologies employ individual controls, multichannel communications, and visual mapping systems to provide real-time battlefield awareness. Such command-and-control functionality can be translated into the future for use by security guards for the protection of assets. Thus, security guards can continually receive detection and surveillance data on a real-time basis, reducing the need for dedicated control room staff. Such technology is already available in mobile devices and to access CCTV cameras, remote alarm assessment, and access control systems.

Therefore, future security control systems will support the user, by providing user-friendly information for direct application for the protection of assets. A modest example is the application of grayscale display screens that are more comfortable to view, but convert to a red color when a detector goes into an alarm state, or another color for other crucial information relevant to the security of an organization.

Mobile Devices

It is expected that in the near to mid-future the use of many mobile technologies will be applied to allow greater communications, interconnectivity, and flexibility of many devices, and security will not be exempt. For example, greater device mobility will be incorporated into static security devices such as cameras, detectors, and the like, using open communication protocols. As the expense of hardwiring sensors into systems can amount to a sizable proportion of a security budget, it is expected that in the near future wireless will totally replace existing wired solutions due to their advantages of network convergence, reduced costs, mobility, flexibility, and convenience. Such connectivity will lead to new and emerging system vulnerabilities that are just beginning to eventuate, but will grow in the near term to midterms.

Smart Phones

The access control industry will soon be adopting near field communications (NFC) as a means of addressing tokens and IDs for security control locations. It will be possible to create, apply, and manage secure ID on NFC-enabled smart phones, where a single device can provide physical access to a home, a workplace, corporate PCs, and the corporate network. Future functions of NFC smart phones can be:

- On-demand credential providers for high-security access.
- The provision of mobile keys for multiple functions to access secure doors, computers, and networks.
- The provision of smart tokens, therefore eliminating the need for other devices for secure access.
- Access to home and other authorized facilities with mobile keys for NFC-enabled locks.

Future Data Access

The rapid increase in mobile professional workers has prompted increasing data security concerns, as a majority of companies neglect to encrypt and back up sensitive data. Also, since remote-access software allows users to run applications from office PCs, employees need not store critical data on removable devices with remote-access programs designed for smart phones and tablets. As online storage is the most secure method of remote backup, the advantages to cloud storage are manifold, and they include minimizing the risks associated with viruses, data theft, and lost devices. Nevertheless, where actual data are stored, how, and in what format they are moved may lead to vulnerabilities that will need consideration.

Robotic Devices

A robot is a mechanical device that has some level of virtual intelligence to perform tasks according to instructions or remote control. Some robots have a human form for performing tasks; however, the great majority of robots are machines that are designed to best perform the task for which they were intended. Robots are being employed in a range of tasks, including industry, defense, serving, manufacturing, and landscape development. They are used to perform tasks in the place of humans because of:

- Dangerous and unpleasant locations such as in nuclear reactors.
- Warfare on land, in the air, and underwater.
- Too expensive to employ humans.
- Highly repetitive jobs such as in the manufacture of vehicles.

Robots engaged in the protection of assets will be involved in both dangerous and repetitive tasks that are unsuitable for humans. Such tasks as perimeter barrier patrolling, explosives neutralizing, smart airport baggage examination, virtual management of major defense-in-depth strategies for national infrastructure, and intelligent imaging of people for recognition in large facilities, are appropriate for intelligent mechanical devices. The future for robotics in security is strong, and is expected to exponentially increase in applications over the next few decades.

Unmanned aerial vehicles (UAVs) or automated drones have become common place in the military environment, extending into border surveillance and law enforcement. It is highly likely that within the short term, organizational security will be using such devices in the protection of critical infrastructure such as oil and gas facilities, off-shore platforms and other remote location facilities. These systems will be able to provide automated patrols, response, and surveillance of large and multiple sites over large areas.

The emerging technology of nanorobotics, which engineers machines or robots of which the components are in the scale of nanometers (10^{-9} meters), have future potential for security and asset protection. These robots are designed and built from molecular combinations, and have specific tasks to fix components in usually much larger systems. Nanomachines are still very much in the research and development stage, and are expected to mature as applications over the next two decades. It is expected that nanomachines will be initially applied to medical technology for the identification and destruction of anomalous cells such as cancer. Nanorobots will also be applied to the detection of toxic materials in systems and in the environment. Applications of nanomachines to security may take the form of the molecular robots being active in explosive detection and neutralization, identification of materials and components in security systems, the identification of prohibited substances, and the tagging of items, materials, and substances.

Control Applications

Monitoring and control applications will increase as the expectation of very cheap wireless sensors become available for portable detectors. It is expected that technological advancement is achieved when the cost of the battery is the single largest cost item of a wireless device. And beyond this achievement will be when the battery may be replaceable by ambient power–scavenging devices that will remove the need for a traditional disposable battery. A self-powered sensor device creates the ability for new measurement applications—for example, sensors could be fully embedded in building surfaces to monitor persons and activities. These devices can measure properties in the host material that currently cannot be accessed easily or continuously by external measurement probes. Thus, a mass of self-powered sensors embedded into material will also act as a physical barrier to resist penetration.

Facility Plant and Equipment

As well as the sensor system applied to barriers for the protection of assets, the sensor system will also be applied to monitoring plant and equipment for the diagnosis of early plant failure and degradation of energy efficiency. Present research and technology development focuses on maximizing the energy extraction of mechanical energy by adaptive techniques that sense and adjust to a given vibration frequency and amplitude to maximize power. That is, the search for different ambient sources for the extraction of electric power will greatly increase the efficiency of power consumption in the energy system. For example, mechanical vibration can be converted to electric power by induction, piezo-electric materials can generate a potential voltage when mechanically strained, and thermo-electrical power generators will use the Seabeck effect, commonly used in thermocouple probes for temperature measurements when a temperature differential of a few degrees Celsius can generate power in the microwatt range. These energy-scavenging strategies will enable sensor networks for security and plant monitoring to be self-sufficient in standalone systems.

Integrated and Intelligent Systems

Intelligent buildings that have been developed from current building management systems, and energy management systems will in the near to mid-future result in a single integrated system that monitors, controls, and manages all functional systems within a facility, site, or city block. For example, the ability to share car parking, building energy, and pedestrian access ways will allow a city block to provide a far safer environment for its occupants. The ability to provide intelligence feedback into such systems removes the need for staffing and allows a far more reactive building, as it responds to the internal and external environments. Nevertheless, such dynamic control introduces potential and developing threats and vulnerabilities. These issues include the greater use of wireless devices and telecommunications for ease of connectivity, greater and increasingly open architecture, extended system communications, and artificial intelligence. As a consequence, many of these issues are addressed in later sections.

Smart Sensors

Future sensors will gain more intelligence in their function within a system to detect the presence of persons and protect the assets of an organization. The near future will witness the ability of single sensors to perform multiple functions for security and financial benefits. For example, a passive infrared detector can be applied to the detection of unauthorized intruders, and also as an energy-efficiency measure controlling air conditioning and lighting to an area. Such a system could also be used to count the number of people who pass a given control point. However, such functionality may have some vulnerabilities, and so careful sensor design will be needed to ensure that the security function is not compromised. That is, both integration and interaction within the sensor network, and the optimum locations of the sensors, will need to be considered. The issues of unwanted and false alarms are always a consideration, and so system design is paramount to avoid reducing the effectiveness of the security function. Again, in the near future an example of a multi-use single sensor can be a florescent lamp also functioning as a detector, using the electromagnetic field of the tube as a capacitance sensor, and with minor modification can be used as a metal and dangerous goods detector in public places. Nevertheless, the future development of artificial intelligence for better discrimination of detection signals among much noise will be the single-most effective advancement in sensor technology.

Future designs of sensor systems will readily accept additional devices and are driven through a need for less technical expertise on a particular system. These future designed *plug-and-play* systems to readily accommodate the integration of a variety of sensors and still maintain compatibility will greatly enhance the effectiveness of the security detection strategy. As a corollary to the plug-and-play approach, manufactures will design many functions into a single device, which can be activated according to the service level required by the client. Such devices will be suitable for the international market with manual or toggle switches manipulated to achieve the required performance of the device.

Application of IP

As the Internet becomes a strong communications platform, *Internet protocols* (IPs) provide flexibility of dial-up capability to control and monitor devices anywhere in the world, and it is possible to make fine performance adjustments and conduct fault diagnosis. Thus, with limited infrastructure outlay, remote facilities can be efficiently monitored and controlled in a cost-effective manner. The future can expect great expansion in the application of the Internet for effective connectivity via remote control and automation of entire security protection systems. However, vulnerabilities can be expected within the context of applying IP, as third-party data networks may not be reliable against extraneous attack. Other issues, such as the quality of the public infrastructure, network routing, and software firewalls, will need to be considered with future development of Internet connectivity for security device control.

We may expect that all items will eventually have an IP embedded into their electronics, suggesting that every item in the office and home will be networked and connected. For example, currently items such as mobile phones, tablets, and gaming consoles are now commonly connected with interactivity encouraged by the manufacturers. Also white goods, such as refrigerators, are becoming network-connected, as there are usable benefits achieved by such connectivity. For example, monitoring the contents of the refrigerator allows for deficiencies to be identified and self-ordering systems can replace items when low or out of shelf-life. These integrated systems will add convenience for the user and a business opportunity for the retailers. It is not such an extension to consider that brown goods, such as kettles, irons, and household devices, will also have connectivity, much like televisions and other media devices.

Cloud Computing

The National Institute of Standards and Technology (NIST) describes *cloud computing* as

"Cloud computing is a model for enabling ubiquitous, convenient, on-demand network access to a shared pool of configurable computing resources (eg., networks, servers, storage, applications, and services) that can be rapidly provisioned and released with minimum management effort or service provider interaction." (Mell and Grance, 2011).

Thus, cloud computing provides computation, software, data access, and storage services that do not require end-user knowledge of the physical location and system configuration. This development in computer data storage has provided a windfall for system users since they do not require extensive computer training and knowledge. Therefore, the application of cloud computing will continue to increase in use, but most corporations also will continue to use a mix of data modes for effective control. These modes will include traditional computing, virtualized data centers, private cloud, and public cloud, therefore requiring a mix of on-premises security and cloud-based security.

Also it is expected that security technology vendors will have to add cloud-based delivery to their service offerings, and will have to make investments in both cloud-based infrastructure and developing technology that can scale and adapt to a threat and its criticality. The reliability of web-based networking is a limiting factor of any cloud-based offering and there has to be an investment in load balancing, denial-of-service protection, redundancy, and other function areas to ensure necessary service levels. The testing and certification of security solutions will need to be enhanced in the future with the increase in complexity of systems.

Whole of Spectrum Detection

The extension of sensing technologies into the whole of spectrum detection, including an extended range of electromagnetic frequencies and acoustic frequencies, will greatly contribute to the reliability and validity of these devices in the detection of intruders. By operating detection systems in dual- or multiple-spectrum frequencies, the likelihood of detection is increased and the probability of interference is reduced. The trend for detection technologies appears to support the whole of spectrum detection to counter attempts to corrupt visible light detection technologies.

An advanced approach to *video motion detection* (VMD) of intruders on a large site is the *advanced exterior sensor* (AES) system, which is shown in Figure 10.1 where the three sensor technologies of thermal infrared imaging, visible light imaging, and microwave radar are integrated into a system (Ashby and Pritchard, 2004). The AES scans a full rotation in about a second and provides images of each sensor technology after each rotation (Figure 10.2). In the near to long term, the whole of spectrum detectors will become integrated solid-state devices, making them smaller, cheaper, and commercially available.

Using different combinations of sensor frequencies, this system has the future capability to be applied at airport runways, oil refineries and gas facilities, and other infrastructure locations where large open areas are present.

Laser scanning systems will play an important role in future intrusion detection systems, where multiple lasers with a range of wavelengths will have the capability of locating and analyzing the movements and presence of adversaries (Figure 10.3). Unlike current

FIGURE 10.1   AES with three sensor technologies of thermal infrared imaging, visible light imaging, and microwave radar are integrated into a system. *(Reprinted from Pritchard, 2004.)*

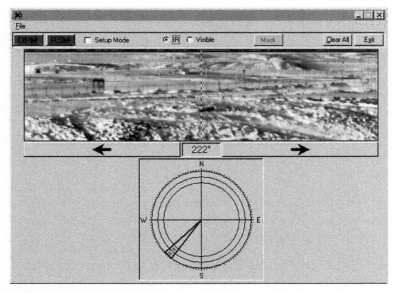

FIGURE 10.2   AES output images in thermal infrared and microwave radar frequencies. *(Reprinted from Ashby and Pritchard, 2004.)*

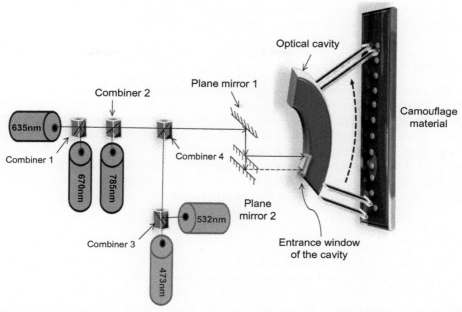

FIGURE 10.3 Schematic representation of a multilaser intrusion detection system with multiple beam divergence from an optical cavity. *(Reprinted from Venkataraayan, 2012.)*

mechanical laser scanning systems, near- to mid-term detectors will be solid-state with no moving parts. Reflected radiation from the intruder will provide (Venkataraayan et al., 2012):

- Location, speed, and direction of movement of the person.
- Analysis of fabric being worn by the person.
- Detect the presence of metals being carried.
- Skin tone.

Future *smart intrusion detection systems* will integrate with biometric methodologies to detect, recognize, and perhaps identify the individuals as intruders. Thus, systems that are based on imaging and photonics will become indistinguishable from each other as integration between previously discrete systems will be produced.

High-Frequency Security Cameras

The recent development of cryogen-free terahertz (THz) security cameras operating at EM frequencies below 1 THz allows imaging of objects such as weapons and explosives that are hidden from view. Previously, these systems required superconducting elements within the camera to reduce the electronic thermal noise that interferes with high-frequency images. This leading-edge technology will develop in the next decade to better detect hidden objects on people and in locations, and also will have the ability to determine an object's chemical composition at a distance. THz radiation is absorbed and emitted by many organic compounds such as explosives and drugs and will be able to be detected by THz security cameras. As such, these detection sensors will become an important technology in the security domain.

Acoustic Surveillance Sensors

A range of acoustic surveillance technologies have become available for police services and military to locate sound sources and gunfire. Wide-area acoustic surveillance is achieved through the positioning of acoustic sensors throughout a coverage area of typically 25 square kilometers. Sensors are matched to audio analysis software that identifies and locates the unique signature of gunshots and other loud explosive sounds in real time. The development of acoustic ID location systems will have considerable impact on future applications in security technology through ID of vehicles approaching barriers, physical attacks on barriers, and the acoustic surveillance of intruders into secure facilities.

Smart Barriers

The defense-in-depth principle uses layers of barriers in a physical security design to restrict access to the major assets of an organization. The purpose of a barrier is to prevent the penetration of an area by intruders. However, as barriers can be defeated with sufficient time and resources, then the purpose of a barrier is to delay the progress of the intrusion sufficiently for a response team to intercede and apprehend the intruders. Barriers can be located at the perimeter as a fence or wall, or located in the interior of a facility as a wall, door lock, or a safe door and lock. Although intrusion may occur by accident, penetration of the physical barriers by force or stealth is disastrous for the physical security design. Thus, strategies need to be devised to enable physical barriers in a protection-of-assets approach to become more intelligent in delaying the progress of an intruder through areas being protected.

The future of smart barriers has commenced with a variety of detection technologies incorporated into the fabric or materials of the barriers to detect when and where the barrier is under attack. However, it is expected that in the near term, serious integration of a range of other technologies will be integrated into barriers to deter and delay progress through the facility. Such integrating technologies could include:

- Enhanced deterrence technologies such as strobe lighting, klaxon alarms, and early encounter imaging systems.
- Fight-back technologies such as electrified strands in a fence, capsicum spray or other irritant substances to retard people, sticky substances to delay intruders, anti-climb surfaces, and the direction of water and other liquids onto the attack region.
- Intelligent fabric in the barriers that will offer passive resistance to penetration but can self-repair, sense an intrusion attack and fold onto the attacker, and flexible fabrics that can collapse and delay climbing.
- Sense the presence of individuals while approaching the barrier to enhance the strength of the barrier at that location.

Currently, the quality of a barrier is determined by the strength of materials from which it is constructed. In the near to mid-future it is expected that the materials of barriers will be extended from those of metals and concrete to plastics and composite materials, which will be both tough and compliant to enhancement. The smart barriers will provide much more assistance to a security manager through greater delay times, and earlier and more accurate warnings of an intrusion attack.

Enhanced Algorithms

There has been a significant progression in the ability of software and hardware designers to implement *smart* algorithms. Such algorithms have been in both development and application for many years, but the efficacy of these systems has improved over the last few years. Combined with improving hardware using technology such as photonics, these algorithms and their ability to operate in the real world are highly likely to significantly improve and become far more commonplace in security technologies.

By combining artificial intelligence (AI) decision-making techniques with data-intensive applications such as automated video surveillance leads to a number of benefits, in particular, as they begin to be effective in application. Thus, image-based systems will benefit from improved learning systems that will evolve over the next decade. Unlike the human operator, past automated surveillance systems had limited or virtually no ability to assess the field-of-view context. Therefore, enhanced algorithms will promote better decision-making techniques in terms of context and remove the past limitations of such AI systems.

Again, a current system under laboratory development has the ability to detect a person's pulse through his or her skin using a remote camera. Researchers at MIT have developed the video processing software that identifies tiny changes, such as a person's breathing or blood flow, from a few frames (Franzen, 2012). This technology has the capacity to analyze a person's vital functions, and determine whether he or she is under stress, as well as other biometric data such as facial recognition and personal characteristics.

FUTURE OF INTELLIGENCE

Security intelligence is intended to provide a relative security advantage by better protecting the assets of an organization. That is, intelligence provides the knowledge about adversaries and their attack methods, which will allow planning to neutralize the effect of their imposition on the organization. The security manager will be better prepared to design and develop security planning for the entity. In terms of security, the intelligence cycle is the process by which information about threats to an organization is gathered and assessed, to determine the likelihood that it will eventuate (Chapter 8). The intelligence cycle is a process by which information is gathered, analyzed, and activated to remove or reduce the threat level to the organization's assets.

Futures in Intelligence

However, alternative futures of intelligence can be considered to challenge current assumptions and strategies in the intelligence domain. Futures in intelligence can be considered in several aspects according to themes that present appropriate approaches in the next decade. Themes to consider for modified approaches to intelligence are:

- Threat Complexity.
- Human Resources.
- Organizational change.
- Systems development.
- Methodologies.

Threat Complexity

The threat environment is thought to become more complex in terms of the number of near-term tangible threats and mid- to long-term less tangible threats. That is, threat is expected to become more difficult to manage in the future due to many negative driving forces in the natural environment. The management of threat would become more demanding in the future with tangible and intangible threats both impacting on national and corporate security. It may be that a growing threat complexity may impede an intelligence and security function only focused on the current environment. That is, intelligence and security functions suffering from policy inertia and strategic drag can be expected to cascade down to mediocrity.

Human Resources

Human generation change over the next decade is expected to contribute to both management and operational changes. As current managers leave the industry and current operators promote to management, it is expected that different generational management styles will be imposed on the intelligence domain. Because intelligence is considered as a people-business, the quality of the management and operations depend entirely on the training and style of engagement of the generational changes in the people involved. Claims have been made that the future generation of managers and operators have diminished institutional loyalty and reduced respect for corporate knowledge.

Organizational Change

The need for future change in organizational structures will result from a long engagement with slow-moving systematic threats. That is, adaptive organizations will need to overcome institutional inertia for effective intelligence response to be achieved. Unfortunately, a reaction to the problem has been an increase in the numbers of intelligence staff, which resulted in a lack of shared understanding of the role of intelligence. This effect has contributed to a lack of effectiveness of community-wide intelligence capability development. Future changes could witness new organizational structures with some core functions being outsourced to the private sector and higher education facilities. Other organizational structures may emerge that permit intelligence analysts to self-organize through knowledge management models that satisfy the need for vitality and enthusiasm.

Systems Development

Current intelligence systems have a lack of connectivity and both logic and administrative impositions on information flows and wider collaboration. The future of the development of intelligence systems will require explicit future-proofing of systems, which can only be achieved at considerable expense and commitment. Therefore, technological innovation and the desire for free-flowing information would be expected to weaken well-established information security protocols. It would be expected that larger, perhaps national, information networks will become available for interrogation of data to produce intelligence for organizations. Thus, computer-assisted analysis, as the major technology driver, will complement human analysis of data in the production of intelligence.

Methodologies

An expectation of new theories of practice and types of analyses will be developed for analysts to apply in the production of intelligence. As intangible targets become more pervasive, the need for smarter, more efficient processes and techniques for intelligence production will be obligatory. The new threat environment will need practice and analysis incorporated from newer domains of decision science, network theory, and knowledge management. It is expected that as intelligence becomes more pervasive in society, then the community will exhibit a more risk-averse behavior. That is, the prominence of intelligence in the community may produce a societal attitude of a reduced awareness of security risk. Such an outcome may cause an enhanced vulnerability to crime in the community, and require increased law enforcement.

Alternative Futures

Alternative futures of intelligence can be postulated according to the foreseeable trends that are available for consideration in the time frame available. Thus, future scenarios can be postulated according to the possible environments for an organization determined by its development trends. However, the range of scenarios is produced by the certainty (or uncertainty) of the variables that will generate the alternative futures. The study of alternative futures allows us to examine and challenge the assumptions about plausible future developments. The scenarios attempt to address the rhetoric questions of:

- Where will intelligence be in a decade?
- How are we going to get there?
- Who will be involved?
- What have we learned from the past?

Peppler (2006) reported on the Intelligence 2006 conference, which considered the future of intelligence, and developed a number of future intelligence scenarios for the next decade or so. The selected scenarios of *transformation, adaption*, and *status quo* demonstrate the variety in possible outcomes from futures studies of intelligence, and present a foundation for challenging the assumptions associated with current processes and practices.

Transformation

As current old models and methods lose their potency, intelligence researchers and practitioners will seek new knowledge to transform people, processes, organizations, and systems according to the future environment. The need for change has been driven by the people of the intelligence communities who have been valued for their individual contributions, and their influences on the wider intelligence community. The capability of intelligence organizations has been dependent on the people of the organization, but the transformation scenario with capability deficiencies in the organizations can be modified by strong partnerships with the private sector. Future-proofing of intelligence capability can be achieved by contractual arrangements with private and academic partners. Therefore, the future transformation of the intelligence industry will witness the revival of methodological skills of creativity and innovation. The accessing of cross-disciplinary concepts to new threats will expand the future methodological approaches that can be applied to adversaries. Thus, the intelligence community's investment in strategic analysis and estimative intelligence will ensure a future-focused context for planning and decision making.

Adaptation

There is an expectation that the future will witness even more of what is occurring at the present; by intelligence analysts adapting models and practices that make people, processes, organizations, and systems more robust with the need for change. That is, as the threat environment continues to become more complex, the requirement to adjust models and practices to meet the challenge will be paramount. It could be claimed that adaptation is an exercise in pragmatism as new threats will determine better outcomes.

The many dimensions of emerging threats will require better organizational structures within organizations and between organizations. Flexibility in adjusting to new scenarios can be achieved by innovative practitioners from higher education and private organizations contributing to the intelligence knowledge of the entity. The sense of collaboration between like intelligence teams in government, higher education, and corporate entities will provide new approaches to intelligence processes.

Status Quo

Perhaps the future scenario for intelligence is that little or no change is to occur in the near term with current models and practices maintaining currency in the quest for intelligence. With an absence of strategic vision for the future, the status quo will continue to provide the processes for the production of intelligence, only relying on evolutionary change to modify approaches. This approach will ensure that immediate and urgent requirements for intelligence will be met, but will not account for future unspecified threats that may not be challenged by new models and practices. That is, without major structural change it can be expected that current approaches will be inadequate for future threats. The maintaining of the status quo in the future can expect diminishing returns for effort and resources expended.

Outcomes

The alternative futures of intelligence in the protection of assets appear to indicate the need for change to address the expected new types and levels of threats to organizations. It is imperative that change to the intelligence function remains in advance of the threats to organizations. It is proposed that the intelligence structure both within and between organizations becomes less organization-centric, and more engagement is created through collaboration channels. The future-proofing of intelligence capability may be achieved through partnerships extending beyond traditional organizations. Finally, innovation in models and methodologies in intelligence may be the only real competitive advantage in a changing threat environment.

PROFESSIONALISM

A primary trend for the security industry at the national and international levels is an increase in particular types of crime, at a rate that will see volumes of activities within the industry doubling every few years. The security industry has become an integral part of business enterprise and human activities, whether these are wealth-creating activities or people congregating for leisure or living. The trends and functions of the security industry to meet the needs of the community will be gained through enhanced professionalism and security education and training. The structure and management of future security organizations will demand professional security consultants and managers. In reality, the assets of the future will be protected by highly technical and management skilled individuals in combination.

The future of security seems to have a tendency in the international context for private security supplementing the law enforcement agencies in crime prevention in the community. Trends indicate that advances in multiple facets of security between private and government sectors will enhance asset protection. In the near to mid-terms, the security industry will witness a period for progressive and innovative companies to professionalize security management in the community.

Recognized professional vocations are characterized by identifiable features of distinction and functions of operation. Some of the characteristics of a profession that will apply in the security sector are:

- An educated workforce.
- Sufficient maturity and organizational infrastructure to be self-regulating.
- Adopts a proactive leadership position in security matters.
- Professional responsibility is extended to clients within the security sector.
- Capable of a visionary perspective in national planning strategies.
- Workers at all levels in the security industry have skilled knowledge, which is continually maintained.

Nevertheless, security is an amalgam of disciplines that is moving inexorably toward professionalization yet eludes a consensus definition. In the present, identifying who or what defines a security professional remains as difficult and elusory as a comprehensive definition of security that captures all of its modern facets and many actors (Griffiths et al., 2010). Such an issue is unlikely to change in the short to midterm, but there has to be progression to achieving such definition.

The view of elevating security to the status of a profession provokes polarized opinions; however, there are elements to identify a security professional. These elements include agreed and enforced standards of behavior/ethics, standards of education, formal requirement for professional development, a college of peers, and a distinct body of knowledge (Griffiths et al., 2010). The future professionalizing of the security sector will require an enormous restructure of the industry and a quantum change in educational programs for managers and technologists (Smith, 1996). As a consequence, the future of the security sector will benefit from education of the workforce by:

- A higher-quality service can be provided for clients.
- Training and education represent the most cost-effective solution.
- Skills development provides a higher status profession.
- Knowledge management within an organization will increase management and technical skills.
- The standardization of procedures and techniques will be achieved with an industry-wide educational program.

The short to midterm future of security as a profession is dependent on the uptake of professional educational programs at the managerial and strategic levels. The future enhancement of professionalism in the security industry is dependent on the industry to develop structures and programs to service the future needs of the community.

Human and Social Factors

Human and social factors will have a greater impact on organizational security, although such assessment in these areas is more difficult as there is not necessarily an explicit cause and effect. Organizational security will not be affected first hand, but rather second and often third hand. As a consequence, such issues, like an increasing risk-adverse society with greater wealth, are likely to lead to greater security, but such an effect is slow and environmentally based.

Risk-Adverse Society

Society is becoming more adverse to risk, both actual and perceived. Although all activities carry some form of risk, there will be ever-greater demands for increasing a reduction in risk exposure, from cultural, social, community, corporate, and individual bases. Such adverse-risk views can proceed beyond the point of overall benefit and become counterproductive, to all facets of society. As the predictive nature of risk management and security improves, the expectation of protecting against risks will increase, although protection against probabilistic risks such as acts of nature will not increase greatly. Rather, risk related to human activities in what is made, how it is used, and who has control are likely to increase over time. In other words, some technologies will cause adverse reaction whereas others will be embraced. What is accepted or rejected is likely to be those that cause a moderate level of dread and therefore are not perceived as a social benefit.

Terrorism

The issue of terrorism will remain with society for the short to midterm, and many will use terrorism to enhance the need for greater security, driven by political, geo-environmental, and other broader social factors. Nevertheless, the nature, cause, and expression of terrorism and application of security will change over time, resulting in quite a different future that we view today. The changing concept of terrorism may incorporate eco-terrorism (against private organizations), cyber-terrorism (hacking, identity theft, and fraud), cybernetic terrorism (robotics), and corporate terrorism (ransom, public reputation). Thus, as the concept of terrorism changes into the future, the countertechniques to minimize or neutralize the process of terrorism will evolve and develop. However, no matter what the future of terrorism may produce, the analysis of risk and threat of terrorism will always be paramount in the security of the community through the protection of assets.

Security Education

The future trends and functions of the security industry to meet the needs of the community will be gained through enhanced professionalism, security education and training, progressive security management approaches, technological sophistication, and industrial intelligence. Much of these opportunities will become available through an understanding of the importance of information and information exchange for the protection of assets at the corporate and community levels of security. The traditional academic disciplines have evolved and developed over centuries to reach the state of refinement as we now find them. These traditional academic disciplines of astronomy, mathematics, medicine, and more recently environmental science, exhibit a set of characteristics by which each can be designated as a discipline. These characteristics include:

- *Body of knowledge*: A well-defined and inclusive body of knowledge.
- *Structure of knowledge*: Internal structure of knowledge achieved through logical relationships between concepts.
- *Concepts and principles*: The building blocks of knowledge in a discipline.
- *Theories*: Predictive in function and model the description of the outcomes.

At this stage, security science lacks the validity of the characteristics of the traditional disciplines. However, the future of security science as an academic discipline will depend on the trends in security research to enhance the characteristics of a discipline. It is expected that evidence-based research will play an important role in the professionalization of security. Some emerging theories to drive understanding in security include the concept of entropy applied to security in terms of risk and threat, and that of security decay as a mechanism for understanding the degradation of effective security in an organization.

Privacy

The expectation of an individual's privacy will reduce over time. Such a view opposes others, where there is the expectation that individuals will have a heightened expectation of privacy, tempered by a willingness to indulge in privacy-benefit trade-off (Cannataci, 2010). It is suggested that this view will not be the case; rather, the concept of privacy is a first-world idea that will significantly reduce over the short to midterm. Future generations will be less concerned with their individual privacy than past generations, driven by ever-increasing connectivity using wireless technology, sharing and social media, the exponential quantity of data, the willingness to post data, and the ever-increasing use of mobile technology as a commodity. Thus, connectivity will be a disposable item that is used and disposed, with a clear understanding of the footprint that individuals are leaving behind.

Smart System Integration

Security risk analysis and human behavioral studies will be applied to analysis to determine if an intruder represents a threat, based on the determined motion and behavior of the person. These smart integrated systems will assimilate the human behavioral characteristics into the measure of threat, where threat will be used to inform the likelihood in the process of risk analysis. Such an approach could allow the system to learn by monitoring the environment, therefore raising or lowering the risk level as the dynamic environment changes. Once a predetermined risk level is reached, an early warning signal can be generated that results in a response aligned to the threat.

Again, surveillance has taken on an increasingly important role in tandem with the rise of new approaches to govern and influence cross-border mobility. Unmanned aerial vehicles, machine-readable travel documents, electronic passports, biometric screening, and trusted traveler programs are among the most prevalent techniques in which borders are becoming subject to surveillance for the purposes of smart and swift management of international cross-border flows of people, commodities, and information. In addition, the emergence of international migration management has become a notable development that traverses throughout the use of new border surveillance and management techniques. These trends in migration are the result of larger institutional developments in intergovernmental relations and international political economy.

MANAGEMENT

Risk Management

The concept of risk management as a formal discipline emerged throughout the corporate sectors and has become a well-established discipline. The Risk Management International Standards Organization (ISO) 31000:2009 standard, considered the international benchmark, will continue to be propagated throughout the corporate world. However, this standard has been questioned for its suitable for security risk management, as it neglects to raise and integrate specific security risk concepts such as threat, vulnerability, and criticality (Brooks, 2011; Cubbage and Brooks, 2012; Dali, 2011). Security risk management will develop as a standalone risk management process, incorporating core security risk concepts of threat, criticality, and vulnerability.

Corporate Governance

Security managers must have a sound understanding of corporate governance principles to ensure that the security function is integrated into the corporate governance framework

(Cubbage and Brooks, 2012), otherwise security will become subservient to governance. The security industry needs to gain considerable ground toward professionalism in the near to mid-future, or it will be incorporated into the governance or risk department. Such an outcome will restrict the ability of security to develop into a professional practice area, resulting in security maintaining its external image of guards and guns.

Greater Executive/Director Compliance

In the mid-future, there will be greater obligation on corporations to have *reasonable and sufficient* security in place. When security fails, the level of security will have to conform to what may be considered reasonable by an independent entity such as the courts (Cubbage and Brooks, 2012). As health, safety, and environment (HSE) and risk management have developed and been embedded into organizations, these processes have been mandated by legislation to ultimately be the responsibilities of the board, executives, and staff. It is expected that security will follow a similar path as HSE and risk management, and will be legislated as an executive responsibility.

Security Standards

It is expected that the future will determine that the community, commercial, and national security industries will be guided by security standards that are a result of the professionalization of the protection of assets. Presently, standards in security are both optional and piecemeal, and as a result there is no rigor in the context of the performance of security products and services. However, the near future will witness a more extensive range of security standards across security technology and security practices, with quality outcomes being presented. The application of standards to practice and performance is critical for national and international licensing and registration programs. By relying on standards, security device manufacturers and security service providers can provide equipment, technology, and services that meet the requirements of the national governments and national industry organizations. Also, by complying with domain standards the industry users can easily source quality products from across the globe. Thus, standardization of technology and services reduces costs for delivery of the protection of assets.

Therefore, the proliferation of standards for the future in the security industry will provide a number of benefits for the industry and the consumer:

- Standards will impact quality, lead-time, manufacturing flexibility, and supply-chain management.
- Standardization and conformity assessment lead to lower costs by reducing redundancy, minimizing errors, and reducing time to market.
- Demonstrating compliance to standards assists products and services to cross borders and reach international clients. Thus, standards make international operations possible, ensuring that devices manufactured in one country can be sold and used in another.
- Organizations not only reduce the economic risk of their research and development activities by standardization, they can also lower their overall research and development costs by relying on previously standardized technologies.

Thus, standards in security have an important role to provide a formal risk management framework to ensure that the technologies and services are effective for the situation. That is, the security standards produce the criteria within which the security technology or security service can be tested or evaluated. Without such a formal framework, the evaluation of technologies and services can produce inappropriate equipment that inadequately protects against risks, poorly integrates with organizational operations, is rejected by the users, and potentially impacts on overall organizational performance.

CONCLUSION

Security has a critical role is all aspects of the nation, business, and leisure, and as a result should be given serious consideration for its future directions and trends. The futures of security can be determined by a number of trends or predictions according to present and past performances. For security to adopt a particular trending direction, decisions should be made to steer the development of aspects of security along a particular path for predictable outcomes.

The future outcomes for security technologies in the near-term are reasonably well defined, but mid- to long-term predictions are much less certain as new science will impact on future technology development. Much less predictable in the future will be the managerial and social contexts of security in the community, as political and administrative decisions will have far-reaching impacts on the nature of society and the role of security within the community.

However, with reasonable certainty the need for future development of the security industry toward a recognized profession will be achieved to acquire some structure in to the chaos of the current security industry. The quest for professionalism will require well-established security education programs that advance the understanding and performance of security as a service to the nation and the community. The development of these education programs is embryonic at this stage, but will gain maturity in the next few decades. The discipline of security science will become established with time, and therefore the professionalization of the security sector will advance.

Further Reading

Friedman, G., 2009. The Next 100 Years: A Forecast for the 21st Century. Double Day, New York.

References

Ashby, R., Pritchard, D.A., 2004. Sensing beyond the perimeter: The advanced exterior sensor (AES). In: Proceedings of the IEEE 38th Annual 2004 International Carnahan Conference on Security Technology. Albuquerque, NM, pp. 182–188.
Brooks, D.J., 2011. Security risk management: A psychometric map of expert knowledge structure. International Journal of Risk Management 13 (1/2), 17–41.
Cannataci, J.A., 2010. Data protection vision 2020: Options for improving European policy and legislation during 2010–2020. Council of Europe Recommendation R (87)15 and ETS Convention 108. Directorate General of Human Rights and Legal Affairs, Strasbourg.

Cubbage, C., Brooks, D.J., 2012. Corporate Security in the Asia Pacific Region: Crisis, Crime. Fraud and Misconduct. Francis and Taylor, Boca Raton, FL.

Dali, A., 2011. Global survey on ISO 31000 risk management standard. Retrieved October, 18, 2011, from http://www.linkedin.com/groups?mostPopular=&gid=1834592.

Franzen, C., 2012, June 7. See like Superman? MIT scientists make it possible. TRM. Retrieved June 11, 2012, from http://idealab.talkingpointsmemo.com/2012/06/mit-explains-technology-behind-superhero-vision.php?ref=fpb.

Griffiths, M., Brooks, D.J., Corkill, J., 2010. Defining the Security Professional: Definition through a Body of Knowledge. Paper presented at the *Proceedings of the 3rd Australian Security and Intelligence Conference*, Perth, Western Australia.

Mell, P., Grance, T., 2011. The NIST definition of cloud computing. Special Publication 800–145, National Institute of Standards and Technology, U.S. Department of Commerce, Gaitherburg, MD.

Peppler, B., 2006. The future of intelligence. National Security Practice Notes November 2006.

Pritchard, D.A., 2004. Personal communication.

Smith, C.L., 1996. Developments in security technology. Malaysian Safety and Security Journal 6, 19–26.

Venkataraayan, K., 2012. PhD thesis. Edith Cowan University, Perth, Western Australia.

Venkataraayan, K., Askraba, S., Alameh, K.E., Smith, C.L., 2012. Multi-wavelength laser sensor for intruder detection and discrimination. Optics and Lasers in Engineering 50, 176–181.

Watson, R., 2008. Future Files: 5 Trends That Will Shape the Next 50 Years. Nicholas Brealey, Yarmouth, ME.

Index

Note: Page numbers followed by *f* indicate figures and *t* indicate tables.